D1635977

Migration, Social Change, and Health

Craig R. Janes

Migration, Social Change, and Health

A Samoan Community in Urban California

Stanford University Press, Stanford, California

1990

Stanford University Press
Stanford, California
© 1990 by the Board of Trustees of the
Leland Stanford Junior University

Printed in the United States of America

CIP data appear at the end of the book

Preface

Stress is a popular term with manifold meanings in both lay and academic settings. In both contexts stress has been elevated to the status of a primary explanatory variable for a wide variety of illnesses. In popular discourse stress emerges from the many and sometimes conflicting demands that are placed on people in their day-to-day lives, hence the sayings, "I'm burnt out," "I'm stressed out" or even "I can't cope." Analysis of these sayings and the contexts in which they are used suggests that stress is conceived of as individual responses to external conditions.

But in the intellectual domains of biomedicine, public health, and related fields (especially psychology), a different kind of discourse arises: a vocabulary focused exclusively on individual responsibility and physiologic process. As Allan Young (1980) argues, notions of stress in this literature are shorn of historical or sociological relevance. Stress as a process stems from incomplete or "failed" coping with environmental factors that seem to arise disembodied and almost randomly. Thus appropriate/inappropriate coping, troublesome "life events" (which being rather ordinary and everyday are something that everyone experiences; that one should experience such events more than another is simply accidental, like being hit by a bus), anger reactions, and the like are given explanatory prominence. The issue here, of course, is not where stress comes from, but how people respond to it. Following this position to its logical conclusion, we may then assume that "dealing with stress" involves learning new coping behaviors, reaction patterns, and the like. The problem is, after all, a person's own fault. This particular orientation stems from the mechanistic, particularistic epistemology of biomedicine that has tended to bound cause within individual bodies. Research on stress deriving from this paradigm (even if it does challenge the dualism of mind and body) rarely engages analysis of the intersection of individual and sociohistorical context.

But there is a smaller literature on stress, one that has roots in sociology, anthropology, and social epidemiology (or "social medicine"), that offers a reasonable alternative to the reductionist trap of biomedicine. This literature offers as a counterpoint the view that stress can be understood only in terms of social-structural changes in the inconsistencies and conflicts in which individuals play the role of victims in scenes over which they have little or no control. The problematic in this particular equation is one of uncovering paradox, conflict, and disorders in the social fabric. Inductively, and indeed logically, this social-structural position has much to recommend it. It has developed along with medical ecology, a discipline that has successfully stretched public health models to include environmental and behavioral variables. Moreover, there is a convergence between the intellectual discourse on structural stress and the popular discourse on the disorders of modern living. This lends the perspective a certain prima facie salience insofar as it parallels and reflects individuals' day-to-day lives. Finally, an approach that focuses on socio-environmental rather than, or in addition to, individual factors is more amenable to preventive intervention (e.g., Ratcliffe et al. 1984).

The perspective offered by this book falls in line with this more environmental approach. I take the position that although stress occurs in the context of individual experience, to understand it fully requires linking such experience with a system of social relations and social change. I thus focus on mediating processes, such as social performance, status, role, social class, and economic resources, in an effort to understand the way in which migration and consequent social changes ramify throughout the groups involved and impinge on the lives of individuals.

The root of such an effort is basic ethnography. Through increasing levels of specificity, beginning with a discussion of the macrosocial forces that impel migration, I show how individuals experience social change as a series of conflicts and as paradoxes in which they acquire innumerable material benefits but struggle to meet their own and their families' needs. Once these factors are derived from the ethnographic material, they are applied in a quasi-epidemiologic framework to patterns of disease risk. This manner of presentation is not unique, but it will perhaps be new or unfamiliar to readers with public health or behavioral medicine backgrounds. To these readers, and for students of anthropology, let me assert simply that the goal of ethnography as an approach to epidemiology is to impart a sense of real people in day-to-day situations and to counterbalance the use of abstract quantitative models.

The reader may wonder at the choice of Samoans as a study population. The group was selected for far more than the usual anthropological reasons (which often as not seem to reduce to serendipity). Samoans have been migrating in large numbers to industrial, urban centers for nearly 30 years now. Sizable communities have been established in New Zealand and Hawaii and on the U.S. mainland. At the same time Samoans have maintained a viable, rural, and distinct lifestyle in their home islands. Both migrant and nonmigrant communities have been studied extensively by anthropologists, offering a rich mine of information from which to construct an analysis of social change. Moreover, research by members of the Samoan Migration Project (Baker et al. 1986) over the past ten years provides an abundance of data on health and health risks. These data are used extensively in this book and add a comparative dimension to my study of one specific migrant community. Finally, although Samoans possess a distinct and largely unambiguous repertoire of responses to the dominant American culture, they are in many senses representative of the growing numbers of non-Western immigrants in American cities. By understanding the processes by which the health of Samoans is influenced, we may learn something about migration and health in general.

There is also a personal reason for choosing to work with Samoans. From the time I first began research in the community with Ivan "Guy" Pawson in 1979, I was attracted to Samoan culture by its grace, its puzzling paradoxes, and the fascinating ways it had been molded to the urban, American context. Although I now live far away from the people I studied, I remain committed to them in far more than an intellectual way.

Like all studies, this one has a particular intellectual genealogy that needs to be traced. As with genealogies based on kinship, reference to my intellectual ancestors is a way of establishing my own identity as a scholar as well as establishing academic membership in a particular group. The work of early social epidemiologists like Norman Scotch, John Cassel, and S. Leonard Syme provides an important theoretical backdrop to this book. Their work stimulated my own thinking about the relationship of social change to disease and kept me from swerving from the "structural course" I have followed. The fine work of J. Clyde Mitchell, Elizabeth Colson, and others on urbanization and migration provided the theoretical context for my focus on social relations and social roles in the context of change. More recently, I owe a great deal to the work of Bill Dressler, who to my mind is one of the most important anthropological scholars working in behavioral medicine and on the very leading edge of the study of social change and health.

Not only is a book the product of intellectual kin ties, it is also the end

product of a long dialogue. This dialogue is both personal and intellectual, and involves many people: friends, family, advisers, teachers, colleagues, and critics. Without their help, support, and input, the research
and the book would never have been possible. It is with a great deal of
pleasure that I extend my formal thanks to these people for the important
role they have played in this work.

Few have assisted and supported me as much as Joan Ablon. Her
wisdom and spirit were in many ways the guiding energy behind my
graduate work at the University of California, San Francisco. I would like
to acknowledge especially her help in organizing and conducting my
fieldwork. A superlative fieldworker who is guided always by a strong
ethical sense and a spirit of humanism, she will always be my most important role model. I also owe special thanks to Elizabeth Colson. Her work,
teaching, and quiet wisdom taught me much about the craft of anthropology. She was particularly instrumental in helping me gain an understanding of migration and resettlement. I feel particularly honored to
have been able to work with her.

For helping me articulate my ideas on stress and health, I am indebted
to Ted and Nancy Graves, Fred Dunn, Dorothea Leighton, and Bob
Hackenberg. For supporting my interest in Samoans, giving valuable research suggestions and opportunities, and providing research assistant-
ships, I thank Guy Pawson. I also thank Paul Shankman and Karla Rolff,
who at various points made valuable comments on the research and later
the writing of the book.

Many Samoans assisted me with advice, logistical support, and, most
important, friendship. I am especially indebted to Vaita Utu, who helped
me establish myself in the community, contacted informants on my behalf, and taught me much about what it was like to be a Samoan in urban
America. I thank Chief Tuimavave Aoelua for his patient instruction in
Samoan and the rudiments of formal etiquette; and Falefasa Tagaloa for
her help and support throughout the project, and her assistance in intro-
ducing me to important members of the community. There are many
other Samoans in California and Samoa I would like to acknowledge by
name, but my commitment to maintaining the anonymity of my informants precludes this. I thank them all for participating in the research
and allowing me to become, at least for a short time, part of their lives.
Fa'afetai lava lo tou fesoasoani; fa'afetai lava lo tou agalelei!

I owe most to my wife Linda and my daughter Enessa. I thank Linda
for giving me the time and encouragement to pursue my dream, and for
being my social support when I needed it the most. To my daughter
Enessa I dedicate this book. She arrived during the fieldwork, and though
she complicated things a bit, she put the whole experience into perspec-

tive. I will always cherish memories of writing parts of this book with her on my lap, at first as a baby and usually asleep, and later as an energetic child wanting to play with the computer keys.

The research described here was supported in part by a grant from the National Science Foundation, #BNS-8204572. The Graduate Division of the University of California, San Francisco, supported portions of the fieldwork with grants of "Patent Funds," and supported my travel to and from Samoa in 1982. Computer time was kindly made available by the UCSF Computer Center and the Department of Computing Services, University of Colorado, Denver. The writing was supported in part by fellowships from the Graduate Division at UCSF and the Soroptimist Club, Sierra Pacific Region.

Finally, I thank my colleagues in the Medical Anthropology Program at UCSF, the Prevention Research Center in Berkeley, California, and the Department of Anthropology of the University of Colorado, Denver, for their patience, support, and encouragement during the many phases of writing, research, and analysis that went into this book.

C.R.J.

Contents

Figures and Tables

Migration, Social Change, and Health

Introduction

It is often with a great sense of promise that migrants embark on their life-changing excursions. However great the promise, and however great the probability that anticipations will be fulfilled in a new land, migration exacts a psychological toll. Individuals must learn new skills, develop new problem-solving strategies, and reinterpret the ideals held from their cultures of origin in what is likely a far different environment. This is especially true of the current waves of migrants coming to the United States from Third World societies. The paradox entailed in this process, and the problem on which this book focuses, is that though migration may on the whole improve the socioeconomic lot of the people who move and be perceived as a desirable alternative to conditions at home, it exacts a price that is evidenced in higher rates of mental illness, cancer, and cardiovascular disease.

But just how the social and cultural discontinuities embodied in cross-cultural migration affect health is still imperfectly understood. This may be due to the persistence of artificial disciplinary boundaries that restrict the collaboration of health and social scientists. Social scientists, in particular anthropologists, have been interested for some time in the adaptation of migrant groups to complex urban settings and have developed a few theoretical constructs for understanding the patterns of this adaptation. Unfortunately, until very recently these models have not been extended to explain variation in adaptive strategies among migrants and its implications for the health of the individual. Similarly, health scientists, particularly epidemiologists, have studied the health consequences of migration without directing any significant attention to migration as an important "intervening" variable. The major problem in bridging these disciplinary perspectives, and therefore developing a holistic perspective on migration, social change, and disease, lies in creating adequate definitions of such commonly used explanatory concepts as "Westernization," "acculturation," and "stress." An approach to migration and health is needed that integrates social science and epidemiologic perspectives.

The research discussed in this book represents an effort to integrate anthropological and epidemiological approaches in analyzing the links between migration, adaptation, social and cultural changes, and health. Particular emphasis is placed on the antecedents and correlates of stress and the relationship of stress to important health indicators. The research population is a Pacific Island group of Polynesian descent that began migrating in substantial numbers to California in the 1950's. For most of the period of high population mobility, especially in the two decades from 1950 to 1970, Samoans in the islands sustained a largely rural, agrarian, and marine economy that was well integrated with a thriving and conservative cultural system.* This environment, the techniques for exploiting it, and the cultural system derived from the social prerequisites of this technology could not be more different from the milieu of the urban United States. The study of Samoan migrants thus offers a natural laboratory for exploring the degree to which environmental discontinuity ramifies throughout the cultural system migrants bring with them, and how individual responses to that discontinuity and to cultural change affect health.

Because one goal of this study was to integrate anthropological and epidemiological tools, concepts, and theories, the methods applied to the study of migration and health, and the resulting manner of data exposition, are unique. The methodological strategy involved two goals. On the first level the intent was to explore migration and its sociocultural sequelae, using the tools of basic ethnographic research. On the second level, the intent was to codify those sequelae in a way that tested available epidemiologic hypotheses and yet ensured some grounding in the ethnographic data. The presentation of data in this book closely follows the sequential research steps necessitated by this twofold agenda. The reader is first invited to explore the process of Samoan migration and the adap-

---

* Economic "development" in the islands has brought about a significant decline in subsistence activities, and wrought changes in the various cultural institutions that supervise land use. Today American Samoa, which supplies most of the U.S. migrants, depends heavily on funds provided by the U.S. government, circulated through public employment, some forms of direct welfare to individuals, and a thriving entrepreneurial economy. Wage labor has replaced farming and fishing as the primary economic activity of most men, thereby eroding the leadership role of the extended family leader, the *matai*, who gained much of his power through his control of family lands and supervision of subsistence activities. The people of Western Samoa, an independent country, remain far more dependent on subsistence agriculture and fishing and are thought by anthropologists and Samoans alike to be far more "traditional." About one-fourth of the migrants to the United States are from Western Samoa.

tation of Samoans to the particular economic, political, social, and cultural environment of urban California. Data of importance for understanding disease and health-care issues are developed out of this excursion and applied in subsequent chapters to an analysis of particular health problems.

Throughout the book the focus is on understanding and describing what Dunn and Janes (1986) term "causal assemblages," rather than on specific linear cause-and-effect relationships between "independent" and "dependent" variables. This focus is based on a theoretical model that posits health as an outcome of the interaction of man's natural and social environments; that is, from an "ecological" point of view. In this perspective migration and health are conceived as a problem in human ecology. In the following sections I develop this particular approach in the context of related work in anthropology, sociology, and the health sciences.

Migration, Stress, and Health

The epidemiological literature on migrants is well developed. Migrants present often ideal "natural experiments" for assessing the relative weight of hereditary and environmental factors in the etiology of many, particularly chronic, noninfectious diseases. The logic of these studies is to start out with known differences in the rate of specific diseases between two populations and choose a migrant sample with the intent to "maximize interpopulation variability in the environmental factors and to minimize genetic and other factors on which the migrants are presumed to be highly similar to the residents of the country from which they came" (Kasl and Berkman 1983). Analytically, the focus is on sorting out, using multivariate methods, the relative contribution of changes in known risk factors to changes in disease rates. For the most part the intervening processes of migration, adaptation, and social change are not dealt with directly. Their impact is simply inferred as the unexplainable difference in disease rates between home and host societies.

The great majority of these studies indicate that within a generation, migrant groups from rural non-Western cultures to Western urban centers experience striking increases in the incidence of several noninfectious diseases (e.g. Antonovsky 1979; Cassel 1975; Haenszel 1970; Hull 1979; Wessen 1971). The majority of research has focused on cancer mortality and cardiovascular disease mortality and morbidity, especially hypertension. Mental illness, patterns of health-care utilization, and overall levels of health have received comparatively little scrutiny. Mental illness in migrants has been studied almost exclusively in the context of clinical populations (Hull 1979; Sanua 1970). Patterns of overall morbidity and health-care utilization are difficult to measure because of typically vast differences between health-care systems in the societies of origin and destination, and because health is clearly influenced by type and level of care (Kasl and Berkman 1983). The work on cancer is quite advanced, but researchers have chosen to assess the relative effects of hereditary factors and exposure to environmental agents (e.g., Haenszel and Kurihara 1968; Haenszel et al. 1972; Knudson 1977; Mancuso and Sterling 1974). The work was never intended to explore the etiologic significance of migration itself (Kasl and Berkman 1983).

Much of the research on heart disease and related risk factors, however, has included some examination of the impact of migration. The most voluminous literature contrasts blood pressure levels and hypertension rates between stable, rural, underdeveloped areas and changing, industrialized urban areas. Because many of these studies start with the assumption that high blood pressure and heart disease are physiological indicators of the stresses inherent in Western industrialized society, significantly more attention has been directed to elucidating the particular psychosocial underpinnings of variance in morbidity rates. Consequently, this literature provides a richer theoretical resource for understanding the impact of migration than does any other body of epidemiologic or social science research.

Any study of the relationship of environmental change and individual health must begin by considering what psychophysiological processes are thought to lead to—and constitute—stress. Beginning with the writings of Wolff (1953) and Selye (1956), stress has been seen as an outcome of the individual's appraisal of external events that are in some way threatening. These external stimuli are commonly termed "stressors." In the presence of stressors the individual is thought to strive for homeostasis by taking appropriate corrective actions. If these fail, and the perception of stressors persists, the individual is believed to be under stress.

Three variables are important to consider in this equation. First, it is necessary to determine what kind of external events represent stressors. Second, given the existence of potential stressors, the variable individual perceptions of what are and what are not stressors—and thus their salience in producing stress—must be considered. Finally, and perhaps most important, it is critical to identify what constitutes positive "corrective actions," and what personal or social resources a person may marshal in effecting equilibrium. These resources, consisting of biochemical, physiological, psychological, social, or cultural attributes, are thought to buttress "host resistance" (Antonovsky 1979; Berkman and Syme 1979; Kaplan et al. 1977; Levine and Scotch 1970; Pilisuk and Froland 1978).

Because stress is an aspect of the human experience with which most people can, in some fashion, identify, the syndrome has perhaps inevitably been used to explain all sorts of health problems—ranging from problem drinking to the common cold. The wholesale use of stress as an explanatory concept, however, has had the unfortunate result of producing a wide variety of differing definitions and understandings of just what it is. At the same time research on the physiological sequelae of the stress process—what Selye (1956) originally identified as the "general adaptation syndrome"—has lagged far behind the correlative studies of supposed environmental antecedents of stress and health outcomes. At present the actual process of stress, including the full range of psychophysiological phenomena present—from cognitive perception to specific biochemical and biomechanical changes—can only be surmised.* Fairly consistent cross-cultural observations that sociocultural change is related to disease prevalence after known risk factors have been statistically controlled offers prima facie evidence for stress as an etiological element. Just what stress is in psychophysiological terms, however, remains problematic (Vingerhoets and Marcelissen 1988).

It has been the task of social epidemiologists and social scientists interested in the health aspects of change to clarify the links between macrosocial processes and individual experience. Many theories have been advanced to explain the relationship between environment, social structure, individual experience, cognition, and stress, but for our purposes they may be reduced to three general groups: (1) those that posit stress as an outcome of the individual's appraisal of life changes or events (e.g., Dohrenwend and Dohrenwend 1974); (2) those that see stress as an outcome of "cultural incongruity," where the essential predictability of social life is compromised by new or competing cultural systems (e.g., Cassel 1975; Marmot and Syme 1976); and (3) those that locate stress in the patterns of inconsistency or discrepancy arising when new statuses become available to individuals who do not have the resources or experience to fulfill the behavioral expectations associated with those statuses (e.g., Dressler 1982, 1985). The last explanation has been found to be most salient when modernization or acculturation pressures lead to a change in the class structure (Dressler et al. 1987a, b).

These three models are not necessarily competing or mutually exclusive. Indeed, each is based on the idea that status/role change or incongruity produces stress (see Mestrovic and Glassner 1983). The differences are primarily a matter of scale, ranging from a focus on groups and

---

* Joel M. Hanna of the University of Hawaii is currently attempting to link psychosocial measures of stress to biochemical changes in several groups of Samoan migrants. This research represents a major effort to elucidate some of the links between culture, psychology, and physiology.

subgroups (cultures or communities) to a focus on individuals. The perspective taken in this book is that though stress is personally experienced, it is influenced most profoundly by the particular social, cultural, and historical context that people find themselves in. To organize the particular theoretical questions that stem from this perspective, I use a definition of stress that is based on sociological concepts of status and role (e.g., Gore and Mangione 1983; Kandel et al. 1985; Merton 1949; O'Nell and Selby 1968). I call this "social stress."* Because definitions of stress differ widely from one investigator to the next, and one discipline to the next, I offer the following brief outline of the concept as I use it in this book.

Individual behavior is typically organized according to more or less general sets of social expectations. Expectations that are situationally and/or interactionally specific are known as "role expectations," as opposed to those that define general social categories, such as class and gender, which may be termed "status expectations." The distinction between the two is not theoretically critical so far as stress is concerned. Both kinds of expectations define who a person is, what is expected of that person under given circumstances, and what goals are appropriate. It should be clear that the biosocial categories of age, sex, and socioeconomic position determine in large part the range and content of status and role expectations. Stress as I define it stems from three processes that are linked to the wider social context: deficiencies of social, economic, or psychological resources that compromise role performance; the acquisition of new statuses or roles that are unfamiliar and/or conflict with other social positions the individual occupies; and hindrances placed on the acquisition of desired statuses/roles. Further, the condition may be either relatively acute (e.g., the stresses produced by major life changes) or chronic (e.g., the stresses produced by status inconsistencies as a result of *in situ* modernization; Dressler et al. 1987b). Social support in this model describes the relative availability of information that increases people's ability to learn and adequately perform new roles, or represents direct, instrumental aid that provides resources necessary for status/role acquisition and performance (Kahn and Antonucci 1980; Mechanic 1974).

Though ubiquitous to human social life, stress increases, at least potentially, with exposure to rapid change. With the technological and socioeconomic changes that result from migration, urbanization, and the integration of formerly subsistence-based communities into the worldwide market economy, new statuses are prized, new styles of life are held up as desirable by dominant or elite groups, and a society's division of labor may be transformed (Dressler et al. 1987a). At the personal level, such

* I prefer this to the more common "psychosocial stress," as better reflecting my emphasis on social environment and individual status and role expectations, rather than individual cognition or stress appraisal.

changes inevitably generate conflicts over status and role expectations; they may also increase the number of important life events that result in major status or role change. Modernization typically includes the development of class or status hierarchies where the most desirable social positions are those most closely identified with capitalist institutions. Access to these desirable "modern" statuses demands educational and economic resources that are in short supply and typically available only to specific subgroups. It is the problems associated with gaining or maintaining an expensive status that result in the most pernicious stress.

Migration as a Problem in Human Ecology

A model of human ecology proposed by Moore et al. (1987) is useful for organizing factors related to health and disease in a migrating population (see Fig. 1.1). In this model two levels of organization are differentiated: the societal and the individual. The first level, which we might call the environmental system, embraces both the local cultural system of which the individual is a member—the community—and the wider environment in which that system functions. In the context of migration, one's community is that of other migrants, and its functioning is based largely on their characteristics, as well as the circumstances under which they migrated; and the wider environment is now the cultural system of the host society, containing a different set of economic and social institutions to which the migrant community must adapt if it is to survive. Of course there is an interplay between the two cultural systems, but it is typically the migrants who are under the greatest adaptive pressure, particularly in the case of rural people coming to a complex, urban society.

In addition, it is important to recognize migration as a historical process. Migrants rarely arrive all at once with all cultural institutions intact. They filter into a particular locale, and the success of the firstcomers' strategies influences later arrivals. As the migrant community grows, with its own demographic and cultural characteristics (voluntary migrants are often quite different from their countrymen), two things tend to occur. First, the migrants, now a "community," develop particular urban social and cultural patterns. Second, an array of potential adaptive strategies and social statuses becomes available to individuals to pursue as they see fit. So, though a migrant community of some sort might develop, it is important to note that migration enables the individual to choose among behavioral options, and it is these options that may or may not involve stress.

Students of migration have observed that certain elements of migrant and host societies appear to dictate the relative success (generally defined in economic terms) of migrant societies. For example, whether migrants

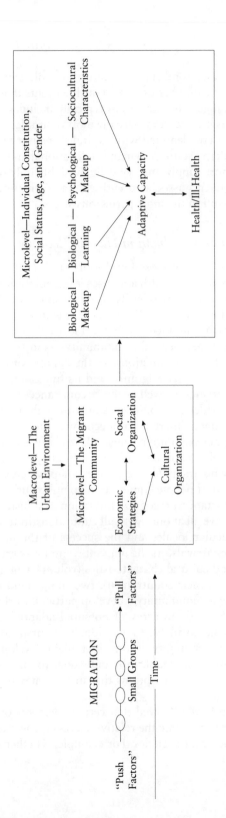

Fig. 1.1. A biocultural view of migration and health. Adapted from Lorna G. Moore, Peter W. Van Arsdale, JoAnn E. Glittenberg, and Robert A. Aldrich, *The Biocultural Basis of Health*, copyright © 1980, reissued 1987 (Prospect Heights, Ill.: Waveland Press, Inc.).

are young or old, whether they are well educated and have job experience, or whether they come with kin with whom they can share resources, dictates what will happen after they arrive. The economic conditions of the host society and the availability of helping social institutions are equally important. If few jobs are available for the unskilled and the uneducated, and these are the predominant characteristics of the migrants, survival will be a problem, at least in the short run. If the migrants are discriminated against for racial or cultural reasons, this too will have a deleterious impact.

In the context of the theoretical model of stress discussed above, one of the more important aspects of host-migrant society interaction is whether individuals are put into situations where they are under pressure to achieve or maintain a status—that is, they subscribe to a cultural value that makes such a status desirable—but have no resources for doing so. Such status may be defined as desirable in terms of either the host or the migrant society. Does one aspire to be a celebrated leader of one's community, or does one search for achievement in Euro-American terms?

The second organizational level embraces the mix of endogenous and exogenous factors that comprise the individual's constitution. The key question in understanding a person's responses to stressors in the environment is whether he or she possesses the adaptive capacity, or "resistance resources," that would buffer such stressors. The potential for individual adaptation rests on four interacting factors: biological makeup (the interaction of genes and environment as the person develops); biological learning, or the history of responses to environmental insults and the resulting "immunity" (or lasting damages) those responses entailed; psychological makeup, or the interaction of biology and society in the development of cognitive abilities, personality, and emotional resources; and social and cultural characteristics, or the person's interaction with others in the social environment, as well as the beliefs and values that motivate individual behavior.

What most stress researchers have concerned themselves with, almost exclusively, is the interaction of the last two factors; that is also my main concern in this book. However, it is important to underscore Caudill's assertion (1958) of many years ago that stress arises in each of the domains noted above: biological, sociocultural, and psychological. It is also probably true that people possess biological resources that either result from their genetic makeup or from early experiences with stress. It is thus important to consider the nature of other than purely psychosocial stressors and resistance resources, particularly nutritional stress (e.g., obesity), exercise patterns, and cardiopulmonary stress (e.g., smoking, atherosclerosis). Of particular importance to understanding the etiology of hypertension in Samoans is obesity, and in Chapter 7 I consider the inter-action of obesity and psychosocial stress in some detail.

Samoan Migration and Health

Like many rural migrants from non-Western cultures to Western cities, Samoans manifest a much-changed pattern of diseases. Less prone to the parasitic/infectious diseases that are comparatively important causes of morbidity and mortality in their homeland, they now fall victim to the chronic and degenerative diseases characteristic of their Western hosts. The correlates of this epidemiological transition have been analyzed by members of the Samoan Studies Project, a large, multiple-objective study of Samoan modernization and migration (Baker et al. 1986). From 1975 to 1978 researchers focused on communities in American Samoa and Hawaii and conducted general surveys of body morphology, blood pressure, and self-reported health problems. These surveys were followed by more intensive but limited studies of work capacity, food habits, blood bio-chemistry, attitudes toward body size, and genetic structure. Studies on these features were also undertaken in Samoan subpopulations at extreme ends of the modernization continuum—California and Western Samoa. In 1979 I joined this project, and with Ivan G. Pawson conducted a number of health surveys in the California Samoan population.

The most striking characteristic Samoans manifest when exposed to modernization is a rapid increase in body mass (weight/height$\times$100) and rapid weight gain. Our surveys revealed that the level of obesity among Samoans in California is as great as any known in the world (Pawson and Janes 1981, 1982; Janes and Pawson 1986). Body mass is clearly associated with place of residence and by inference, level of modernization. The lowest body mass is found among rural Western Samoan agriculturalists, the highest among urbanized California and Hawaii Samoans. Figure 1.2 illustrates these data. Gradations in body-mass levels across the sub-populations is mirrored by body fatness (skinfolds) where such measurements were made.

The sources of such massive weight gain in the modernized subpopulations are not known. Studies of the growth and development of Samoan children have revealed few growth-related differences between them and children of European ancestry. Indeed, comparison of the Western Samoan figures with the U.S. means for the same age groups suggests that there are few differences, at least until middle age (Pawson 1986). However, based on data from American Samoa, Samoan children evidence a rapid weight gain in the first four months of life (Bindon and Zansky 1986). Baker and Hanna (1986) speculate that some environmental factor, prob-

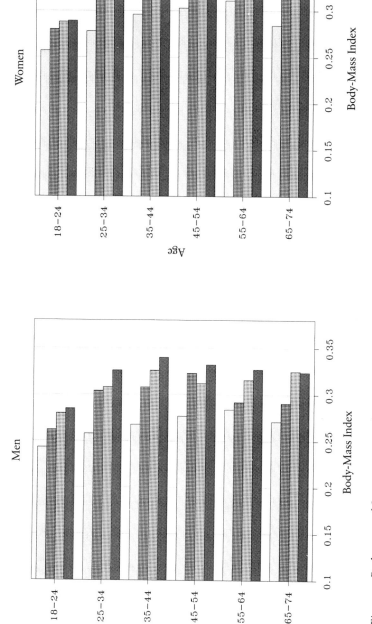

Fig. 1.2. Body mass of Samoan men and women by subpopulation. Based on data in Ivan G. Pawson, "The Morphological Characteristics of Samoan Adults," in Paul T. Baker, Joel M. Hanna, and Thelma S. Baker, eds., *The Changing Samoans* (New York: Oxford University Press, 1986).

ably nutritional, sustains this weight gain during infancy into the adolescent years in the more modernized subpopulations.

Studies of Samoan diet have been undertaken in differentially urbanized communities in Western Samoa, in the remote Manuan village of Ta'u, and among a small sample in Hawaii (Hanna, Pelletier, and Brown 1986). In Western Samoa Pelletier (1984) studied three groups of men: rural residents of Upolu (village of Salea'aumua), wage laborers employed in physically demanding occupations, and sedentary workers employed in Apia. Although the three groups differed from one another in body mass and adiposity, Pelletier found no difference in the proportion of macronutrients consumed. Protein, fat, and carbohydrate comprised approximately 10, 30, and 60 percent of the men's diets, respectively. Overall calories varied by subgroup, however, with, as one would expect, the more active consuming more than the more sedentary. Differences in caloric intake corresponded with energy expenditure in each of the subgroups with one important exception: adherence by the sedentary workers to the custom of Sunday feasting (*to'ona'i*) resulted in an excess of energy intake that was not compensated for during weekly activities. The continuation of Sunday feasting in the modernizing and migrant populations, which will be discussed in Chapter 5, suggests that it may be a determinant of overnutrition in these settings as well. Pelletier (1984) concludes that differences in body mass and fatness reflect differences in energy expenditure rather than energy intake.

Studies of residents of Ta'u, a village in the outlying Manua group of American Samoa that is considered "traditional," and of Samoans living on Oahu, Hawaii, yield comparable findings. No consistent patterns in macronutrient consumption were found that reflected the migration/modernization experience (Bindon 1984; Brown et al. 1984). The major dietary change occurring with modernization is a greater diversity of foods, a pattern consistent with modernization in other parts of the world. The level of obesity in Samoan subpopulations appears to be related more to systematic differences in energy expenditure than to diet (Bindon 1981; Pelletier and Hornick 1986).

One important question is whether obesity carries with it the same risk for morbidity and mortality in modernizing subpopulations as it does in populations of industrialized countries. In the Samoan Studies Project much of the research on morbidity patterns has focused on cardiovascular risk factors. Diet and physical activity influence health not only through adiposity, but through the mechanism of fat transport in the blood. Investigators have scrutinized blood lipids among various subgroups in Western Samoa, American Samoa, and Hawaii (Hornick 1979; Hornick and Hanna 1982; Lukaski 1977; Pelletier 1984; Pelletier and Hornick 1986).

Several of the studies focused on the relationship between diet, body morphology, physical activity, and plasma lipid concentrations.

A comparison of Western and American Samoans with migrants to Hawaii shows few differences in total and HDL cholesterol concentrations for men or women.* Although the urban populations exhibit somewhat higher total cholesterol levels, the variation across the subpopulations is less than might be expected from other studies of modernizing populations (e.g., Reed and Stallones 1970). The most striking finding is that despite the modernizing Samoans' obesity and high intake of saturated fats, they have significantly lower cholesterol and triglyceride levels than people of European heritage (Pelletier and Hornick 1986). These results suggest that the obesity-cardiovascular disease link in Samoans is somewhat less direct than has been suggested for Caucasian groups.

The characteristic that has received the greatest attention from researchers has been blood pressure. At the time of this writing (1987), blood pressure measurements had been made on some 3,000 Samoan adults, in settings ranging from rural agricultural villages in Western Samoa to urban California. Together with measurements of sociodemographic characteristics and body morphology, these data permit a rather detailed look at the relationship of modernization to blood pressure within and across populations.

Figure 1.3 illustrates the mean blood pressures by age for subpopulations of Samoan adults. The groups studied were the residents of two villages in rural Upolu (studied in 1979) and 23 villages on Tutuila (1976); eight communities on the island of Oahu, Hawaii (1975–77); and members of seven communities (churches in urban California (1979–83). This book is based on 104 of the adults included in the California subsample shown in Table 1.1.[†]

Table 1.1 shows the prevalence of hypertension among the Samoans living in Western Samoa, Tutuila, Hawaii, and California. The age-specific rates of definite hypertension are based on the standard epidemiologic

---

* Cholesterol in the blood plasma does not occur in a free state, but is carried by lipoprotein fractions. Lipoproteins are conjugated proteins consisting of simple proteins combined with lipid components. The lipoproteins are of varying density; epidemiologically significant are the so-called "high density" (HDL) and "low density" lipoproteins (LDL). In humans, serum cholesterol is carried primarily by the low-density lipoprotein. However, some cholesterol is carried by the high-density lipoprotein, and the proportion of HDL to total cholesterol varies among individuals and between populations. Although the mechanism of action has yet to be defined, the proportion of HDL cholesterol to total cholesterol has been found to be *inversely* correlated with atherosclerosis, and thus heart disease. That is, the higher the HDL-cholesterol fraction, the lower the risk of disease. Studies conducted in the United States suggest that higher HDL fractions are positively correlated with, among other things, exercise.

† See Janes and Pawson (1986) for a description of the different stages of research conducted in the California Samoan community.

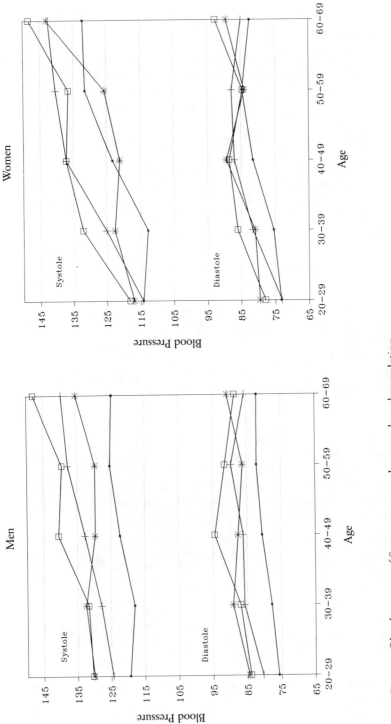

Fig. 1.3. Blood pressure of Samoan men and women by subpopulation. Based on data in Stephen T. McGarvey and Diane E. Schendel, "Blood Pressures of Samoans," in Paul T. Baker et al. (see Fig. 1.2).

TABLE 1.1
Prevalence of Definite Hypertension Among Samoans in Western Samoa,
Tutuila, Hawaii, and California by Age Group

Group	18–34 years	35–54 years	55+ years	All ages
MEN				
Western Samoans	122	79	41	242
Hypertensives	3	6	7	19
Percent	2.4%	7.6%	17.1%	7.9%
Tutuilans	132	121	88	341
Hypertensives	9	35	23	67
Percent	6.8%	28.9%	26.2%	19.6%
Hawaiians	115	94	46	255
Hypertensives	20	27	11	58
Percent	17.4%	28.7%	23.9%	22.7%
Californians	36	84	46	166
Hypertensives	6	34	12	52
Percent	16.7%	40.4%	26.1%	31.4%
U.S. hypertensive rate	5.9%	19.1%	35.3%	21.0%
WOMEN				
Western Samoans	131	90	58	279
Hypertensives	1	8	9	18
Percent	0.7%	8.9%	15.5%	6.5%
Tutuilans	169	167	83	419
Hypertensives	6	38	21	65
Percent	3.6%	22.8%	25.3%	15.5%
Hawaiians	96	107	40	343
Hypertensives	12	26	8	46
Percent	12.5%	24.3%	20.0%	13.4%
Californians	57	65	37	159
Hypertensives	2	15	12	29
Percent	3.5%	23.1%	32.4%	18.2%
U.S. hypertensive rate	3.0%	18.0%	43.6%	23.5%

SOURCES: Western Samoa, Tutuila, and Hawaii, Stephen T. McGarvey and Diane E. Schendel, "Blood Pressures of Samoans," in Paul T. Baker, Joel M. Hanna, and Thelma S. Baker, eds., *The Changing Samoans* (New York: Oxford University Press, 1986); California, Craig R. Janes and Ivan G. Pawson, "Migration and Biocultural Adaptation: Samoans in California," *Social Science and Medicine* 22 (1986): 821–34 (the data include the 104 men and women discussed in this book); U.S., Terence Drizd, A. L. Dannenberg, and A. Engel, "Blood Pressure Levels in Persons 18–74 Years of Age in 1976–1980 and Trends in Blood Pressure from 1960–1980 in the United States," *Vital and Health Statistics*, series 11, no. 234, DHHS Pub. No. (PHS) 86–1684 (Washington, D.C.: Government Printing Office, 1986).

NOTE: Definite hypertension is defined as a systolic pressure greater than 160 mm/Hg and/or a diastolic pressure greater than 95 mm/Hg.

criterion of systolic blood pressure greater than 160 mm/Hg or diastolic blood pressure greater than 95 mm/Hg. Table 1.1 indicates that the proportions of hypertensives among the migrant and urban subpopulations, particularly in the 35 and over age groups, are strikingly high in comparison with the rural Western Samoan group. Of particular interest is the comparison of the Samoan rates to the rates for the 1976–80 U.S.

population, which are representative of the high rates of hypertension found in Western, industrialized nations. In the 35–54 age group the rates for the urban and migrant Samoan subpopulations exceed those for the United States. It is this aged 35–54 Samoan cohort that has been subject to the greatest degree of social and environmental change in the form of urbanization, development, and migration (see Chapter 2).

One notes in Figure 1.3 an overall association of place of residence with blood pressure. For most age groups there is a clear gradient in both systolic and diastolic blood pressure from least to most modernized groups. The Hawaii group, though, does not generally fit into this modernization gradient; in most cases, Hawaii Samoans have blood pressures similar to the Tutuilans'. The anomaly is most probably due to the tremendous variation in both the Tutuilan and Hawaii Samoans' living circumstances (ranging from rural to urban), and thus considerable variance in exposure to "modernizing influences" (McGarvey and Schendel 1986), including exposure to stress. Although the data tend to point to the important role of obesity in the distribution of high blood pressure in all the subpopulations studied, variation between the subpopulations in the significance of obesity as a risk factor (see Pawson and Janes 1982) suggests that additional factors should be considered risk factors for hypertension both in interaction with and independent of body mass.

Because stress had not been analyzed intensively and in detail in relation to blood pressure or other health indicators in the early phases of the Samoan Studies Project, I undertook in 1982 to assess the relationship of migration, social change, stress, and health in the California Samoan community. Since the community was suffering economically, I hypothesized that stress played a significant etiological role in the high rate of hypertension noted above and possibly also in the levels of general ill-health in the community.

Data Collection

My fieldwork with the migrant community of the San Francisco area began in earnest in early 1982 and was largely completed by the fall of 1983. From 1983 to 1985 I continued to work in the Samoan community, in a variety of capacities, and was able to collect a significant amount of ethnographic data to supplement that already gathered. In the first of these two stages of data collection, I was interested in conducting the kind of community ethnography that is typical of anthropological research. I also wanted to sketch out culturally specific adaptive patterns in qualitative terms. To this end I chose a "community" and became involved in it as a participant-observer. The concept of community is often a difficult one to define in urban settings, but happily, it was easy enough in this case: Samoans themselves define the church congregation as an urban village (see Tofaeono 1978). I selected a large and well-established congregation that by all accounts (from Samoans as well as anthropologists) was typical of others in the area. It was of the Congregational denomination (formerly the London Missionary Society) and was affiliated with the Samoan Congregational Church organization, not its American (predominantly white) counterpart. As part of this community I participated in group events and at one point accompanied a group of migrants when they returned to Samoa for a visit. Consequently, I not only was able to observe their change in behavior, but could also compare their accounts of island life with my own observations.

In August 1982, while still quite involved in community life, I began the second phase of my research—to interview formally a representative sample of Samoan adults. I was interested not only in obtaining information that would permit testing the stress-health relationship, but in gathering quantitative data on economic issues, household composition, and kinship-based activities. All together, I interviewed 115 adults from 70 households selected at random from the lists of several Congregational church congregations. To maximize variance in blood pressure and other health indexes, individuals younger than 30 were excluded.* In addition, I selected a nonprobability "opportunity" sample of members of other religious denominations, particularly Mormon. I never found a migrant who did not claim membership in some church, though there was significant variation in church participation. All things considered, the sample was a representative one of Samoans in the San Francisco area. Probably more of my informants were from the remote American Samoa islands of Manua than is true of the general population, but as I will discuss later, point of origin is obscured by other, more significant cultural factors, such as extended residence and employment in the urbanizing areas around the main port town of Fagatogo. Table 1.2 gives the ages and age of migration of the 104 people in the final sample.

The formal interviews focused on migration history, housing and employment history, helping networks both during migration and after, so-

---

* This study gives quantitative data on only 104 of those informants, 47 women and 57 men. Eleven interviews were not coded for lack of data because of language problems or the informant's reluctance to answer important questions. These excluded interviews were primarily of older people who had been on the mainland just a short time. Since the interviews were incomplete, it is difficult to tell if their exclusion biases the sample. I believe that it does not, since the migration of the elderly is a fairly recent phenomenon, and they constitute a small minority of the total population. Their significant presence in my sample is a result of the fact that the elderly are more likely to be at home and thus be included in a household sample than younger individuals.

TABLE 1.2
Age and Age at Migration of 104 Bay Area Samoans

Category	Men (N = 57)		Women (N = 47)	
	Number	Percent	Number	Percent
Age				
30–39	13	22.8%	15	31.9%
40–49	17	29.8	11	23.4
50+	27	47.4	21	44.7
Age at migration				
0–11	0	0%	2	4.3%
12–20	7	12.2	8	17.0
21–30	26	45.6	14	29.8
31–40	12	21.1	9	19.1
41+	12	21.1	14	29.8

cial networks, involvement in cultural affairs, household income and expenditures, an inventory of life difficulties (like a stressful-events scale but specific to the Samoan context), routine leisure activities, and self-reported health problems. The interviews ranged anywhere from one to five hours; most were completed in one sitting. Blood pressure and other medical data were obtained at the conclusion of the interview. Chapter 7 describes in greater detail the different measures of health used in the study. (For the interview schedule, see the Appendix, pp. 175–82.)

After the conclusion of these interviews, I maintained contact with the Samoan community and with the majority of my informants. Though involved in other activities and other kinds of research by then, I continued to learn about the Samoan community and was able to fill in a few of the gaps left by my earlier ethnographic research. These data are included where appropriate.

The two sets of data I gathered not only allowed me to test the stress-health relationship, but permitted scrutiny of the process of cultural adaptation to urban American society. The chapters that follow chronicle this process, beginning with the determinants and contexts of Samoan migration to California (Chapter 2). Chapter 3 discusses the settlement and initial adaptation responses of the migrants and shows how these changed over time. Chapters 4–6 examine stateside Samoan society, focusing specifically on those institutions and processes that affect health. Chapter 7 deals with the stress-health relationship, and Chapter 8 evaluates the role of social support and other cultural resources in buffering the effects of stress. Chapter 9 turns from a focus on stress to the matter of health-care utilization, focusing in particular on the interaction of Samoans with formal American health-care institutions, and how this interaction may affect morbidity and mortality patterns. In Chapter 10 I return to address the idea of stress as an explanatory variable in the Samoan community as well as other changing societies.

TWO

From Village to City: Samoan Migration to California

The Samoan archipelago lies at the western edge of the "Polynesian Triangle," between 13° and 15° south latitude and 168° and 173° west longitude (see Fig. 2.1). The inhabited islands are of volcanic origin, and in American Samoa particularly, the habitable coastal fringe is overshadowed by steep, rugged mountains shaped by volcanic activity. At the westernmost part of the chain lie the two largest islands, Savaii and Upolu; together they contain approximately 1,100 square miles of land, of which only a small fraction is suitable for cultivation. Upolu, the more fertile of the two, supports a population in excess of 100,000. Upolu, Savaii, and the two tiny islands of Manono and Apolima that lie between them constitute the independent country of Western Samoa.

Some 80 miles to the east of Upolu lies Tutuila, the main island of American Samoa. Tutuila is a long and mostly narrow strip of land with a spine of extremely steep and rugged mountains. These mountains drop precipitously in many places, to form small valleys and narrow coastal strips, where the majority of the population lives. In the total land area of 50 square miles, there are scarcely more than a few square miles of cultivable land. As one rides along the single coastal road, it is not uncommon to see taro plantations growing on nearly vertical canyon walls. The most striking feature of Tutuila, and one that figures prominently in its colonial history, is the large, well-protected, and deep-water harbor at Pago Pago. In 1984 Tutuila supported a population of about 30,000. By then, cash income from two tuna canneries plus the considerable influx of money for U.S. government programs had resulted in a considerable shift away from subsistence agriculture.

Some 80 to 100 miles off the eastern tip of Tutuila lie the small islands of the Manua group: Ofu, Olosega, and Ta'u. Though the three together support only a small population of just over 2,000, Manua (the group is

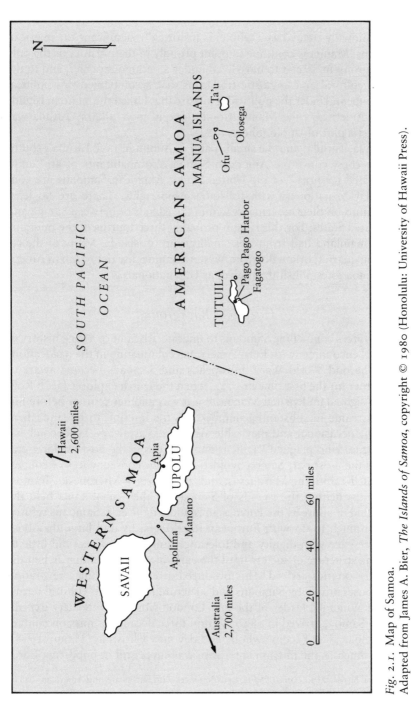

Fig. 2.1. Map of Samoa.
Adapted from James A. Bier, *The Islands of Samoa,* copyright © 1980 (Honolulu: University of Hawaii Press).

conventionally treated as a whole) is historically significant to American Samoans. Manuans continue to point proudly to their history as the only island group in Samoa to have lived under a paramount chief, and to the unique cultural and linguistic traditions that accompanied this political development. Under the political structure that linked the Samoan islands before American rule, Manua stood alone in most affairs; Tutuila was then just a part of Upolu (Shore 1982).

Manua, Tutuila, and the small island of Aunuu just off Tutuila's southeastern coast constitute American Samoa. As inhabitants of an "unincorporated territory" of the United States, American Samoans are considered U.S. nationals with full citizenship rights. There are no legal restrictions on their movements within the islands or between Samoa and the United States. For this reason probably three-fourths of the migrants to the mainland hail from this small group of islands. Many of the remaining quarter, originally from Western Samoa, use ties to kin in American Samoa to establish themselves as U.S. nationals.

Historical Background

The forces compelling Samoans to migrate arise out of a long history of colonial encounters with Euro-Americans culminating in the dislocations of the Second World War.* Europeans and Samoans became aware of each other for the first time in 1722, when the Dutch explorer Jacob Roggeveen sighted and visited Manua. But it was another century before Europeans came in substantial numbers. In the interim, to be sure, there were the occasional and inevitable arrivals of castaways, beachcombers, and rogues who plagued Pacific island societies in the post-explorer era. But for the most part Samoa avoided the tragic consequences of contact that befell Tahiti, the Marquesas, and some parts of Micronesia. To most Europeans neither the islands of Samoa nor their inhabitants held the same kind of allure as the Polynesian islands to the east. Samoans refused to have much to do with European interlopers; by and large they bore their presence with dignity and tolerance. European contact did little to alter the structure of society until the early nineteenth century, when the first missionaries arrived. This produced a revolution, but a revolution led almost entirely by Samoans and structured in Samoan cultural terms.

John Williams, leader of the first London Missionary Society expedition to Samoa, arrived in 1830. Within three decades of mission contact the Samoans had become wholly and devoutly Christian (Tiffany 1978). But as much as the mission enterprise was successful in importing Euro-

* Good historical accounts of Samoan experiences with Europeans and Americans can be found in Gray (1960) and Keesing (1934).

pean Christian ideas and some institutional characteristics of the European religious system, missionaries were singularly unsuccessful in keeping Samoans from shaping Christianity to suit their own tastes. As Oliver (1961: 213) notes in his comprehensive cultural history of the Pacific:

In Samoa, where religion was never so highly institutionalized as elsewhere in Polynesia, the mission teachers simply replaced native priests in the new system, and the *matais* [chiefs], formerly the families' intercessors with supernatural forces, simply became deacons in village churches. Ultimately the Protestant congregations developed into peculiarly Samoan native-church organizations, possessing many local twists in doctrine and practice.

Following close on the heels of the missionaries were Europeans with more secular goals in mind. German, British, and to a lesser extent, American entrepreneurs established trading posts in the islands with the goal of exploiting Samoa's natural and human resources. Conflicts inevitably occurred between the trading nations, and by the 1880's these had reached crisis proportions. The fortuitous interference of a hurricane in 1889 kept the three powers from an armed confrontation, and cooler heads prevailed. Britain eventually withdrew to pursue interests elsewhere in the Pacific, Germany extended government control over the Western islands of Upolu and Savaii, and the U.S. military took over Tutuila and Manua. Germany surrendered control of the Western islands to New Zealand after the First World War, and in 1962 Western Samoa was granted independence.

Until the beginning of the Second World War, American Samoa was governed by the U.S. Navy with a kind of benign neglect. Local entrepreneurship was not supported; social, educational, and public health services were provided only sporadically and often paid for by the Samoans themselves; there were no attempts at social or economic development; and the Samoans were kept isolated, left largely to go about their own business. Oliver (1961: 334) comments:

Paternalistic naval rule had ill-prepared the Samoans for participation in the hard competitive world they would have to face unless they were to be kept always as museum pieces. . . . So dependent, in fact, had they become upon Naval facilities in every aspect of living that [Samoans] formally requested of a congressional commission that the United States create a trust fund of one million dollars for the benefit of American Samoa, asserting that generous handouts of this nature constituted the "practice and policy all over the world by all governments"!

But for the most part Samoans steadfastly went their own way and sought their own satisfactions. In both Samoas the changes wrought by a century of Western domination were slight. Samoans tended to take what they wanted from the aliens, but acceded not at all to demands made on them by governments in areas that were not perceived to be their business. In fact, as anthropologists have suggested, the Samoan response to pressures for change has been conservative; external forces or opportunities for innovation often resulted in a new consolidation and reaffirmation by Samoans of their own cultural values (Keesing 1934; Rolff 1978; Shankman 1976). As the Second World War approached, it could thus be said for both Samoas that they had survived the worst aspects of Western cultural domination without "losing their numbers, their strength, their dignity, or their zest for a good controversy" (Oliver 1961: 220).

The war had a sudden and profound impact on Samoan society. It was not so much the actual conflict that caused this upheaval as the presence of vast numbers of mostly American troops, accompanied by the products of a highly technological society and its monetary largesse. The concentration of American troops was especially high on the small island of Tutuila, which was a major staging and supply depot for American military forces. Within weeks after Pearl Harbor, Tutuila was transformed from a sleepy outpost to a major military installation. Military leaders feared for a short time that Japan might attack Samoa for its harbor facilities, and the U.S. invasion of Guadalcanal was staged in part from the Navy facilities at Pago Pago.

Tutuilans lived in a virtual armed camp, where American Marines at one point reportedly outnumbered them. Manua did not share this fate, but it was deeply affected nevertheless, for substantial numbers of its young and middle-aged men were drawn to Tutuila to participate in war-related activities. Many worked as stevedores on the docks, and others worked on road building and construction crews. Nearly 1,000 men joined the "home guard" (the Fita Fita), or a reserve Marine unit called the Samoan Marines (Malini). Schools were closed and buildings commandeered for use as barracks and supply depots, and for other purposes. A paved road was built along the south coast from one end of the island to the other. Roads were also thrown across the steep mountain interior at a few places, bringing remote villages to within a day's walk of the port town of Fagatogo.

The infusion of large quantities of cash into the Samoan economy had direct and long-lasting effects. The copra industry ceased during the war, but an unprecedented amount of money from military-related wage labor found its way to nearly every family in American Samoa. The presence of U.S. troops with little to do but spend money brought a new wave of prosperity to local merchants and provided a ready market for Samoan crafts. The war brought, in no uncertain terms, a monetary economy into American Samoa and left it relatively rich. "The [American Samoan] government's surplus, carefully invested, made it one of the few governments in the world which was more prosperous in 1945 than it had been in 1941" (Gray 1960: 245).

After the war many Samoans returned to their subsistence activities and the world they had known; but Samoans and Samoa would never be the same. Young men who had seen Hawaii and points beyond were anxious to see more of the world. Many members of the Fita Fita and the Malini chose to migrate to Honolulu or California to enlist in the U.S. armed services. For a time the U.S. Marines and Army guaranteed reimbursement of air or boat fare to Samoans who could pass the entrance exams.

Samoans had also acquired a taste for material assets far beyond their ability to pay. Young people crowded into the rapidly growing Pago Pago area looking for wage-paying jobs to satisfy their appetite for American clothes, canned foods, beer, and motion pictures. But falling exports and rising import prices seriously affected the local economy, and the number of wage-earning jobs available to Samoans was sharply reduced. The majority of remaining positions were with the U.S. Navy or supported directly by Navy funds. It became apparent to many future-oriented Samoans that migration to Hawaii or California was the alternative of choice for anyone seeking a job, an education, or escape from what some perceived as the chafing confines of village life.

Life in the villages was also affected by rising population. Public health programs that accompanied the war effort improved village sanitation and all but eliminated filariasis.* Accessible clinic facilities were established in nearly every district, and Samoans became increasingly aware of the benefits of medical care. The death rate fell from 24 per 1,000 in 1912 to 8 per 1,000 in 1949. The annual birth rate stayed at 40 children per 1,000 through this period, resulting in a threefold population increase between 1900 and 1950, from about 6,000 to nearly 19,000 persons. For the first time Samoans experienced some crowding and a need to expand their subsistence activities. For young men and women, particularly, the competition for positions of status and prestige became fierce. And to those young men who bridled under the authority of the family chief, migration became an attractive alternative to staying at home and pursuing status and prestige along conventional paths (Gray 1960; Lewthwaite et al. 1973).

The Navy's decision in 1951 to terminate its operations in Pago Pago

* A chronic disease caused by a mosquito-borne parasitic nematode (in Samoa: *Wuchereria bancrofti*). Typically, the parasite infests the lymphatic vessels and organs, the circulatory system, and subcutaneous tissues, resulting after some time in about 5 percent of the cases in the condition popularly known as elephantiasis. Filariasis is still endemic in some parts of the Pacific but has been virtually eradicated from both American and Western Samoa (see Desowitz 1976).

and transfer civilian personnel and their families stateside served more than any other to trigger the massive migration of American Samoans to Hawaii and California. With the Navy went many of the remaining wage-earning opportunities. When the last transport called at Pago Pago in 1952 to pick up dependents of military men and civilian employees who had been transferred to Hawaii, authorities were faced with something of a rush: almost 1,000 Samoans embarked for Honolulu to join relatives or to enlist in military service.

By 1960 Samoa was seized by migration fever. It was not just military experience, education, or employment that migrants sought, but something far less tangible. Many people left with nothing else in mind save for the idea that migration was necessary to secure a future for themselves and their families. Gifted young people were encouraged to migrate for further education in Hawaii or on the mainland, and others were simply propelled by the belief that all things in Samoa were inferior to what was to be had on the mainland. By the early 1960's it was clear that migration was becoming institutionalized as a rite of passage for young Samoans. In 1962, for example, the prerequisites for being elected to a chiefly title, especially a high one, had expanded from a knowledge of ancient lore, speaking ability, and political savvy to include education, wage-earning experience and ability, and status as a migrant (Holmes 1964). Consequently, promising young men in line for higher titles went abroad for the requisite education and job experience. One man I met on my trip to Tutuila in 1982 said he had been sent to Fiji to learn skills as a medical practitioner, then to Hawaii, where he eventually earned a master's degree in sociology. He returned to take one of the highest titles in his district and became one of the most powerful men in the government of American Samoa.

Emigration was so great by 1970, particularly in the productive age categories, that subsistence agriculture nearly disappeared. Income from remittances, local government employment, a growing tuna-canning industry, small-scale entrepreneurial activities, and other wage-earning opportunities had made it possible for many families to purchase much of their food. Today, agricultural labor is universally disdained by young men, and local fisheries have declined because of overfishing. Consequently, most food is now imported from Western Samoa, Hawaii, and the mainland. Canned food and drinks have replaced products native to Samoa. When I observed the market in Fagatogo on several occasions in the summer of 1982, I found very limited amounts of local produce or fish for sale; what little was available was imported from Western Samoa. One man, a migrant who gave me a tour of Tutuila, showed me his now-overgrown family lands, saying at one point along the way "someone should really take care of this land, but everybody is in San Francisco. . . . Those who stay here are too busy or too lazy to climb up the mountain. It is easier just to go to the store."

The first migrants to leave Samoa were predominantly young and male, reflecting the large numbers of men who left to join or work for the military (Lewthwaite et al. 1973). A military career was not seen as appropriate for young women. By the late 1950's the ratio of men to women migrants had equalized, but the age of the migrants remained young— between the ages of 18 and 30. Though few sociodemographic data on Samoan migration exist, my data suggest that the very first cohort of migrants was mostly made up of single males. Within a few years, by the late 1950's and early 1960's, these unmarried male migrants were replaced by young couples and women moving to join now-established spouses or families. Many unmarried young women also came to help their relatives with child care and household chores. This trend continued, though the average migrant leaving Samoa after 1970 tended to be older. I met elderly parents in several households who had recently migrated to live or visit children and other kin.

In sum, the Second World War worked profound changes on Samoan society. The most evident and lasting effect was the infusion of cash into a subsistence economy. This led directly to what Lewthwaite, Mainzer, and Holland (1973) call a "revolution of rising expectations." Once Samoans experienced the luxuries and freedoms that a cash income provided there was no turning back. When the Navy left in 1951, taking with it the majority of island employment opportunities, the dam was broken. Yet during this time Samoans remained largely committed to those aspects of their culture they considered superior: kinship and family, religion, systems of leadership, and family rituals and events. As they had done throughout their colonial history, Samoans integrated what they liked about the new with what they admired of the old.

To be sure, urbanization and the monetization of Samoan society introduced some cultural variability into American Samoa.* The most evident differences are in the political system, due primarily to an erosion of the leaders' (*matai*) authority over their extended families. This is a consequence of descent groups' shifting away from dependence on agricultural land for subsistence, which the matai controls, to reliance on wage income. A source of steady cash income gives the wage earner considerable

---

* Curiously, cultural variability in Samoa—both within American Samoa and between it and the Western islands—has not been subject to much detailed examination (witness Freeman's [1983] attack on Mead in which he argues that the entire archipelago is culturally homogenous). Franklin Young (1972) compares American and Western Samoans, but at the time of this writing the only examination of variation within American Samoa in any detail dated back to 1955–56 (Ember 1964).

economic and thus political independence. Much of the cultural differentiation that exists today can be traced to the extent to which villages, and within them families, have been incorporated into the cash economy (see, e.g., Ember 1964). Today, as in the past, the center of capitalist economic activity is in the urbanized zone surrounding Fagatogo.

Fa'asamoa: The Cultural Background of Samoan Migrants

The basic social and political unit of Samoan society is the village (*nu'u*), or in the case of very large villages, the subvillage (*pitonu'u*). Villages were historically—and are still largely—autonomous. Intravillage conflicts and disputes are adjudicated by councils consisting of titled family heads, or matai. Village-wide associations of young men and women (the *'aumaga* and *aualuma*) cooperate in carrying out local public-works projects, preparing for ceremonial affairs, and feeding and entertaining visiting groups from other villages. Laws and regulations are promulgated by village chiefs, and violations are handled within the village, though the matai's reduced political control has limited their powers of enforcement somewhat (Ember 1964). Even in villages that have been incorporated into growing urban areas, the autonomy of the village as a political unit, and more important, as an aspect of individual identity, has remained intact (Hirsch 1958; Holmes 1964; Tiffany 1974).

The constituent units of the village are local cognatic descent groups usually referred to by the generic term *'aiga*. This word can be interpreted as extended family, household, a kinsman, or simply shared kinship. Shore (1982) suggests that the organization of a village is most appropriately defined as the matai and the set of household "clusters" they head. He calls the cluster the *'au'aiga*, or literally "group of kin." But this is a somewhat awkward usage, is not much more precise than 'aiga, and is confusing when applied to Samoan kinship structure as it exists outside the islands. I follow convention here and use the term 'aiga to refer to a village's cognatic descent group. For a group of related 'aiga, or the entire body of people to which a person can trace consanguinity, I use the anthropological term kindred. The generic English term family is used when it is necessary to distinguish the nuclear family from the 'aiga or a personal kindred. These distinctions are not quite so important for describing the social organization of a Samoan village, but they are crucial to understanding how Samoans organize themselves outside Samoa; hence they need to be preserved in this study.

Most members of an 'aiga are close cognatic kin and affines, but there are often more distant kin in temporary residence, for people are wont to exercise rights to hospitality and membership in any 'aiga to which they can trace kinship. Membership in an 'aiga provides individuals with cooperative use of land; they also have the potential of attaining leadership status, since membership confers access to a title in the 'aiga. Membership in an 'aiga is never fixed. Anyone belonging to a local 'aiga also belongs potentially to many others as well. These may be dispersed throughout several villages. But many potential memberships are not activated because, "it would be most difficult, if not impossible, for an individual to meet the political, economic, and psychological obligations involved in maintaining active memberships in all 'aiga to which he could conceivably claim consanguinity" (Tiffany 1974: 36). Individuals generally collapse the number of links to other local descent groups by simply referring to relationships as falling on "sides." It is common to hear the father's side of the kindred referred to as the "strong" side (*itu malosi*), and the mother's as the "weak" side (*itu vaivai*), indicating some preference for patrilineality. In actuality, however, people typically activate ties with the local 'aiga in which they are raised and remain in it unless marriage and/or profit dictates doing otherwise (Holmes 1974; Mead 1930; Shore 1982; Tiffany 1974).

'Aiga are identified with a particular village. Although some members may be living elsewhere, the core of the 'aiga—often centered about brothers—remains in the village, occupying land that belongs historically to its matai. The most important dimension of Samoan descent and social organization is that membership in a localized segment is maintained through active participation, and that one's potential membership in other groups is allowed to lapse or remain latent until activated for some purpose. Migration is one way that Samoans use latent kinship ties. Ritual and social activities also bring together, for a time, dispersed members of an 'aiga; most important are rites of passage such as marriages or funerals and formal meetings where successors to a vacant title are chosen by the full kindred (*'aiga potopoto*; literally, "assembling kindred"). All 'aiga members are bound by mutual rights and obligations that include participation in kindred events and economic or political support when it is needed.

Each local 'aiga has its own matai, vested with the power to make economic decisions affecting the family, particularly the use of land, and to represent the family in the village council and as a spokesman on special occasions requiring formal oratory or a ceremonial exchange of goods. A highly ranked matai may be the leader, symbolically, of the entire dispersed network of cognatically related kin.* All matai are also hierarchi-

* Political ranking in Samoa is too complex to go into here. Speaking very generally, matai titles vary in rank according to the seniority with which descent can be traced from an apical ancestor. A senior matai may be related to junior titles and often has the discretion to appoint these lesser title holders. Shore's (1982) account of Samoan politics is the best to date.

cally related to other matai in a village political system. Shore (1982: 59) describes the matai as

a person empowered through possession of a chiefly name or title, with authority (*pule*) over lands and people. The power of the chief lies not so much in the personal qualities of the holder (though these can significantly affect the title's power and dignity), but rather in the title itself; a name confers power on its holder. All chiefs share a number of characteristics, including possession of a title, pule within both kinship groups and villages, and a general honor and dignity that attaches to his title. Matai are also importantly different from each other in terms of rank, general prestige, and power, and in the kind of power they possess.

Each title gives its holder control over lands currently under cultivation and within the village where houses are located. The matai approves and commissions the building of houses on the village lands he controls. In theory one title may overlap with another in terms of landownership, but in practice residence and use have precedence over theoretical political rights (Mead 1930). Matai also have authority over the actions of individuals within an 'aiga. This authority takes the form of assigning tasks related to feeding the 'aiga and keeping up the structures and garden lands. Also important are village or ceremonial events in which the 'aiga participates. Contributions for funerals, weddings, church dedications, and so forth, as well as allocating labor for cooperative village projects, are under the control of the matai. Finally, the matai is responsible for the behavior of his descent group and culpable for the delicts of its members.

The title a matai holds indicates the kind and extent of power he has in relation to other matai in the village and district. Some matai are called *ali'i*, which has no exact English translation but is usually defined as "nobleman," or one who possesses the power to command. Others are called *tulafale*, theoretically orators for the ali'i, who wield the active "executive power that we [Americans] recognize as explicitly political" (Shore 1982: 59). The categories of tulafale and ali'i are exclusive; that is, the rank of a matai title is determined in relation only to others within the same category. The ranking of the most senior matai, of either category, is typically related to historical and/or mythological relationships to, and lines of descent from, a senior ancestor or group of ancestors. "High" titles can often be traced from apical ancestors; lesser titles have more obscure origins and are often defined by their relationship to a senior title in the same 'aiga.

The principles of cognatic descent give individuals the choice of activating ties to different 'aiga and thus of maximizing their access to economic and political position. The utmost in authority, power, and prestige in this society hinges on its matai system. Access to titles is open to most men who possess the motivation, intelligence, personality, and skills for leadership. Although women can and do occasionally hold titles, their power on the whole resides in their ability to veto the election of men to titles. Women participate in the decision-making process.

The village and district hierarchy of chiefs is represented in a formal stylized system of address known as *fa'alupega*. The fa'alupega may serve, as suggested by Mead (1930), as a mnemonic for ordering rank relationships based on a hypothetical meeting of a "great fono." However, terms of address are not determinate or invariant, but open to change and restructuring depending on the speaker's purpose and the context in which they are used. Fa'alupega remain extremely important to this day, and on the mainland migrants, particularly those in leadership positions, must remember with great accuracy the fa'alupega of the many villages and districts that sponsor traveling groups to California and Hawaii. A poorly remembered or presented fa'alupega at the conclusion of a welcoming speech is an insult to the visitors and causes the speaker and the group he represents great shame.

Samoan villages are very public places, and it is in the public sphere that Samoans emphasize the proper organization and orderliness of behavior. Individuals are expected to abide by a set of precepts that carry legal and moral force. "In a well-run village, life is *maopoopo* (well-ordered), and the lives of its residents are *puipuia* (protected or, literally, 'walled in') by customary institutions" (Shore 1982: 118). Samoans rely on the publicness of behavior to deter antisocial acts and ensure conformity. The public pronouncement of crime and punishment, as well as village gossip, is a powerful instrument for social control and conformity. One of the major changes that occur after migration is the dispersal of 'aiga members into private, "single family" dwellings that are relatively impervious to the prying eyes of other Samoans. Although 'aiga members are aware of a large portion of their relatives' lives, and the church provides an urban setting where gossip and public opinion continue to be powerful methods of social control, individuals have ample opportunity to escape the confines and constraints of the public Samoan world. This appears to be particularly important to adolescents, who by virtue of school and school activities are able to escape the control ("eyes") of their parents and relatives. Public pressures for conformity to ideal behavioral patterns can be expected to weaken substantially with urban living.

In this sketchy account of Samoan culture and society (and often in more detailed accounts), the impression of a fixed and invariant social system may be erroneously conveyed. In fact Samoan social and political organization is so flexible that despite a half-century of anthropological scrutiny, writers continue to debate and confuse certain basic issues (see Freeman 1983; Shore 1982). These debates appear to stem primarily from the tendency of scholars to "fix" Samoan social action in space and time, to construct a static and normative view of Samoan social structure. However, as Shore (1982) argues, Samoan social organization is context-dependent; apparent contradictions can often be explained by "looking to the relations" of who is present in a certain situation, and for what purposes. Samoan society also has an open and flexible quality that puzzles outsiders looking to describe some invariant truth about social behavior.*

To migrants the Samoan cultural system provides a framework for interpreting urban life and organizing social relations. Although Samoa has changed dramatically since the Second World War, many aspects of Samoan culture remain remarkably strong and vibrant. People learn the history of their titles and 'aiga; basic principles of kinship are still understood; the formal political system remains largely intact, though functioning primarily on a symbolic and ritualistic level; and the norms and values that inform interpersonal relationships remain the basis of Samoan social behavior. Migrants not only bring this system of knowledge with them but apply it in forging their new communities. That they do so in an environment that could not be more different is a testimony to their creativity, as well as the at least immediate adaptability of their principles of social organization.

The Migration Process: Personal Stories

Migration is often framed as a consequence of factors (primarily economic) distributed along two dimensions: those that "push" individuals from their societies of origin; and those that "pull" them into specific societies (Lee 1966). As we have seen, for Samoans the dynamics of push and pull began with the Second World War. During and subsequent to the war, rising population, restricted access to status, and new desires for education, goods, and travel impelled islanders to leave in increasing numbers. Although the characteristics of the migrants have changed over time, the context has remained relatively invariant. These aspects of social and demographic change constitute what Mitchell (1959) has defined as the *necessary* conditions of migration. Necessary conditions are not, however, *sufficient* to describe individual acts of migration. For this pur-

---

* The complexities of Samoan social organization are beyond the compass of this study. There are many excellent works that cover various aspects of Samoa and Samoan society, including Mead's research in Manua (1928, 1930), and Holmes's restudy of the same village (1958, 1974). Shore's more recent analysis (1982) of social action and politics in a Western Samoan village is quite complete. For some of the more specialized studies on kinship, economics, urbanization, social change, and psychology, consult the References Cited, pp. 183–92.

pose, let me present three personal histories that highlight the general characteristics of Samoan migration and show how both the process and the personnel have changed over time.

TAUSUA

When the Second World War began, Tausua was lured, like many other men of his village, to Pago Pago to work as a stevedore. There he came in contact with U.S. Marines just arrived to guard the island. He was so impressed by the uniforms and the stories he heard of the Marines' reputed toughness and courage—attributes Samoan men admire—that when a friend told him that the government planned to organize a reserve outfit of Samoan Marines, he eagerly volunteered. Although Tausua dreamed about going abroad, the Samoan Marines spent the entire war stationed on Tutuila. There they underwent basic training, assisted the Americans with a number of public works projects, and guarded military property. When the war was over the unit was disbanded, leaving Tausua with nothing to do but return home. However, he had met a girl from a nearby village, and for lack of a consistent plan for the future, they chose to marry. The formal ceremony was held in late 1946. The couple moved into the main town of Fagatogo, where Tausua was able to get occasional jobs working for the government or helping local merchants.

During this time Tausua remained attracted to the idea of being a soldier, but he knew that to enlist he would have to find the boat fare and travel to Honolulu. Fearing that once Tausua left Samoa he might never return, his wife was very much against his leaving. Finally in 1951, in the face of Tausua's constant complaining and pleading, his wife acquiesced. He was able to pay his boat fare with wages he received for his stint in the Samoan Marines and was duly inducted into the U.S. Army. Tausua tried to get his wife and children to come with him at this time, but his wife was afraid, saying, "What if something should happen to you? We would be all alone in Hawaii without anyone to help us." After the Korean War Tausua returned to Samoa; this time he succeeded in convincing his wife and children to join him in Hawaii. They arrived in Honolulu in late 1953. In 1956 Tausua was transferred from Hawaii to Fort Ord in Northern California, and this time the whole family, already numbering nine, moved together. Tausua left the Army three years later, moved to San Francisco, where he found an apartment in the Hunters Point area, and went to work for a local ship-building company. He was employed there until the late 1970's, when a serious back injury forced him into early retirement. He and his family now live in a modest house they purchased in Daly City.

Tausua helped establish one of the area's largest Samoan Congregational churches, and over the years he has helped many of his relatives to establish themselves. At the time of the interview he had just brought over a nephew so "he could get a decent education."

Tausua is typical of many early migrants to Hawaii and the mainland. Most were young, had some experience with the American military, were highly motivated to travel, and were independent and fairly self-reliant. Tausua, his wife, and others like them were the pioneers on whom scores of later arriving relatives, friends, and village-mates depended for initial housing and employment arrangements. For example, another migrant of Tausua's cohort, Enokati, arrived as part of a group of migrant farm-workers in 1949 to pick lettuce for a Japanese grower in the Santa Clara Valley. They had been recruited by another Samoan who had worked for this grower the two previous seasons. On fulfilling his contract for a season's work, Enokati quit and moved to San Francisco to join a cousin and his family. Once Enokati found a job in the Navy shipyards at Hunters Point, he and later his Samoan wife, whom he met in San Francisco, helped to settle nearly 50 other migrants. In the early days, he claims, "we helped all Samoans, whether we were related to them or not, because there weren't very many of us here."

For women the story is different. Many came with or to join husbands and other relatives. Most of the women I spoke with exercised considerably less control over the decision to migrate than men. For these early female migrants, raising a family in a strange place, with few other kin around, was sometimes a lonely experience.

MALOSI

Malosi always excelled in school and after graduation from the ninth grade, she received a scholarship to the nurse's training facility in Utulei. In early 1946 Malosi left her village of Leone, Tutuila, to live with relatives in Utulei while participating in this training program. Malosi completed her training in four years and then returned to her native village. There she worked in the local dispensary, counseling village women on sanitary methods of food preparation and childcare, treating scores of ailments, referring villagers to the main hospital, and occasionally assisting midwives in the delivery of babies.

In the summer of 1950 Malosi received a letter from a distant relative living in San Francisco, asking her to come and help with a very sick child who needed constant attention. Malosi agreed and arrived in San Francisco in December 1950. Shortly after, she met her future husband. They returned to Malosi's village for the wedding ceremonies but soon returned to San Francisco so that Malosi's husband could join the Army.

In recounting those first years, Malosi said, "We were excited about seeing America, about being somewhere where there was indoor plumbing, and electric lights and appliances. It was like a miracle, what we saw. But we were afraid; we lived in the housing projects then, and we tried our hardest to live the American way. We did not want to show our differences. It was much worse when my husband shipped out to Japan and left us alone. I was afraid and lonely. It was just me and my two oldest kids at that time. But then other relatives came from the islands and we started our own church and started acting like Samoans again." Malosi and her husband are the heads of one of the area's largest and most influential extended families, numbering over 75 members.

The stories of Tausua, Enokati, and Malosi are those of exceptionally bright and accomplished individuals, and it seems likely that this first group was self-selected for these traits. Later migrants typically moved to join established family and church networks and did not suffer the same degree of loneliness Malosi describes, or the fear and uncertainty that must affect all pioneers. Relatives and church-mates, initially at least, housed them, fed them, and in some cases provided a ready-made job. Such are the obvious benefits of kin-linked chain migration—benefits that have accrued to most migrant Samoans since the late 1950's.

The story of a young woman, Agalelei, is typical of these later migrants in terms of motivations, the process by which the decision to migrate was made, and experiences subsequent to their arrival on the mainland.

AGALELEI

Agalelei was born and raised in the village of Ofu, Manua. She grew up in what she calls a "very traditional" way, of poor parents who had little status in the village. She was the youngest of five children, three brothers and one sister. She started school late because she had to care for her parents. Only one sister was left in the village when she was growing up, and the two shared the many household chores. In 1962, at the age of 18, Agalelei finished junior high school and left Manua for the first time to attend high school in Utulei, Tutuila. When she graduated, the 22-year-old Agalelei wanted to do anything but go back to live in Manua. "I was crazy to leave Samoa. All my brothers had gone, and some of my friends and people I knew told me about all the wonderful things over in California. I wanted to see these new places for myself. I thought maybe I could get a better education, too. When my oldest brother wrote me and asked if I wanted to come, well I just jumped at the chance. I was on the plane within a week. I've never regretted it, either. My husband wants to go back; he thinks the life is better there, but me, I don't. There is nothing for me back there. My kids are my future and I'll struggle to keep my kids here and bring them up right with a decent education." Agalelei and her husband lived with her brother and his family until they had a child and moved into a place of their own.

For Samoans of Agalelei's age migration had already become institutionalized. For those with relatives abroad, especially siblings, the move itself was relatively easy: a quick letter to a brother, sister or uncle, and the fare was arranged. Or a person's mother or father would make arrangements with his or her siblings who had previously migrated, and fares and initial accommodations were made available. In cases such as these, young men and women commonly "repaid" the transportation costs by helping their benefactors with chores and child care or by getting a job and contributing wages to their hosts' household.

This has been the pattern throughout the course of Samoan migration to California. Once the community was established by the first pioneers, relatives flocked to join them. The later migrants differed from the first arrivals, moving into a world rendered less foreign by their kinfolk's experiences and accumulated knowledge. When they arrived the social landscape was already familiarly structured around small but growing kin groups and church congregations.

More recently two new kinds of migrants have been arriving. The young still come seeking what they perceive as a better future, to be sure, but they are increasingly joined by those who have been affected by the demographic distortions that decades of emigration by young adults have produced in many villages of Samoa. One of these new groups consists of older men and women who come to be with their children and visit their grandchildren. It is common in some areas, particularly in the more isolated villages of Manua, for nearly all the children of a family to have migrated to either Tutuila or the United States. Aging parents thus find themselves without the degree of familial support they had looked forward to and expected in old age. They either migrate on a permanent basis to areas where children have homes or visit for extended periods. Many also migrate for health reasons, encouraged by children to take advantage of what is perceived as a health-care system that is far superior to Samoa's. Once here, elderly migrants are typically dissatisfied with the quality of urban social life—particularly with the physical distances between households that make visiting difficult. As one man told me through his middle-aged son: "There is nothing to do here. I like it better at home where I can walk to the next house and sit with my friends. We make fishing lures and talk. I miss this. Here I just sit and watch all these crazy people on television."

There are, of course, elderly who are "old-time" migrants, but they have lived long enough in urban areas to be relatively comfortable with city life. They will shortly be joined, in any case, by the first cohort of migrants, who are fast approaching old age. Most of these "pioneers" continue to enjoy the fast and busy life of San Francisco, although a few men approaching retirement admitted to me that they might like to return to the islands to live, for they found they wanted to "relax." I will consider the phenomenon of return migration in the next chapter.

The other new kind of migrant group also consists of older people, who come to the United States, they say, because nothing remains for them in their villages, even though they prefer life there. Matai may have few 'aiga left in the descent group they lead, everyone having gone to the United States. Fewer young men may be about who are willing to care for the plantation, provide food for the households, and cash for necessary trade items. Other, nontitled individuals may face what we call in America a midlife crisis, suddenly finding village life and its rewards unsatisfying in comparison to the urban experiences of friends and relatives. Finally, the loss of a job, political squabbling, or family problems may provide a reason for people to leave Samoa. One man, a junior-rank matai from a small, fairly remote Tutuilan village arrived recently to join his sisters and younger brothers, the majority of whom live in the San Francisco area. When asked why he decided to come, he mentioned poor health (filariasis) and a desire to ensure a "good future for my children." In my field notes I made the following comment:

Tui is fairly typical of a just-migrated matai. Due to a shrinking power base in Samoa they contemplate migrating. They are older and without many job skills, and are a drain on their kin. Tui has attempted to reassert authority over his brothers, sisters, and their children in the conventional fashion, and now expects them to help support him, his wife, and children. Though Tui presently receives supplemental Social Security income, it does not satisfy his and his family's needs.

I later interviewed Tui's older sister, a woman who migrated in the early 1950's. She resented her brother's attempts to assert authority over the 'aiga. She thought it was unfair for Tui to assume leadership because he had not worked as hard as she and her brothers had to "build our lives over here." This kind of criticism was occasionally leveled by long-time residents at matai who they said "took advantage of the family."

In the same category is Ioane, who left Samoa in 1970 at the age of 44.

Ioane says he migrated because he was tired of working at part-time, poorly paying jobs and farming his family's lands. Knowing that he had no chance for a matai title, he asked his brother already established in San Francisco to pay his way over—which he did. A year later, Ioane and his brother pooled their resources to bring over Ioane's wife and eight children. Ioane arrived with only an eighth-grade education, few job skills, and a family of nine to support. In the twelve years that he had been in California, he had worked only one temporary job. His children and his relatives helped where they could to support his household.

Not all recent older migrants are similar to these two men, but there is a noticeable tendency for more recent arrivals to represent a greater potential drain on established households than was the case during the first two decades of Samoan migration. This has not gone unnoticed by the Samoans themselves, and they offer a variety of perspectives and opinions on the problem. Said one young woman, a daughter of one of the first migrants, "Most of the Samoans who come over now go on welfare. They do not have the skills or motivations my parents' generation had when they came over. They have no grasp of how to manage money." A well-established man who migrated in 1959 later told me essentially the same thing:

In the last ten years more and more Samoans coming over here are going right on welfare. When I first came, nobody did that; it would be a great shame. [*Why do you think this is?*] Well, there are many reasons. You know, back home it's an easy life now. The government has lots of money and you don't have to work hard to get it. You just have to know someone. Some of these Samoans also live for a while in Hawaii. You know those Hawaiians, they taught Samoans all about the welfare. When these people come over here they go right on the welfare just like they did in Hawaii. Also, there are a lot of older people coming over here now, people who are too old or too sick to work. The family has to care for these old guys.

The idea that the "easy life" of Samoa contributes to the economic situation of contemporary migrants is an interesting one. What the man had not perceived was that the economy of California had changed significantly between 1960 and 1980, making employment for Samoans and other groups with minimal education and technical skills scarce. I discuss this in the next chapter.

The Migration Process: Characteristics of the Sample

To place the foregoing stories in context, we need to see how representative they are of the sample as a whole. Did these migrants come from the same parts of the islands as the bulk of the migrants in the San

Francisco community? Do other migrants come directly to the mainland, as Malosi did, or spend time in Pago Pago or Hawaii, like Tausua? What reasons do other migrants give for leaving Samoa? And just how do those later to come differ from old hands like Agalelei?

The first question, of where migrants originated in the archipelago, has an important bearing on the problem of adaptation. As the historical and case material previously presented indicates, different islands have undergone varying degrees of change depending on their exposure to external influences. Manua, for example, has been comparatively isolated from events affecting the larger islands to the west throughout the history of Samoa, including the precolonial period. Even though many of its young men and women were drawn to Tutuila for employment during the Second World War and then for education in the postwar years, the village economic system has persisted to a degree unique to American Samoa. Today a substantial number of families still obtain a good portion of their food supply from plantation and sea.

As a consequence Manua remains less Americanized than Tutuila, despite extensive contact between the two areas. In his restudy of Mead's work in Manua, Holmes (1958: 65) remarks: "It can truly be said that no additional outside stimulus to culture change exists today in Manua that was not present in 1926." Holmes also supports Keesing's supposition that the lack of social change in Manua is sustained by the practice of giving titles later in life. This creates a gerontocracy that tends toward conservatism and acts to discourage "innovation or outlet for youth's enthusiasm within the native groups" (Keesing 1934: 479). Since the political system derives its primary power and authority from the control of land, and thus of economic resources, it has been maintained to a much greater degree in Manua, where the control of land has remained a relatively important issue. By contrast, Tutuilan society has seen a significant number of changes: crowding; a gradual undermining of the subsistence system in most areas; and more direct contact with Americans, both during and after the war. Yet even on Tutuila the more remote villages are still likely to be much more oriented to the matai system than those villages having easy access to the Pago Pago Bay area.

One might expect that the conservative nature of Manuan society would be one factor impelling people, especially the young, to migrate. Although there are no data on the extent of emigration from Manua, Samoans I have talked to here reckon that many of the men and women in productive age categories have left. Even the high-titled men of Manua spend a great deal of time on Tutuila, where many have posts in the territorial government.

Scholars have hypothesized that these different degrees of change have an effect on patterns of disease morbidity and mortality. McGarvey and Baker (1979), for example, suggest that Samoans may be compared on the basis of their exposure to "modernization," defined in this instance as proximity to the urban concentrations around Fagatogo (Pago Pago Bay area) or Apia (Western Samoa). In their health survey of several American Samoan villages, they found significant differences between people coming from villages identified as "traditional," "intermediate," or "modern" in terms of languages spoken, education completed, job experience, and blood pressure. According to the theory currently prominent in social epidemiology that social or cultural discontinuity, experienced as stressors, causes higher rates of cardiovascular disease, migration from a very rural area to the mainland would involve a greater shock—or discontinuity—than migration from a less "traditional" area. Though this factor may be important to understanding the distribution of ill-health among Samoans in California, other factors—intra-island migration, step-migration (see below), age, cohort of migration, and so on—confuse the issue considerably.

Table 2.1 lists the point of origin for my sample. Urban Pago Pago refers to the dense settlements in or around Fagatogo. The villages of the south coast of Tutuila, though outside of Fagatogo, still lie within the densely settled strip from Nuuli on the west to Laulii on the east and have had relatively easy access to the Fagatogo area. The "Other Tutuila" villages have had somewhat less contact with the Fagatogo area and are located in the island's less densely settled regions. The urban Apia area extends about five miles either side of Apia, including the dense sprawl of villages that together constitute the town. Northern Upolu is that area on either side of Apia, from the Faleolo airport on the west to Falefa on the east. The remaining categories are self-explanatory.

TABLE 2.1

Area of Origin of Bay Area Samoans

Area	Men		Women	
	Number	Percent	Number	Percent
Urban Pago Pago	9	15.8%	7	14.9%
South coast villages of Tutuila	3	5.3	3	6.4
Other Tutuila	19	33.3	12	25.5
Manua	21	36.8	16	34.0
Urban Apia	2	3.5	4	8.5
Northern Upolu	2	3.5	1	2.1
Other Upolu	1	1.8	3	6.4
Savaii	–	–	1	2.1
TOTAL	57	100.0%	47	100.0%

The table shows that a substantial part of the sample comes from Manua. This is a result of the sample selection process. As described in Chapter 1, participants were selected at random from two church congregations. They were at one time a single congregation, founded by a core group of families originating from Manua. As more and more relatives migrated, the proportion of Manuans thus remained relatively high in comparison to migrants from other areas. Otherwise, based on the population of the various areas of American Samoa and the estimated migration of Western Samoans, the proportion of migrants from these different areas appears to be representative of the California Samoan population. For example, in 1980 the Pago Pago Bay area accounted for 28 percent of American Samoa's population. However, probably only half of these people were originally from that area, the rest either coming from outer villages or migrating from Western Samoa (Park 1979). My data are based on village of origin; that is, where the individual spent most of his or her first eighteen years.

The migrants rarely came direct to San Francisco; most stayed for a time in some other place before moving on. The Pago Pago area has always been a magnet for those seeking jobs, education, and adventure, and many of the migrants I interviewed had lived and worked there for a time. Fully 81 percent of both the men and the women made at least two moves, and 34 percent of the men and 26 percent of the women made as many as four before arriving in San Francisco. Of course these figures only approximate what is by nature a complex process. For example, most migrants from Manua, especially before the late 1970's, lived for a time on Tutuila if for no other reason than to attend high school. For those with easy access by road to Pago Pago, a quick bus ride was all that was necessary to get into town; they had no reason to migrate to Pago Pago itself. These people may have moved directly to San Francisco. Thus it is inappropriate to assume that individuals falling within the crude categories cited above are similar in any fundamental way with respect to migration experience. What these figures do indicate, however, is that the population is on the whole a mobile one.

This finding bears significantly on the cultural variability in Samoa and the differing "traditionality" of migrants. Given the extent to which migrants moved about before settling in San Francisco, it is questionable to assume that those from a "traditional" area like Manua would adhere more to a Samoan lifestyle than those who hail from the Pago Pago area. Again, these are details that can hardly be evaluated on the group level; they represent processes unique to the life history of each migrant. I suggest that a person's decision to adhere to Samoan customs or participate in Samoan events and 'aiga activities is not likely to be determined by the village where he or she grew up.

TABLE 2.2

Primary Reason for Migration

Reason	Men (N = 57)		Women (N = 47)	
	Number	Percent	Number	Percent
Education of self, spouse, or children	22	39.0%	10	21.3%
Adventure or curiosity	8	14.0	7	14.9
Employment/money	8	14.0	0	0
Military	6	10.5	0	0
To accompany or join family (not always own choice)	3	5.0	19	40.4
Because of own or spouse's health	4	7.0	8	17.0
Trouble in family/village	4	7.0	1	2.1
Other	2	3.5	2	4.3

TABLE 2.3

Age at Migration and Marital Status by Cohort of Migration

Cohort of migration	Mean age at migration		Marital status	
	Years	Standard deviation	Single	Married
1940–1959				
Men	24.7	4.9	13	5
Women	23.3	9.5	7	4
1960–1969				
Men	30.3	13.4	12	11
Women	29.6	13.4	8 [a]	8 [a]
1970–1983				
Men	40.2	10.0	2	14
Women	43.0	14.0	1	17

[a] Incomplete information on two cases in this group.

The stories presented in the previous section illustrate a few of the reasons migrants chose to leave Samoa, and the set of different characteristics and motivations typical to each cohort. As part of my formal interviewing I asked informants several questions about their reasons for leaving Samoa, as well as about the events surrounding the actual decision to migrate. Although everyone had a concise reason to offer for migrating, this reason was developed in retrospect; one might thus expect people to offer an idealized—or at least more well-thought-out reason—for migrating than may have been the case at the time. The data presented in Table 2.2 reflect reasons given an outsider at a later date and thus do not necessarily represent the actual deciding issue at the time of migration.

The evident differences between men and women in the areas of employment and education suggest that women exercised less control over the decision to migrate than men. Over 40 percent of the women migrated primarily to join other family members or were brought over by relatives to help with household chores, work, or go to school. Only a few men reported having not made the primary decision to migrate, and most indicated that they were motivated by a specific goal: education, money, joining the service, and so forth. Two patterns emerge when these data are considered on a cohort-by-cohort basis. For both men and women health issues as a motivation to migrate did not become important until recently, illustrating the advancing age of recent migrants. For men early migrants were more likely to be motivated by joining the military, since there were no recruiting offices in Samoa until the late 1960's.

The fact that women were less likely than men to have made the primary decision to migrate may be related to differences in marital status. Table 2.3 presents a breakdown of marital status and age by cohort of migration.

Men were less likely to be married when they decided to migrate (27 of 57 single, against 16 of 47 for women), and for both sexes early migrants were somewhat less likely to be married than the later ones. This fact explains differences between men and women with regard to motivations: women were much more likely to either accompany or join spouses.

Table 2.3 also illustrates the trend toward older migrants with each progressive cohort. It is important to note, however—as indicated by the standard deviation statistic—that there is a greater degree of variability in age among the later cohort. In other words, while migrants in this cohort tend on average to be older, a significant number of young people are continuing to migrate.

THREE

Settling In: Opportunities, Challenges, and Stresses

The first migrants did not select cities at random but settled where there were military bases or dock facilities. San Francisco was not only an important Navy port, but until the 1970's also had large shipbuilding and repair facilities at Hunters Point and Mare Island. San Francisco's Presidio and Fort Ord, near Monterey, are the two major Army bases in Northern California. It was these military facilities that first brought Samoans to Northern California, paving the way for later migration. In Southern California the first settlements were at Oceanside, National City, San Diego, and Long Beach. Once established, these communities became powerful magnets for those considering leaving Samoa. This is the typical growth pattern of chain migration, in which "prospective migrants learn of opportunities, are provided with transportation and have initial accommodation and employment arranged by means of primary social relationships with previous migrants" (MacDonald and MacDonald 1964: 83).

Because of the scarcity of affordable housing in San Francisco, migrants did not move into any one neighborhood or district, but went wherever there was inexpensive and available housing. When my informants were able to move out of relatives' homes, many moved into public housing located in the southerly parts of the city: Hunters Point, Portrero Hill, and Visitacion Valley. Once they had jobs, many migrants of the 1960's and 1970's purchased their own houses, primarily in the same areas of the city. Most of the more recent arrivals, however, faced with rising house prices and rents, have been forced to remain in subsidized public housing, and none of the recent migrants I met had been able to purchase their own houses. Outside of the city of San Francisco, major concentrations of Samoans can be found in the cities of South San Francisco, Daly City, San Mateo, Oakland, San Leandro, East Palo Alto, San Jose, and Milpitas.

Ablon (1971a) estimates that the Samoan population of California numbered between 15,000 and 20,000 in 1970, but by the estimate of Lewthwaite, Mainzer, and Holland (1973), the figure would be much higher; they suggest that as many as 40,000 Samoans probably then lived on the mainland, and another 12,000 in Hawaii. In 1980 Samoans were identified as a distinct ethnic category in the U.S. Census for the first time, permitting a rough estimate of the size of the population and its general demographic and socioeconomic structure. These data suggest a much smaller population than that estimated by Lewthwaite et al. (1973). Table 3.1 gives the California population by county, and Table 3.2 shows the population by age and sex.

In 1983, in connection with pending legislation extending "Native American" status to Samoans in the United States, the U.S. Department of Labor commissioned a study of unemployment and poverty among them. One outcome of that study was a detailed examination and criticism of the census by demographers. Using known emigration rates, baseline population figures, and estimates of births and deaths, the authors of one paper suggest a 10 to 17 percent underenumeration (Hayes and Levin 1984a). This would put the 1980 population in California at between 22,000 and 24,000.

Allowing for natural increase and immigration, the Samoan population in 1984 probably numbered about 30,000.* One problem with underenumeration lies in determining just what segment, if any, of the population was not counted. One might think that those less likely to answer any census—the poor, less educated, or fearful—would be underrepresented. Also older people on extended "visits" may not have been counted. Given the almost-certain skewing of the census, figures on socioeconomic status should be used with some suspicion.

It is apparent from Table 3.2 that, like most migrant populations, the Samoan population is comparatively young. This is a consequence of two factors: a high rate of immigration of relatively young adults and a very high birthrate. The majority of the censused population reported they were born in the United States. The median age of 19.4 years makes Samoans the youngest of any Asian/Pacific Islander minority in the United States. The median age for Samoans in Hawaii is even lower: 17.5. The table also shows a balanced sex structure. Both sets of data imply a sig-

---

* Based on an annual rate of natural increase of 3 percent and the immigration of about 900 people a year (Hayes and Levin 1984a). The figure assumes that the proportion of migrants going to the various states has remained constant.

TABLE 3.1

Samoan Population in California by County, 1980

County	Number	Percent of total
Northern California		
Alameda	619	3.1%
San Francisco	1,799	9.0
San Mateo	1,672	8.3
Santa Clara	1,037	5.2
Southern California		
Los Angeles	8,049	40.1
Orange	2,008	10.0
San Diego	2,807	14.0
Ventura	366	1.8
Other	1,732	8.6
TOTAL	20,089	100.0%

SOURCE: U.S. census data supplied by California State Census Data Center.

TABLE 3.2

Samoan Population in California by Age and Sex, 1980

Age	Total	Male	Female
<1	547	261	286
1–9	4,641	2,370	2,271
10–19	5,122	2,582	2,540
20–29	3,807	1,868	1,939
30–39	2,650	1,329	1,321
40–49	1,568	840	728
50–59	1,002	528	474
60–69	502	233	269
70+	250	93	157
TOTAL	20,089	10,104	9,985
MEDIAN (years)	19.4	19.4	19.5

SOURCE: Same as Table 3.1.

nificant future growth in the young adult population, particularly in the 1980's and 1990's. Since this is the age where many will be attempting to enter the labor force, it is appropriate at this point to consider the community's current economic situation and see how it changed over the three decades 1950–80.

Socioeconomic Characteristics

When Ablon (1971a,b) conducted her research, she found nearly all the adults fully employed. The majority of men were working in local shipyards, heavy manufacturing industries, the armed services, the Merchant Marine, shipping and warehousing, and service industries. Many women worked as nurse's aides in hospitals, convalescent homes, and residential facilities for the aged (Ablon 1971a: 92). By and large these represent occupations where, at least before the mid-1970's, people willing to work hard could get jobs even if they had relatively few technical skills and less than a high school education. Employment opportunities were also in industries and settings with which many migrants had prior experience. It was not until the 1960's that a high school education was universally available to Samoans. By all indications—my own sample plus census figures—the median level of education for all migrants is under eleven years. Even among the later cohort of migrants, the median level remains less than twelve years. Only about one-fourth of all Samoans living on the mainland possess a high school education or greater. Adult Samoans also typically have problems speaking good English, barring them from occupations where effective communication skills are required. They have thus gravitated to industries and occupations where technical skills, education, and language abilities are of comparatively little importance.

The attitudes of employers were also favorable to the early migrants to California. They suffered none of the stigmatization their countrymen endured in Hawaii.* Indeed, for many years the Samoans of San Francisco were not known as a distinct ethnic group outside their own neighborhoods. Since the mid-1970's, however, a growing number of newspaper stories and television programs has made the Samoan community much more visible. While the tone of some of these presentations suggests that Samoans are just another poor migrant minority, the majority perpetuate a romantic and idealized image of them. Regardless, Samoans in California have not been subject to employment discrimination to the extent that Samoans elsewhere have. Ablon (1971b) suggests that Samoans made good employees because they were quite willing to work long and hard hours, were diligent in their tasks, and were able to accept supervision easily—being accustomed to a traditional system of rank and status that gave titled leaders control over their work and the products of their work. Once the first migrants had established themselves in industry, new arrivals were quickly provided not only temporary lodging, but information about jobs and available housing. I was told several stories of how migrants were accommodated by their established relatives, but the best and

---

* The Samoans themselves recognize that they are a more visible and stigmatized group in Hawaii, and occasionally identify troublemakers in the community as "from Hawaii." There are no scholarly analyses of this phenomenon; it would certainly make for an interesting and important comparative study.

most representative statement of this process is cited by Ablon (1971b: 390–91):

Tui, his wife Seve, and their three children are met at the airport by Tui's brother and taken to his apartment. Tui has three brothers in the area and these together paid the advance necessary for the family's flight. . . . One of Tui's brothers has lined up a job for Tui in the shipyard where he works, and he helps him with the necessary union technicalities. . . . By the fourth week [after arrival] Seve has a job as a nurse's aide in the convalescent home where another of Tui's sisters-in-law and two other relatives work. . . . At the end of three months, Tui and Seve had paid back their transportation expenses and move to an apartment of their own down the block.

Tables 3.3–3.5 show how chain migration functioned to provide for the initial needs of the migrants. Table 3.5, presenting data on initial employment, refers only to actual direct assistance: accompanying someone to an interview, helping fill out an application, taking the person to a

TABLE 3.3

Duration of Residence in Another's Household on Arrival

Duration	Men		Women	
	Number	Percent	Number	Percent
<1 month	3	5.3%	1	2.1%
1–5 months	10	17.5	9	19.1
6–11 months	14	24.6	9	19.1
1–5 years	16	28.1	14	29.8
5+ years	12	21.0	11	23.4
Not applicable/none	2	3.5	3	6.4

TABLE 3.4

Composition of Household of First Residence

Composition	Men		Women	
	Number	Percent	Number	Percent
Lived alone, own household	1	1.8%	0	—
Migrant and accompanying family lived in own household	0	—	3	6.4%
Lived with immediate bilateral kin already established in joint or extended household	28	49.1	27	57.4
Lived with other relatives already established	24	42.1	15	31.9
Lived with friends or acquaintances	2	3.5	2	4.3
Military housing	2	3.5	0	—

however. The Employment Development Department (EDD) of California routinely evaluates employment outlook in an annual planning guide; by its figures San Francisco showed a general shift away from production to managerial and administrative positions between 1970 and 1982. In 1982 the EDD acknowledged that many production facilities for major Bay Area manufacturing firms had been relocated either elsewhere in the state or out of the state and country altogether. Only apparel manufacturing was experiencing growth in 1983, and significant declines and job losses were forecast for ship repair and other heavy industries that remained in the San Francisco area. Transportation and warehousing industries also came on hard times in the 1970's. Most area steel firms closed down early in the decade, and the shipbuilding facilities at Hunters Point ceased operations shortly thereafter. These were industries that had employed a large number of Samoans and provided them with relatively high wages and excellent benefits. Also significant is the increasing competition Samoans face from other immigrant and nonimmigrant groups who, like most Samoans, do not have the technical skills to compete for jobs requiring substantial education and experience.

It is clear that this industrial decline will affect not only new migrants and young adults, but long-time residents as well, though seniority can be expected to protect some employees. The National Office of Samoan Affairs estimates that between 40 percent and 50 percent of young adults are unemployed, and the range is only slightly lower for older adults (NOSA n.d.). The employment picture is no better for those reared on the mainland. Area high schools report a significant dropout rate for teen-aged Samoans, and this is thought by community leaders to result in significant under- or unemployment. Young Samoans suggest that family pressures on children to find jobs as soon as they are able to supplement household income is one reason for the high dropout rate. But most of the jobs available to sixteen- and seventeen-year-olds do not offer good pay or security. In their needs-assessment study of a Samoan community in Los Angeles, Shu and Satele (1977: 69–70) found that 29 percent of adults were unemployed. In a study of Samoan unemployment in San Francisco and San Jose, Roblin (personal communication, 1984) found that over 40 percent of the adults were unemployed, and of these, half had lost jobs within the past year. Among my sample, total unemployment was approximately 30 percent for able-bodied adults (23 percent of men and 45 percent of women). But this sample, as indicated in Chapter 1, may not be wholly representative because I did not draw equally from all age groups. U.S. census figures for 1979 show that 11 percent of Samoan working-age men and 10 percent of women were unemployed for all of 1979, and that only 40 percent of the men and 55 percent of the

women were employed a full 50–52 weeks. Samoans of both sexes have
the highest unemployment rates of all Asian and Pacific Island groups in
California, with the exception of Asian Indian women (Hayes and Levin
1984b). The low rate of full-year employment suggests great job instability and reflects the poor financial condition of the major industries
and occupations where most Samoans are employed.

The meaning of these figures in personal terms can be seen in the following two cases: one of a man who arrived in the 1950's, and the other
of a man who arrived in the late 1970's. Both cases illustrate the effects of
worsening economic conditions on the personal level and present with
greater clarity the difficulties unemployment poses for the community as
a whole.

PATI

Pati migrated to San Francisco in 1955. His brother, a construction
worker, paid his way, and when Pati arrived, his brother took him
down to the union and helped him find a part-time laborer's position.
Within a short time, Pati tired of the hard and unsteady work and
found himself a full-time job in a warehousing and shipping firm near
the airport. He married a girl he met through his brother's church and
began a family. In 1961 Pati purchased a home in Daly City for about
$20,000.

For the next twenty years Pati worked hard. He and his wife brought
over her immediate family, plus several nieces, nephews, cousins, aunts,
and uncles. "There were never less than fifteen people in this house, but
we didn't mind. We knew we could help, so we did." Unfortunately for
Pati, in 1981, just after he turned 54, the company he worked for suddenly moved its operations to Salt Lake City. The company offered to
relocate Pati, but he could not conceive of leaving his family: "How
could I leave this area where my children and family are? Especially my
wife, she couldn't do it, it would kill her." Even with a pension at 55,
no certain thing when we spoke, Pati knew that it would not be nearly
enough to meet all house expenses. The family qualified for food
stamps and AFDC (Aid to Families with Dependent Children) for the
younger children and two recently adopted sons, but it was still barely
enough. Pati was eager to find another job, but his union representative
told him it would be hard to get him one because of his age. Worse yet,
neither Pati's nor his wife's family was any better off. Pati's children
were still in school, and his only surviving brother was retired. On his
wife's side, the sister whom they had often asked for help in the past
had also lost her job, and her husband was disabled. Pati and his wife
were helping several others, but they had to stop. They could not even

contribute much to church any longer, and this really bothered Pati. Because he felt shamed by not being able to contribute as much as he would like, Pati had reduced his church attendance and curtailed his participation in church-centered affairs.

This is not the only story of this type I heard from informants. In this case it is important to recognize that the loss of a job by a man of the age and standing of Pati affects not just his household, but the entire web of kin with whom he is involved in mutual cooperation. This group may act as a buffer in times of economic need, but only so long as the members have enough resources to help one another. Pati's family may marshal enough to support him temporarily or lend assistance in an emergency, but to Pati the lack of resources was most troubling because he could not contribute as much to the church and consequently was withdrawing from church affairs. Also troubling was his loss of a provider identity that had over the years given him prestige in the community as well as a great sense of personal satisfaction.

Although more recent migrants do not have to face difficulties stemming from a changing economic status vis-à-vis other family members, the effects of unemployment and poverty are just as profound.

VAI

Vai comes from a relatively well-educated Manuan family. Many of his brothers have been to college, and two sisters are nurses. Two of Vai's brothers hold prominent positions in the government of American Samoa, and a third is a minister in Western Samoa. Vai began to follow in the footsteps of his siblings but had to turn down a scholarship to Santa Clara University in California because he was the youngest son of the family, and his father needed him at home to serve the 'aiga. After several years of working as an untitled man in Manua, Vai was able to extricate himself from village life. He moved to Tutuila, where he found a good administrative job with the public works department. He enjoyed this job but quit in anger when a returning migrant was appointed to a supervisory job he himself was in line for, "just because he had lived in the States." With a new wife, Mele, and a growing family, Vai had to find other work. He did not want to return to Manua, where he felt he had absolutely no future. He decided to join the Navy and in 1975 left Samoa for the first time. After basic training in California, he was assigned to Honolulu, where his wife and children joined him.

The Navy did not turn out to be a good experience for Vai. He did not get the training he wanted and was transferred to Alaska, where he spent most of his time sitting at a desk doing what he perceived as meaningless work. He left the Navy in 1978 and returned to Honolulu, where he worked several part-time jobs but found nothing permanent. In 1979 he and his family decided to come to San Francisco, where Mele had sisters and Vai had an uncle to whom he had been close as a child. They lived with Mele's sister for a few months, then moved in with Vai's uncle because he had more room. Vai's uncle helped him get a job working on the waterfront for a ship-repair company, but the work was unsteady. When the company went out of business in 1982, the union could do little but put Vai "on call." He and his family felt intrusive in his uncle's house and badly wanted to find their own place. Rents were much too high, but they did qualify for and eventually received an apartment in a public-housing project. Vai does not like living in the project but says, "at least there are a lot of other Samoan families moving in around here."

Vai, Mele, and their six children now live as best they can on $800 a month in AFDC and food stamps. They get help when they need it from his uncle and Mele's sister. Vai is not quite sure what to do. At 35, he feels "stuck": "I'm very mad that I never pursued my education. Things are not as easy as they were a few years ago. To be anything, you got to have some college. I wish I'd never come here, but I think I'm stuck where I am. I've got six babies. . . . What can I do?" Vai and his wife have a big family in the area, and they are often asked to contribute for funerals and other events. They give what they can, knowing that if they help the family, the family will help them.

What is especially striking about this story is the fact that even though Vai's education, job, and military experience make him more employable than most of the migrants of the 1950's and 1960's, he found employment and housing extremely difficult to find. Moreover, unlike Pati, he has always been in a dependent position in relation to the rest of the family, and he realizes that he has little choice but to remain involved in the network of 'aiga exchange, even if it means being short of money occasionally. By being involved, Vai and his wife know that they will be helped by the family should an emergency arise.

These two stories illustrate the effects of worsening economic conditions on a few Samoan households. But have all households been equally affected? What is the general economic standing of the Samoan community in San Francisco? We can begin to answer those questions by looking at Tables 3.6–3.8.

Table 3.6 shows the percentage of Samoan households falling in various income categories. For purposes of comparison, total figures for all

TABLE 3.6

Total, Median, and Per Capita Income of Samoan Households in
California and Bay Area

Category	California, 1979		Bay Area Samoans, 1979[a]	1982–83 sample[b]
	All	Samoans		
Household income (percent)				
<$5,000	11.5%	12.1%	14.2%	3.2%
$5,000–9,999	14.8	14.7	14.6	4.8
$10,000–14,999	14.8	16.5	14.3	22.2
$15,000–19,999	13.3	18.0	12.2	25.4
$20,000–24,999	12.0	12.0	13.5	12.7
$25,000–29,999	9.4	10.3	15.1	12.7
$30,000–39,999	12.1	9.9	10.2	14.3
$40,000+	12.1	6.4	5.9	4.8
Median (dollars)	$18,248	$16,616	$17,856	$19,000
Per capita (dollars)	$8,295	$4,081	$4,128	$2,793
Mean household size (persons)	2.7	5.0	5.9	7.8

SOURCE: Same as Table 3.1.
[a] San Francisco and San Mateo counties.
[b] 63 households surveyed 9/82–10/83.

Californians are listed in column 1. Although in the aggregate, Samoans do not appear substantially less well off than all Californians, the average Samoan household contains nearly twice as many people. At just over $4,000, the Samoan per capita income is less than half that for all groups.

Moreover, as Table 3.7 shows, Samoans have the lowest per capita incomes of all Asian/Pacific Island migrants in Hawaii, and except for Vietnamese, the lowest in California. The per capita income for my sample of 63 households, $2,793, is significantly lower than the census figure and is comparable to the Hawaiian Samoans' income. My sample is probably slightly poorer than the general Samoan population, since I did not sample households headed by younger people, where one would likely find fewer household members and thus higher per capita incomes. On the other hand, it is equally probable that the census selectively under-enumerated those households where the members had less education and thus lower incomes. In addition, I counted people staying in the household on extended or semipermanent visits, who were likely to have been excluded in the census. In any case, by whatever measure, it is evident that Samoans are on the whole very poor.

When the sample's per capita income is broken down by cohort of migration (Table 3.8), it is interesting to note the great difference between the first-cohort and third-cohort migrants. This is a striking illustration of how both changing economic conditions and changing characteristics of the migrating population have affected the community. In particular, men

TABLE 3.7

Per Capita Income by Race/Ethnic Group
in California, Hawaii, and Bay Area

(*Dollars*)

Group	California, 1980	Hawaii, 1980
White	$9,109	$8,762
Black	5,710	5,437
Japanese	9,567	9,475
Chinese	7,946	9,422
Filipino	6,625	5,375
Asian Indian	8,159	10,165
Vietnamese	3,315	2,813
Hawaiian	7,169	5,328
Samoan	*4,081*	*2,729*
1982–83 sample	*2,793*	–

SOURCE: Geoffrey Hayes and Michael J. Levin, "A Statistical Profile of Samoans in the United States" (unpublished manuscript, Northwest Regional Educational Laboratory, 1984).

TABLE 3.8

Average Per Capita Income by Cohort of Migration

Group	Cohort of migration 1945–1959	Cohort of migration 1960–1969	Cohort of migration 1970–1983
Men			
Number	18	23	16
Average income	$4,107	$2,568	$2,393
Standard deviation	1,790	1,358	1,490
Women			
Number	11	18	17[a]
Average income	$2,839	$2,629	$2,225
Standard deviation	1,386	919	1,273
Total			
Number	29	41	33
Average income	$3,626	$2,595	$2,306
Standard deviation	1,739	1,173	1,364

[a]Incomplete information on one case in this group.

in the first cohort have a much higher per capita income than any of the other groups. Although women's per capita income declines with each successive cohort, the difference between the 1945–59 and 1970–83 cohorts is not great. There are several explanations for this gender difference: Samoan men's access to high-paying jobs when the first cohort migrated; the lack of access to such jobs in all cohorts for Samoan women; and the presence in the sample of single women who head households or who are married and/or live in households where the male wage earners migrated later.

As a result of the changing economic circumstances, more families are turning to welfare as their primary means of support. This appears to be a relatively recent trend, for Ablon (personal communication) notes that at the time of her fieldwork few, if any, families received public assistance. My informants reported essentially the same thing, commenting that accepting welfare was considered until recently—and is still considered by some—to bring shame on the family. They also report that whereas in the early days of Samoan migration, people with money problems were sent back home by their relatives, who did not want to support them, the same relatives are now helping new arrivals apply for welfare and public housing. About 15 percent of the sample depended solely on welfare for subsistence; another 10 percent received supplementary public support in the form of direct payments, food stamps, or medical care.

Aside from the fact that economic conditions have placed even well-respected members of the community on welfare, this change in attitude can be traced to Samoans' increasing knowledge of and sophistication in using American social-service resources. One relatively new community organization provides bilingual assistance and counseling in welfare matters, and a representative will accompany needy families to the welfare offices. Migrants who have been on the mainland for some time are now proficient enough in English to help their kin. When asked about welfare, informants typically evinced the attitude that "welfare is all right for people who really need it." Still, the relatively low ceiling amounts, given the typically large numbers of dependents in the Samoan household, mean that most families remain poor. The 1980 census found nearly a third of Samoan households in California living below the "poverty line," as defined by the U.S. Department of Agriculture. In the opinion of many county officials, this so-called 100 percent poverty-line figure, based on the minimum amount needed to buy a "basic" basket of groceries and pay a modest rent and a few bills in a given community, is too low. If they are right, we would expect these households to have difficulty meeting even basic subsistence needs.

One factor contributing to the Samoans' economic difficulties is the California housing market. As I noted earlier, very few recent migrants, even those fortunate enough to have well-paying jobs, have been able to buy houses, as their predecessors did. They must either pay high rents or move into public housing, so along with a decrease in per capita income, the share of income going to housing has increased substantially. Table 3.9, summarizing the sample's housing by cohort of migration, shows the trend away from homeownership with each more recent cohort.

TABLE 3.9
Housing Status by Cohort of Migration

	Cohort of migration		
Housing status	1945–1959	1960–1969	1970–1983
Living in home owned by self or spouse	19	16	0
Living in home rented by self or spouse	4	19	21
Living with relatives	2	1	5
Living with friends	0	0	2
House belongs to a relative, living for free or paying a small rent	4	5	5

That migrants themselves recognize the growing economic differences between cohorts is clear from the early migrants' inclination to distinguish themselves from recent "welfare-oriented" arrivals. Other researchers have similarly found relatively affluent Samoans describing a developing class structure in what was a short time ago a remarkably homogeneous community (e.g., Ablon 1971a, b). Many Samoans gain prestige through expensive family and community activities that poorer households cannot sustain. Thus poorer members of 'aiga networks may withdraw from affairs where status and prestige are validated. Rolff (1978) suggests that many affluent households deliberately limit their participation in extended family networks because they are in a position to pursue status and prestige as defined in American cultural terms.

Regardless of how a Samoan feels about participating in a family network, relative poverty constrains and determines to a great extent his or her opportunities and choices. The more affluent are not only free to choose to stay aloof from their kinsmen, if they so wish, but also have greater access to status in the Samoan community than the less fortunate. Poverty is a significant stressor in more than simple economic terms, leading to a shrinkage of social networks and a corresponding loss of access to positions of leadership. This can create a conflict between a person's desire to participate in family and community affairs and the obligation to meet the needs of his or her immediate household. More important, expensive community, church, and kin group events are central to the social life of the stateside community. These activities bring together dispersed households, reaffirm 'aiga networks, and contribute to a sense of social solidarity and cultural identity (Ablon 1970a). Though economic conditions have not resulted in widespread disaffection or in the excluding of substantial numbers of people from participation in Samoan affairs, the pressure is there, and Samoans feel it deeply. In my interviews the most commonly enunciated worry was over money and financial instability in general. This worry in turn contributes to a growing ambivalence about the value of participating in expensive 'aiga affairs.

Return Migration: Ideology, Process, and Actuality

Samoans return to live in Samoa for many reasons, not the least of which is dissatisfaction with the quality of life on the mainland. Unlike many other migrant groups, though, Samoans do not always envision a return in "glory" to establish themselves with the status and prestige they lacked when they left (Gmelch 1980). A strong ideology of return is not a motivating factor for most Samoan immigrants; only a few maintain their primary social ties and commitments to their native villages. The reasons Samoans give for wanting to return are to retire in the perceived "ease" of island living, where they believe the quality of life is better; problems on the mainland that make returning the most viable option; and an offer by the 'aiga to take a title—particularly a high one.

One reason Samoans do not overidealize Samoa is the frequency and ease with which they return to visit and participate in 'aiga affairs, particularly as they get older. More than three-fourths of the men and women in my sample had returned to Samoa at least once. Most of those who had not returned were either young or too newly arrived to have had an opportunity to return. Additionally, the migrant community is continually infused with visitors from the islands: relatives, formal traveling groups, and entertainment troupes. Improved communications with the islands have brought villages and family back home only a telephone call away. Finally, as individuals get older they assume more responsibilities in their 'aiga and often have occasion to return to Samoa, for example, to represent the family in land disputes or for church dedications, the election campaign of a relative, or an assembly of the whole family to select a successor to a title. In many ways Samoa and San Francisco constitute a single social field in which there is a substantial circulation of members.

Such experiences serve to prevent a strong idealization of village life. Only a handful of informants said they had definite plans to go back and live in Samoa permanently. Some of these were experiencing economic and family difficulties on the mainland, and others were interested in simply retiring and relaxing in a social environment they considered superior to San Francisco. There was no apparent pattern. Most of those queried suggested that they thought they would like at some time to return but were unclear on when that might be. A common response was, "When my children are settled and I'm ready to retire." Other qualifications consisted of having enough capital saved up to start a small business or build a nice American-style home. About one-third of the sample indicated that they had absolutely no desire to return and were content just to visit. More men than women showed a strong desire to return, and here access to status or a wish to exercise chiefly prerogatives was a primary motivating factor. One man, just chosen by a branch of his family in Western Samoa to be given a matai title, said, "I'm crazy to go back. I love the cultural things, the way of life. But my wife says no. She says she can never live apart from her children and grandchildren." In addition to wanting to be near family, women who wanted to stay on the mainland vouchsafed that modern conveniences made life much easier for them.

There are no particular characteristics that distinguish those who wish to return from those who do not. The man just quoted is a well-educated person who worked most of his life as a skilled civilian laborer in the Navy shipyards. But others with less education and fewer job skills also expressed a desire to return. I did not investigate this matter in any depth, but my guess is that the men who perceive a high status for themselves on returning are those who would like to move back to their village on a permanent basis.

In any case, it is interesting to note that many, if not most, Samoans actively maintain rights to land in Samoa. A few have even built large American-style houses in their villages. In one instance, four brothers, two living in Los Angeles and two in San Francisco, had just finished building a very large and expensive home in their village on Tutuila. The youngest told me that he did not have any desire to return and did not think his brothers did either. He and his brothers simply wanted "a nice house for us and the rest of the family to stay when we come." In another case a man and his wife returned to support the branch of the wife's family still in Samoa, which was engaged in a serious dispute over family lands. Both said that they prized that land and did not want to let "this other part of the family from Western Samoa get it." Similar disputes are becoming common as the heavy emigration of Samoans from certain parts of American Samoa leaves lands untended. Given the flexibility of cognatic descent in Samoa, other branches of the kindred may move in and establish rights to such land by invoking their relationship to the matai who controls the land (and his 'aiga) and proceeding to farm it. Title disputes also attract the interest of the entire kindred, particularly if the title is a high one. So while the majority of Samoans I spoke to had little immediate desire to return, most mantained their involvement, interest, and participation in affairs of the village and that part of the family still resident in Samoa.

Finally, Samoans do not feel they have to return to Samoa to experience and participate in the aspects of their culture they value. Several people indicated that they believe the stateside community to be more integrated, more religious, and more adherent to *fa'asamoa* (Samoan culture) than the part of Samoa they came from. Though once "more North American than the North Americans" (Mackenzie 1977), Samoan migrants now feel they are in many ways "more Samoan than the Samoans in Samoa." The majority are generally content with their lives on the mainland, and content with an occasional visit to Samoa to reaffirm village ties.

The data in this and the foregoing chapter suggest that while migrants can be said to leave one kind of society for another—which is on the face of it markedly different—there is no one typical experience, no single process of change, and no specific challenge and response that typifies Samoan migration. Samoans have left one social system in the midst of change and entered another where the forces for change are different but no less powerful. The degree to which the motivations and situations that compelled them to leave have changed over the course of the postwar years is matched only by the degree to which urban American society has changed, offering opportunities to some at one time and denying the same opportunities to most at a later time. The migrant community today can hardly be said to be completely homogeneous, even though in some respects and from an outsider's standpoint it may appear to be so.

The pressures for social and cultural differentiation have been significant. One of the most evident bases for that differentiation is economic status. A worsening economic situation in San Francisco, especially since the 1970's, has seriously affected Samoans who, like migrants from parts of Latin America and Asia, characteristically enter the workplace with less than a high school education, often some language difficulties, and few job skills. They now face stiff competition for jobs in a fast-shrinking market. Economic disadvantage is not the whole story, though adapting to a totally cash system of exchange is the one problem raised by all groups of Samoan migrants; equally or more important are social consequences of scarce economic resources. Growing economic problems are exacerbated by a developing community and social organization that demands of its members significant expenditures of time and money. Yet it is this participation that makes a Samoan a Samoan, that defines for him a salient cultural identity, and that increases the solidarity of the church and kin networks to which he belongs. Thus poverty, and the social problems that accompany it, constitute a significant social and psychological stressor.

Still, everyone possesses some capability to adapt and respond to such stressors. Innate or acquired aspects of the personality play a role, to be sure, but the most important strengths derive from the person's immediate social environment. The most important resources are the social and psychological support that is available within a person's social network. For Samoans these resources consist of a well-defined segment of the social world: networks of close bilateral kin, church-mates, and friends. Also important is a sense of cultural continuity provided by participation in the Samoan cultural institutions of church and 'aiga. It is to a discussion of this social world that I now turn.

FOUR

Family and Kinship Relations

Several processes of social and cultural differentiation affect Samoan migrants. Newcomers are able to establish cooperative relationships with previous migrants that are salient in traditional cultural terms. Occurring over time and involving large numbers of related people, the process of chain migration promotes the development of kindred networks. These groups represent a strong force for conformity. On the other hand, the newcomers move into an urban system that encourages them to change their behavior and their ideas. Complicating these issues is the fact that migration is often a selective process, whose characteristics change over time. The unique push-pull factors at any given point result in the movement of certain kinds of people: young and educated, males, dependents, and so forth. Younger people, or those migrating to escape what they perceive as negative aspects of traditional Samoan life, may be more responsive to opportunities for change, just as older people may be a more conservative force. Finally, as we have seen, economic status affects people's willingness to involve themselves in Samoan kindred networks.

Many of the first migrants were more highly motivated and self-reliant than the Samoans who remained at home. Some of these men and women left to escape the confines of the matai system, which seemed to them to place excessive demands on their income and exert too much control over their activities (see, e.g., Ablon 1971a). The first migrants to San Francisco moved into the same general areas of the city, but the housing situation forced them to disperse into various neighborhoods throughout these areas. Though they maintained relations with kin and friends, there were too few families to permit much emphasis on Samoan ways. Most strove to behave like Americans and downplayed cultural differences. It is interesting in this regard to reconsider the comments of a woman cited earlier:

We were afraid; we lived in the housing projects then, and we tried our hardest to live the American way. We did not want to show our differences. . . . But then other relatives came from the islands and we started our own church and began acting like Samoans again. Now our *fa'asamoa* [Samoan culture, Samoan "way"] is so strong that people from the islands say there is more *fa'asamoa* in San Francisco than back home.

Distinctly Samoan institutions began to arise as migration brought in more and more related people. Though adjusted to fit in with the busy lives of working people living in dispersed households, these institutions were nonetheless Samoan in flavor and organization. In a historical analysis of the development of Samoan stateside communities, Rolff (1978: 69–74) distinguishes five kinds of networks, each functioning differently, that were emphasized at varying times as the population grew. These are networks based on friendship, household membership, religious cooperation, kindred participation, and community interest and political action.

Samoans initially formed informal friendship networks. Comments Rolff (1978: 69): "Conscious of their common origins, people were concerned about each other's welfare, and Samoanness *per se*, rather than common membership in an 'aiga." New migrants joined established households, and when these became too crowded, family groups split off to form their own households. The kin ties that had been strengthened in the migration process served to unite individuals in separate households into functioning 'aiga groups. Groups of households, tied together by kinship and friendship bonds, in turn cooperated to establish church congregations. Churches rose in importance, playing the role of village sociopolitical organizations. Eventually the numbers of relatives migrating were sufficient to permit limited ritual activities. Informal at first, these activities were gradually elaborated over time as more migrants arrived and participated. The reincorporation of 'aiga networks was accomplished primarily through the celebration of rites of passage (*fa'alavelave*, literally, "troubles"), such as marriages and funerals. Rolff's fifth category is a social network that cuts across 'aiga or church affiliations to encompass the entire community. Groups of chiefs, civic-minded women, educated young people, and others have cooperated to create self-help voluntary organizations, as well as groups organized for political action. Community-wide networks are a relatively new phenomenon, increasing in size, variety, and importance mainly in the 1980's.

Although each kind of network predominated at different historical points in the development of stateside communities, all are evident today. In this and the following chapters I will discuss elements of Samoan social organization, illustrating the current shape and function of the different social networks. We begin at the lowest level, household and family organization.

As in Samoa, the 'aiga is the basic unit of social organization, although its composition and structure vary considerably across the community. The most evident difference in family organization is the fact that the 'aiga is no longer a localized core of kin under a matai, but has become an amalgam of loosely cooperating, sometimes only infrequently interacting, dispersed households. Thus, for urban Samoans, distinctions between the nuclear family, household, 'aiga, and kindred have blurred.

It is always difficult to fix and describe parts of cognatic kinship systems as if they were determinate things, particularly in the changing urban context described here. In most villages of Samoa, cognatic descent groups are pragmatically restricted to residence, even though constituent members may maintain ties to other groups (see, e.g., Fox 1967: 156). In San Francisco the principle of descent itself has weakened because of a commitment, especially by the young, to life on the mainland. Descent is important for access to land and titles in Samoa. Moreover, whereas in Samoa an 'aiga can be defined as that household cluster under the authority (*pule*) of a matai, the same cannot be said of cooperating clusters of households on the mainland. Outside the ceremonial sphere, matai do not generally lead a well-defined group of households. Household groups do engage in regular economic cooperation, but not nearly to the degree common in Samoa. The most effective way in which to view urban Samoan kinship is as a complex system of ego- or household-centered social networks. One cannot typically distinguish bounded and corporate groups among these networks, but it is possible to define three levels of social relations, representing different spheres of social activity, or sets of personal social relationships, that vary in content and meaning, namely, the household, the 'aiga, and the kindred.

Household Structure and Composition

At the center of Samoan social networks is the household. Households vary in composition, and their membership expands and contracts over time as migration and economic matters dictate. Four general types emerged in my household survey. The first is the conventional nuclear family, consisting of a man, a woman, and their children. About one-fourth of the households (15 of 63) were of this type. There is some evidence to suggest that the nuclear family is an ideal type, or at least becoming so for many migrants. Several people, both young and old, said that it is preferable for a young couple to establish their own household if they can afford it, and especially once they have a child. In a typical case a woman told me that her daughter and son-in-law would live with her and her husband until the couple had a child, when it would be suggested that they move out. Most residential decisions, however, are based on economic considerations. In a cash economy where not everyone has equal access to income, some will be providers, and others dependents. Those who are in dependent positions must rely on those who are not, and this usually means sharing a household.

A little more than one-fourth (17) of the households sampled were three-generation, lineally extended families: a nuclear family unit plus either parents or grandchildren of the household provider and his or her spouse. Because of the aging of the original migrant population and the addition of recently migrating elderly, the three-generation family appears to be a recent development. In several instances a working couple had paid the fare of an older female relative to have someone care for the children. In one such case a man had brought his mother over to stay with his wife and young children while he went on sea duty with the Navy. Like nuclear families, conventional extended families expand and contract as economic needs and personal desires dictate.

In the third category are households consisting of two or more siblings and/or their spouses and children, a pattern that attests to the cultural importance of sibling relationships in Samoa. About one-fifth (13) of the households were of this type. The intensity of relationships between siblings, especially as reinforced by chain migration, is an important feature of Samoan social networks. The tie between brothers and sisters also extends to their children, and it is common for a household head and spouse to support and house several nieces and nephews.

The fourth kind of household is something of a catchall; I call it, after

TABLE 4.1

Household Composition by Type

| | Households | | Members per household | |
Household type	Number	Percent	Mean	Total
Nuclear family	15	23.8%	5.9	89
Extended family	17	27.0	8.4	142
Joint (sibling) family	13	20.6	8.5	111
Grand family	15	23.8	9.7	145
Atypical households				
Widow and children	1	1.6	2.0	2
Divorcé and children	1	1.6	2.0	2
Single person	1	1.6	1.0	1
TOTAL	63	100.0%	7.8	492

Rolff (1978), a "grand" extended family. Typically this is a merging of nuclear family households that involves taking in parents and other bilateral kin as circumstances require. About one-fourth (15) of the households were of this type.

Of the three households that did not fit into any of these four categories, one was headed by a recently widowed woman, one was headed by a divorced man, and one consisted of a single person. Table 4.1 presents a breakdown of household types and the average number of residents in each type.

Core 'Aiga Networks

As in Samoa, many of the consanguineal and affinal ties that join households may be latent for much of a person's life. But individuals maintain close relationships with a core group of relatives. This core group, often based on a sibling set, represents a close-knit household cluster best described as the core 'aiga network. Each spouse will maintain relations with his or her close bilateral kin, but where the core networks are particularly large and well developed, household cooperation and affiliation are often based on the man's ties to his brothers. Though wives maintain their own networks of kin and friends, they are more frequently involved in their husband's 'aiga on a day-to-day basis than the husband is in theirs. This is roughly equivalent to the pattern in Samoa, where wives commonly leave their families of birth to live and participate in their husbands' 'aiga activities. The urban 'aiga network can be defined as a group whose members aid one another in emergencies, engage in day-to-day mutual aid, cooperate in collecting contributions for kindred events, and interact with great frequency.

Because of variation resulting from patterns of affiliation in the migration process, as well as variation in nuclear family size, these core 'aiga networks vary greatly in number, degree of regular cooperation, and composition. The one generalization that seems to hold is that it is centered on ties between brothers. The elder may possess a chiefly title, but this entitles him only to represent the 'aiga on important occasions. Often network members will look to one person as the leader, expected to call meetings and make decisions on family affairs. Blended with sibling ties are those to more distant kin who affiliate by matter of choice with a group of cooperating households. Often these are people who have few siblings in the area, and their relationships to relatives in the core household group are based on friendship, as well as formal kinship rights and obligations.

The fact that sibling relationships are important to the urban family does not represent a significant departure from the Samoan pattern, where groups of brothers may be at the center of a descent group. What is somewhat different is the tendency to truncate kinship networks beyond a relatively close consanguineal circle. Lewthwaite, Mainzer, and Holland (1973) suggest that the process of close relatives helping each other in migrating—usually siblings, first cousins, and uncles and aunts—acted to strengthen these relationships to the exclusion of ties to more distant kin.

An important element of core 'aiga relationships is economic cooperation. People can ill-afford to maintain ties with a great number of potential dependents. The content of relationships to more distant relatives is thus altered to exclude regular economic support, and there is an intensification of relationships with those close consanguineal kin with whom one does have mutual rights and obligations based on a long history of regular economic reciprocity. Although networks of kin outside of the core group are economically significant when events require the cooperation of a kindred group, relatives with whom one is not involved on more than a weekly basis rarely become dependents. Such events typically occur only six to twelve times a year and rarely involve exactly the same set of relatives. Patterns of informal and formal exchange are described and discussed in Chapter 6.

The intensity of relationships within the core 'aiga network is particularly striking.* Contacts with brothers or sisters in the area are far more frequent than nearly any other kin or friendship relationship. People without siblings close by reported fewer relationships with relatives outside of the immediate household and tended to emphasize friendship and religious networks to a larger degree. Siblings and their families often gather on Sundays for a large meal (*to'ona'i*). Decisions on participating in and contributing to kindred-group events are often made in meetings of a group of the households in a core 'aiga network. The network's most important function, however, is the provision of emergency housing and economic support to constituent members or households in need. The psychological benefits accruing from a knowledge that such support exists are also great.

Extended Family Networks: The Kindred

Beyond the 'aiga core group, each household member maintains relationships with other branches of his or her kindred (for example, "mother's kin," "father's kin"). Although a person will interact more frequently with relatives who live close by, kindred networks have no geo-

---

*I follow Mitchell's (1969: 27) definition of intensity: "the degree to which individuals are prepared to honor obligations, or feel free to exercise the rights implied in their link to some other person."

graphic boundaries. People can usually trace relationships to other persons or 'aiga groups wherever there are communities of Samoans. This network represents a set of latent kinship ties that are typically actualized only when life crises (*fa'alavelave*) affect one part or 'aiga of the kindred. These far-flung networks represent the medium by which people locate themselves in the broad framework of Samoan society and define themselves as Samoans. It is common to hear individuals in the course of explaining who they are stress significant kinship relationships with prominent descent groups in Samoa and with the major titles in their village or district of origin. Samoans use many terms to describe these large, diffuse, and largely latent networks; the most common are *'aiga potopoto* ("assembling kindred"; Shore 1982) and *'aiga atoa* ("the entire kin group"; Pitt and Macpherson 1974).

Samoans in San Francisco probably interact more frequently, though on a more formal basis, with distant relatives than is the case in Samoa. On the face of it this appears to contradict the tendency described earlier for individuals to truncate relationships with people outside the 'aiga core. This contradiction can be understood by examining the content of these outside relationships, to wit: paying formal respects to one's relatives by donating money for a special occasion. Such relationships—at least theoretically—entail reciprocity at a later date. One's reputation, as well as that of one's household and branch of the kindred, rests on the appearance of generosity and selflessness in maintaining these obligations. Of course, it remains impossible for all related persons to become involved in any one event. Informants indicated that they would most likely honor obligations to relatives or related 'aiga if (1) they heard of the event in sufficient time to gather a contribution; (2) the relative, household, or 'aiga group was close by or was important enough through prior relationships to warrant travel to, for example, San Jose or Los Angeles; and (3) there was a history of contact between the individuals, households, or 'aiga that entailed some degree of reciprocal obligation.

Because of the financial commitment demanded by participating in these affairs and the pressure to maintain one's obligations, frequent involvement can be psychologically as well as economically taxing. Samoans thus evince some ambivalence about whether such obligations are good or bad.

Relationships with 'aiga groups other than the core 'aiga are emphasized in different contexts and for different purposes. As noted, Samoans conceive of themselves as having "sides" defined by their relationships to different 'aiga groups or parts of their kindred (Shore 1982). Traditionally, the father's side is a person's "strong side" (*itu malosi*), and the mother's side the "weak side" (*itu vaivai*). Individuals also stand in an important relation to their affines, and this part of the kindred is seen as another "side" that entails some responsibility.

In summary Samoan kinship in California can be conceived of as representing three partially overlapping spheres of social activity: the household, the core 'aiga network, and networks of kindred members. These groups are not fixed, but vary with context. People maintain the most frequent and intensive contacts with the members of their own household and other households of close kin. Beyond this, contacts with relatives are comparatively infrequent and formal.

Three San Francisco 'Aiga

To highlight these points and illustrate the broad range of family forms, we may usefully examine some specific cases. The three cases below range from a large, fairly traditional and highly organized 'aiga group to a single nuclear-family household involved primarily in a network of friends.*

THE 'AIGA LEULUA

The San Francisco branch of the 'aiga Leulua originated in the Tutuilan village of Amanave. The first migrant, Onosa'i, was the oldest male in a family of nine children: eight boys and one girl. He had done well in school and worked as a stevedore for a private shipping company in Pago Pago before leaving Samoa in early 1951 "to see the world." When the Navy transferred one of his cousins, with whom he was good friends, to San Diego, Onosa'i was urged to come along for a "visit." He had it in mind to find out about joining the Marines when he arrived but was not really planning to enlist. On a bet with his cousin, who claimed he did not know enough English to pass the entrance test for any of the services, Onosa'i went to the nearest recruiting office, stopped at the first desk, and announced that he wanted to "sign up." It so happened that what he signed up for was the Army. While in training at Fort Ord, near Monterey, he married a young woman from a village close to Amanave who was visiting her sister. The couple established a household in San Francisco, where they knew a few other families. For several years Onosa'i lived at Fort Ord during the week and in San Francisco on the weekends. Though he was occasionally stationed abroad, he was fortunate enough to spend most of his time in the area.

---

* To preserve the anonymity of the subjects, I have not only changed the names of people and villages in these accounts, but also altered a couple of kinship relationships that are unimportant to the story.

After returning from his first overseas duty in Okinawa, Onosa'i wrote to his parents and brothers urging them to come over, and offering lodging and financial assistance. The first to take him up on the offer was Siaosi, the oldest of his younger brothers. He arrived in 1957. Onosa'i urged him to join the Army, but Siaosi opted instead for the Navy. After basic training in San Diego, Siaosi was stationed at Long Beach but spent occasional leaves in San Francisco. In 1961 he left the Navy and joined the Merchant Marine, where he is still employed. He and his family live with Onosa'i.

The next to come, in 1964, was their youngest brother, Ekepati. The military held no appeal for Ekepati, who wanted both to pursue his education and to make a lot of money in as short a time as possible. Onosa'i was stationed in Germany when Ekepati arrived, but a cousin of Onosa'i's wife took the new arrival to his construction union and helped him get a job. Ekepati and his family now live with the cousin in a house three blocks from where Onosa'i lives.

Two years after Ekepati migrated, the next-youngest brother, Vili, arrived. Vili had been a teacher in Samoa, but frustrated by the low pay and poor working conditions, he too left to join his brothers. Vili originally stayed with Ekepati, but once married and established in a good job, he purchased his own home.

Throughout this period Onosa'i and his wife continued to be a powerful magnet for relatives back home. Two of the brothers who chose, for various reasons, to remain in Samoa sent their children to stay with him for purposes of education. Cousins on both sides also wrote asking for help, which Onosa'i and his brothers, being financially able, agreed to provide. Together, Onosa'i and his brothers probably provided fares, initial housing, job information, and general support to at least 25 of their relatives.

The four brothers live in close proximity; Onosa'i and Siaosi share the same house. Together with their wives, children, nieces, nephews, and others, this core 'aiga has 31 members. In addition, fifteen other households frequently affiliate with them on special occasions to form the 'aiga Leulua. This is in fact one of the most well-known and integrated 'aiga in the San Francisco area, consisting of about 100 members. Although each brother and household head makes his own decisions on the management of household affairs and the amount of his contributions to the church, decisions on kindred events are made jointly, with input from other households as the context dictates. Onosa'i controls the 'aiga's affairs with a firm hand and expects his brothers and their families to conform to his wishes in other matters as well. He acts very much as the family's matai and in fact was asked to take an orator title a few years ago, which he accepted. His brother Vili also holds a title descended to him through his mother's brother, but it is junior to Onosa'i's.

The frequency and intensity of relations among the brothers and their households are of a different order from the separate relationships that each adult has with other members of their kindred. For example, each of the brothers' wives belongs to her own sibling networks and 'aiga and honors obligations when required; however, the primary affiliation is to the husband's family. This is a consequence of residential propinquity, combined with the fact that the 'aiga Leulua is more integrated and organized than any of the wives' 'aiga.* On special occasions, especially important holidays, the 'aiga Leulua will get together to share a common meal, to socialize, and more rarely, to discuss an important 'aiga matter.

In this case it is important to remember that the distinctions between the household and the core 'aiga, and between it and each member's kindred network, are by no means invariable. Group boundaries shift by context, and what emerges as a general fact about Samoan social organization may be contradicted in the context of a specific social event, crisis, or environment (see Shore 1982). For example, the last major kindred event that occasioned the cooperation of the 'aiga Leulua was the arrival of a traveling group from Samoa. Onosa'i and his brothers were related to several of its members, as were the wives of two of the brothers and some kindred members who occasionally affiliated with Onosa'i and his brothers. Onosa'i called all of these people and suggested that they make a contribution as a unit. The group then met and decided on the amount each would give toward a group contribution. Onosa'i formally presented the money, termed a *sua*, at the farewell ceremonies. The group activated for this specific purpose was by no means a regularly cooperating unit, merely a network organized for one particular event.

Though the 'aiga network of Onosa'i and his brothers is blended with a much larger group of relatives, the sibling relationships remain primary in most affairs. The households cooperate in many matters and lend assistance to those in need whenever it is necessary. This pattern does not usually extend beyond the primary household cluster unless the need is unusual.

---

* This is not to suggest that women do not participate in or contribute to events concerning their own 'aiga. For example, whenever a relative of one of his sisters-in-law dies, Onosa'i organizes a family meeting and directs each member or couple to contribute an agreed-on amount toward the funeral. In these cases not only are couples a contributing unit, but affinal ties are nearly as strong as consanguineal ones.

In less well-integrated 'aiga groups, though the sibling network remains primary, it does not constitute the basis of a regularly cooperating group like the 'aiga Leulua's. This is illustrated by the consanguineal and affinal relationships of the Salaetua family.

THE 'AIGA SALAETUA

The 'aiga Salaetua originated in the large Manuan village of Fitiuta. Although the 'aiga was said to have once been prestigious, conflicts, less-than-honorable ancestors, and untimely deaths had a deleterious effect. A distant branch had appropriated the highest title and with it some land, so that by the beginning of the Second World War, the 'aiga Salaetua had no status in the village and was poor by Samoan standards. There was little to keep the young and able members at home when the war broke out, and many left to work for the military. Among these first migrants were three brothers, sons of a junior Salaetua matai. The oldest son, Uga, left in 1948 to attend a church school in Western Samoa. His middle brother, Tala, went to Tutuila to attend school in 1950, and the youngest brother, Solomona, followed in his footsteps two years later. Uga eventually became a minister and migrated to Hawaii, where he led a large congregation for more than 20 years. On finishing school in 1956, Tala returned to Manua to serve (*tautua*) his father and work as a *taule'ale'a* (an untitled man). Solomona was chosen for teacher's training school and remained in Tutuila for several years, teaching in various village elementary schools.

But Tala no sooner returned to Manua than he decided to leave. He did not want to have to work hard on his family's land, nor did he want his father to have to do this work either. In a long talk with Solomona, the two brothers discussed the future of the family and the possibilities of migrating. Solomona suggested that it would be good for Tala to enter the service, and then, when he was established, he could send money home and help him and the one sister still in Samoa to come over. Like other prospective migrants, Solomona and Tala believed that the best future for their families lay in migration. But they had few relatives abroad, and no idea of how to find money for fares. Solomona approached an "aunt" (a woman relative on his father's side) who had just received a large settlement of money from her husband's death while in the Navy. She agreed to pay Tala's way and write to some relatives she knew in Honolulu. Tala arrived in Honolulu in 1956, worked for a year cutting sugarcane to pay back his "aunt," and then joined the Navy. As soon as he had saved enough money for boat and plane fare, he sent it to Solomona. Solomona chose to migrate to Los Angeles, where two cousins (father's brother's sons) had moved a year before. Tala was at sea at the time. Solomona got a job on a construction crew and lived with his cousins until 1964, when he lost his job.

By then Tala was stationed in the San Francisco area, so Solomona moved with him into an off-base apartment. The brothers started going to a church in San Francisco, and there Solomona met a woman he married a year later. In the meantime Tala had left the Navy and joined the Merchant Marine, and when the couple found their own apartment in San Francisco, he went to live with them. When their youngest sister, Tufa, graduated from high school, Tala paid her way to join him and Solomona in San Francisco. In 1973 she was married and moved with her new husband into a rented house not far from where Solomona lived. In 1976 the oldest brother, Uga, left his congregation in Hawaii and came to San Francisco because of health problems. He, his wife, his children, and his children's families rent a house in Daly City. Tala married in 1978 and lives with his wife and stepson near Solomona and Tufa.

Within the Salaetua household network there is considerable visiting from day to day, and also a significant degree of mutual financial aid. Both Tala and Uga have had money problems, and Solomona was out of work for a time. There has been a more or less constant flow of money from households with surpluses to those without.

Unlike the Leulua family, however, the Salaetua family is not part of a large 'aiga network. The core 'aiga comprises just the three brothers and sister and their families. Tala, by virtue of his long bachelor-hood and significant absences from the Samoan community, knows few relatives in the area besides his brothers. He has thus only rarely contributed to kindred affairs, and when he has done so, it has been through Solomona or now, his own wife. Solomona is more aware of kindred members living in the area and says he recognizes kinship with three other households. Most of his relatives live in Los Angeles and he sees them infrequently. Interestingly, the networks by which Solomona and his sister Tufa are tied to Samoans outside their immediate family are through their spouses. Solomona's wife is a member of a very large 'aiga in the area; they get together with this group on special occasions several times a year and often contribute when there are life-crisis events. Tufa's husband also belongs to a large 'aiga, and she feels pressure from what she calls these relatives' "insistent" demands for time and money. Uga's wife is from Western Samoa and has no relatives living in California.

In this network we see the same intensity of interaction that characterizes the Leulua sibling network, but the Salaetua siblings do not form the basis of a highly integrated 'aiga. The differences appear to stem from the very migration process itself, which brought few other members of the 'aiga Salaetua to San Francisco, as well as their respective 'aiga histories. By the Salaetua siblings' own admission, theirs was not a large or prominent family in Fitiuta. Moreover, they do not know many other 'aiga outside of a fairly small circle either on the mainland or in Samoa. Instead, members of the Salaetua family are tied by affinal relationships to other, much larger local 'aiga that demand a good deal of time and attention. So far as routine day-to-day affairs are concerned, the core group of the Salaetua 'aiga is simply a network of four siblings. The last life-crisis event in which they acted as a unit was the funeral of their father in 1974. Yet the intimacy, interdependence, and frequency of contact is particularly striking when contrasted to relationships maintained with friends and affines.

In the third case below, we see the opposite end of the spectrum in 'aiga network organization. The Teu household is tied to others in the community more through friendship, clubs, and church activities than kinship.

THE 'AIGA TEU

The 'aiga Teu is the largest of the village of Fagali'i, Tutuila, a small settlement on the remote western end of the island. By 1960 many of the younger members had migrated; several went to Hawaii, some to Southern California, and one to Oakland. One young man, Lopati, unlike his older brothers and sisters, had little desire to come to the United States. He enjoyed life in the village, for he earned enough from a job with the Public Works Department to procure the foods and goods his 'aiga desired. In 1965 he met and married a girl from Tula, a village at the opposite end of the island. Lopati and his new wife, Elisa, soon chose to move closer to the main town of Fagatogo, so that Elisa could complete nurse's training at the hospital. In 1968 Lopati suffered a bad fall on the job that damaged the tendons and muscles in one leg. The hospital did not have the proper facilities to perform surgery, so Lopati was advised to go to Hawaii or California. Lopati and Elisa decided to come to Oakland, where one of Lopati's brothers lived.

After the surgery had been performed and therapy completed, the couple returned to Samoa, but they found life there more dissatisfying than they had remembered it. Lopati's leg had not returned to normal, so he was unable to work at his old job. Nor could he find another that suited him. Life in the village became stifling because of the expectation that Lopati would now work full-time for the matai on the family lands. Lopati and Elisa lasted only a year in Fagali'i before they decided to return to California. Lopati wrote his brother in Oakland, expressing his wish to return and asking for money to help pay for his and his wife's trip. Lopati's brother agreed, and Lopati and Elisa arrived in California for good in 1969. They lived for a year with Lopati's brother and a year with Elisa's sister; then, when their first child was born, they found a small apartment in San Francisco.

Since 1971 the couple and their two children have maintained their own household. They still visit on special occasions with Lopati's brother in Oakland, but the two families are not especially close now. Elisa's sister has returned to Samoa and is unavailable for participation in family events or as a source of support. Lopati has one cousin in the area whom he visits every month or so, and Elisa is distantly related to the wife of one of the Leulua brothers. They contribute to events affecting the Leulua family as the occasion requires and have participated from time to time in 'aiga get-togethers sponsored by the Leuluas. Lopati's brother sometimes calls from Los Angeles to inform Lopati of a death or marriage in the kindred, and Lopati and Elisa will send a small cash contribution.

Unlike other 'aiga, the 'aiga Teu is independent of most other households in the San Francisco area and does not participate to any great extent in kindred affairs. For both Elisa and Lopati the most important relationship is with Lopati's brother in Oakland, who has helped the family with expenses on several occasions. Lopati and Elisa have been without jobs since arriving and occasionally experience difficulty stretching Lopati's disability check and the AFDC they receive for their children. However, Lopati's brother is not heavily involved in *fa'asamoa* because he married a white woman and has purposefully excluded himself from the ceremonial exchange system.

The only real networks that Elisa and Lopati participate in are based on friendship. These networks have arisen in two important social contexts: participation in a Samoan voluntary organization and membership in a local Samoan church. Lopati and Elisa helped start the voluntary organization. Begun by a few interested couples set on organizing the Flag Day celebrations that honor the territorial status of American Samoa, it developed into a sports association that sponsors cricket, softball, and volleyball leagues. Devoted members of their church, both Elisa and Lopati are heavily involved in its social activities, committees, and religious affairs. Lopati is a deacon, and Elisa an active member of the women's association. Through their participation in church activities Elisa and Lopati have developed a wide network of friends. Parties, dinners, and informal get-togethers take up any free time they have remaining from their church and organization activities.

Here is the case of a nuclear household isolated from its kindreds but still thoroughly integrated into the Samoan community. Although nearly all households are involved to some extent in church activities, and many are becoming involved in various voluntary associations, such organizations perform a vital social function for isolated households like the Teus. They not only represent avenues that allow individuals to become integrated into the Samoan community, but facilitate, as in the case of the Teus, the formation of friendship networks.

These cases indicate that some aspects of Samoan kinship have survived in the urban context, even though economic necessity has resulted in a dispersal of households units. These households vary in the degree to which they cooperate with others to which they trace kinship. When the ties are strong, such as those between brothers, a core 'aiga network develops that may in turn function as a basis for a larger, integrated 'aiga grouping. But this development is relatively uncommon; it is more typical for households to be enmeshed in overlapping cooperative networks based primarily on the important relationships between brothers, sisters, and other close bilateral kin. This variability is a result of two important processes: (1) the force for selectivity in migration, that is, the number of close kin migrating to one specific area; and (2) a change in the economic functions of household cooperation from one based on subsistence agriculture to one based on an ideal of mutual aid. The first process has served to emphasize sibling networks or networks of age peers over other kinship ties. The second operates to promote the independence of individual households, thus leaving cooperation to be based on cultural ideals and social pressures, as well as on economic necessity. There is an obvious element of voluntarism involved in the development of 'aiga networks. Networks may develop into highly integrated 'aiga groups or simply embody a few important relationships between close relatives. The personalities of household heads, the economic circumstances of member households, and the occurrence of situations in which 'aiga ties are used for support are also important determinants of 'aiga integration.

FIVE

Community Organization and Leadership

By far the most important institution for integrating dispersed kindreds is the church. It plays a central role in nearly all Samoan affairs, secular as well as religious. It is in the context of the church that one can best see the emergence of a different system of leadership that combines features of both the old and the new. Though other community organizations play a less important role in integrating kindreds, they do function to promote some special interests or fulfill specific needs. Voluntary organizations of this type appear to be a relatively new phenomenon, arising to promote Samoan interests and solve Samoan problems in the American social and cultural milieu.

The Church in Samoa and on the Mainland

Samoans have been devout Christians since the mid-nineteenth century, and church organizations have from that time occupied a central position in the sociopolitical structure of the village. Tiffany (1978: 424) proposes that

the LMS [London Missionary Society] enterprise was successful in Samoa for many reasons, foremost among them . . . its decentralized organization and local congregational approach. . . . In Samoa, the missionaries were confronted with a vigorous sociopolitical system which necessitated their adaptation to an indigenous organization of cognatic descent groups and chiefly hierarchies. . . . Samoa became an arena in which political relations, consisting of labile alignments of chiefs, descent groups, villages and districts, shaped the mission's administrative organization, procedures, affairs and autonomy.

As a consequence of this process churches became politicized, molded by students of the first mission schools into uniquely Samoan institutions. Also subject to reinterpretation were the doctrine and practice of Christianity. Within a very short time the church had become the most important social institution in the village. Though theoretically the local pastor was to remain aloof from and neutral in village political alignments, and remain outside the formal village structure of social control, in reality clergy exerted tremendous influence in these areas. Correspondingly, important lay positions in the church—deacons, committee members, and lay preachers—were occupied by village matai and ranked accordingly. With the introduction of other mission enterprises and religions, denominational affiliation became an important correlate of descent-group affiliation and a point of intravillage political cleavage.

Aside from the role they play in political relations, churches in contemporary Samoa provide an important context for social activities. The entire week is organized around church meetings and affairs: choir practice, youth group activities, women's association meetings, meetings of deacons, pastoral visits to member families, food preparation for the minister, and fund raising.

Under the circumstances it is hardly surprising that many of the first group activities Samoan migrants to the United States organized were based on religion. From the beginning, however, churches were much more than they had been in Samoa: they grew and expanded to fill a void produced by the migrants' loss of not just membership in a local congregation, but village membership as well. The role of the church thus grew to encompass and sanction the wide gambit of activities formerly divided into the secular and religious spheres of life. To a dispersed urban community of comparatively few numbers, the church congregation became the only institution where social interaction and events were possible on a level above that of the core 'aiga network or household. Stateside church congregations thus developed to fill a number of social needs and now function to provide a village-like context for important ceremonies and rituals.

The first church congregation in the San Francisco area was founded in 1957. It was an outgrowth of a network of relatives and friends who met together in each other's homes for regular prayer services and Sunday meals. As more and more relatives and village-mates arrived, these weekly prayer meetings grew. When the group was large enough to support a church and minister, the members decided to affiliate with the United Church of Christ (the American Congregational church organization), which provided financial assistance but required that the services and congregation leadership be organized along American lines. Desiring the more Samoan-type LMS services and organization, four families left a year later to start a new church. For the first year and a half they met in a member's home. In 1959 they received permission from the Congrega-

TABLE 5.1

Northern California Samoan Churches and Bay Area Samoans' Affiliation

Denomination	Number of churches[a]	Affiliation of sample	
		Number	Percent
Congregational (all)	12	87	83.7%
Methodist	3	0	–
Assembly of God	7	2	1.9
Seventh-day Adventist	2	0	–
Pentecostal	3	5	4.8
Other	2	2	1.9
TOTAL	29	96	92.3%
Mormon and Catholic clubs[b]	2	8	7.7%

[a]In Monterey, Santa Clara, San Mateo, Alameda, and San Francisco counties.
[b]Mormons and Catholics attend churches that are not exclusively Samoan, but maintain their own choirs, associations, and clubs.

tional Church of Samoa to start a church and were sent a Samoan minister who had just graduated from the Congregational Church Seminary in Malua, Western Samoa.

As these two congregations grew, subgroups split off from time to time to establish their own congregations. This fissioning was often motivated by political squabbling within the original group, usually along 'aiga lines. But the growth of a network of related 'aiga living at some distance from the church to which they belonged also prompted the founding of a new church in that area. The majority of the first Congregational churches affiliated with the LMS hierarchy in Samoa, which soon established administrative districts linking together congregations started elsewhere in California, Washington state, and Hawaii. Today only three Samoan Congregational churches in the Bay Area remain affiliated with the United Churches of Christ; the rest are associated with the two major Congregational church organizations in Samoa: the Congregational Church of Jesus Christ in Samoa, and the First Samoan Congregational Church of American Samoa. More than half the Samoans in Northern California belong to one or another of the Congregational churches.

The other well-established Samoan denomination, the Methodists, established a church in San Francisco in 1958. It is a large and vigorous congregation. Two smaller Methodist churches have since been founded in Northern California. The Samoans also maintain local Pentecostal, Assembly of God, Seventh-day Adventist, and other fundamentalist Christian churches. In all, there are 29 Samoan churches in Northern California. Table 5.1 lists them by denomination, along with the church affiliation of my sample. A substantial number of Samoans also attend American

Mormon and Catholic churches in the area. At one time the Mormons organized a special Polynesian ward, but this was later disbanded. Most Samoan Mormons now attend the closest church, though one informant indicated that a northern San Mateo county church had attracted a very large Samoan and Tongan membership. Samoan Catholics attend various parish churches in San Francisco and Daly City, but have their own choir, club, and youth group.

Congregation or denominational switching is common; the most frequent causes are disagreements with other church members over finances, doctrine, or the selection of officers; dislike of the minister; and personal disputes. When a large 'aiga or group of 'aiga leaves a congregation, the members usually attempt to start a new church. If the group is not large enough to support a church and minister, it will join another congregation. Marriage and moving to a new residence are also reasons for joining a different church. As in Samoa the decision to affiliate with a particular congregation is more than a personal choice based on religious preference. It is also based on economic and political concerns (Tiffany 1978).

Despite the denominational heterogeneity of the San Francisco community, it is common for church-goers representing different denominations to meet together on special occasions, particularly funerals and the dedication of new church buildings. Ministers representing several of the larger and well-established congregations have formed the Samoan Ministers' Association, an organization developed to address issues pertaining not only to interdenominational communication and cooperation, but to the welfare of the Samoan community in general. Several of these ministers are called on frequently to represent Bay Area Samoans in political and community meetings with non-Samoans. In line with the expanding social role of the church, this ecumenical group serves to communicate information about issues and programs that affect the entire Samoan population.

Samoans reckon that nearly everyone in the migrant community of Northern California belongs to one of the area's Samoan churches, and that a significant majority regularly attend weekly services. This corresponds to my own observations: out of all the Samoans I had contact with—as informants, friends, or colleagues—only one man did not regularly attend church services. But even he was registered as a member of a congregation and occasionally attended dances and other cultural events held at his church. In some ways the extent of church participation is surprising; in San Francisco there is not the kind of social control and pressure that serves to ensure regular religious participation in a Samoan village. Matai do not survey member households to see if someone is shirking his or her religious responsibilities. Individuals are given more freedom in choosing whether to participate, and at what level. Yet 'aiga pressure and the fact that the church congregation provides many opportunities for acquiring leadership status motivate most people at least to attend weekly services. Variation in commitment depends on interest in participating in social affairs and activities. Involvement may be daily or restricted to attending the main Sunday service.

A Bay Area Church Congregation

As part of my fieldwork I attended a Samoan church and participated in the congregation's affairs. This church, the First Samoan Christian Church (FSCC), is a medium-sized Congregational church under the administration of the main church offices in American Samoa.* One of eight congregations in a Northern California district (*pulega*) of the Samoan organization, it was founded in 1962 by five families. Most originally belonged to another Samoan church, but dissatisfaction with the minister led them to leave and form their own congregation. At first one man who had a good education and a thorough knowledge of the Bible conducted prayer meetings in his home. When the prayer group members decided they could support a church, he wrote to the main church offices in Samoa and formally requested permission to found a new congregation. Approval was quickly forthcoming; a new minister and his family arrived within a year.

According to Samoan custom, a pastor (*faife'au*) enters into a ceremonial kinship relationship with his congregation (*feagaiga*), in which the church members provide for the pastor's subsistence needs, and he attends to their spiritual needs. But because of the cost of living in San Francisco, the FSCC's few founding families could not fully support the pastor and his large family at first, so he lived with one of the founders who had just purchased a large home. Later he also took a job in a steel manufacturing firm. The families rented a hall in the city where they could hold services, and each was assigned a monthly tithe of $100 to cover church expenses. Members were also expected to donate as much in cash and food as they could to support the pastor and his family.

The congregation grew rapidly. In 1967 the members purchased an old warehouse that was suitable for holding services, and by 1970 there were enough of them to buy a group of adjacent lots in a residential area and build a church. It was dedicated in a large formal ceremony in early 1972. Throughout these years church members were asked to contribute a regu-

---

*The name, dates, and other identifying information have been changed to ensure the anonymity of the congregation.

lar amount each month to maintain their own property and help support the main church offices and facilities in Samoa. In addition, a special monthly offering was designated to go to the minister and his family. Individual contributions were supplemented from time to time by large fund-raising events like lotteries and dances, which netted significant income. By this time the pastor was able to quit working and turn his full attention to the needs of his growing congregation.

The FSCC organization now consists of a pastor, three lay ministers, and several deacons. A title is not a prerequisite for becoming a deacon as it is in Samoa, but one must be respected by the congregation and be seen as generous, hard-working, and responsible. The FSCC's deacons are elected at an annual meeting of church members. One of them is designated to be the "elder" deacon, essentially the congregation's "talking chief," who represents the church in formal affairs requiring oratory and ceremonial presentation. Other deacons may be appointed to district-wide offices and committees, appointments that entail considerable prestige. The president of the congregation (*ta'ita'i fono*), secretaries, treasurers, and committee members are chosen from the ranks of deacons by a vote of the membership or by appointment of the minister. This group—deacons, minister, and lay preachers—constitutes the FSCC's major decision-making body.

The membership (*'ekalesia*) consists of those who have been baptized and who have applied to the congregation and been accepted as full members. They are also referred to by the term *'au fai ipu*, which refers to their status as communicants ('au=group; fai=do, make; ipu=cup). Visitors and relatives who may attend regularly are known as *uso fa'aopoopo* (literally, "added siblings"). During the time I attended the FSCC, its congregation typically consisted of the members of 61 households plus six to ten regularly attending parents of active members and two or three guests and visitors. Counting entire households, the church had more than 500 members in 1983.

This membership is divided into several subgroups, each involved in a different range of social and religious activities. There is a youth group (*'autalavou*), divided into two sections according to age; a large choir (*'aufaipese*) that includes a separate youth choir; a women's association; and a committee of deacons. Each group has its own meetings, solicits its own contributions, and has certain responsibilities and functions within the church as a whole. Parallels to Samoan village social organization are interesting: the youth group is comparable to the village associations of young men (*'aumaga*) and young women (*aualuma*); the deacons' committee is structured and ranked in a fashion similar to the village *fono* institution; and the women's association is organized much like the *fale tama'ita'i* ("women's house"), made up of the wives of matai. Much as in Samoa women derive their status within the women's association from their husbands' status in the church hierarchy.

The ranking of deacons is most visible at the post-Sunday service meal (*to'ona'i*). The minister sits at a head table either alone or with visiting clergy or the church member who delivered the day's sermon. Perpendicular to that are two tables. At one the men arrange themselves in this order: lay ministers, the moderator (president) of the congregation, elder deacon, other deacon-officeholders, and finally deacons not currently holding an office. At the other table opposite, women are seated in a position roughly corresponding to their husbands' ranks. Usually only a few women attend the to'ona'i, which tends to be a men's affair. The wives and children of many of the deacons help prepare and serve the food.

The church is the scene of much social activity on Sundays. Deacons arrive early to open the church and prepare the facilities for services. When a visiting group is staying with the pastor or important guests are in attendance, a group of men and women arrive early to prepare food for the guests. Sunday school, taught by both men and women, begins at 9:00 A.M. Children are divided into age groups and taught Bible passages and prayers. Although teachers try to give some instruction in Samoan so their charges will pick up the language or at least learn to read the Samoan Bible, most members admit that younger children and those raised stateside have difficulty with Samoan. The desire to teach the Bible outweighs the desire to teach children Samoan, so Sunday-school instruction is often in English, or a mixture of English and simple Samoan.

A prayer service conducted by one of the deacons follows Sunday school. This service consists of several hymns, prayers, and a short message. It offers a chance for deacons to show off their oratorical abilities, and deacons compete to deliver captivating messages. The main church service begins at 11:00 A.M. and lasts approximately one and a half hours. It consists of several hymns sung by the choir, a Bible-reading and comment, a sermon delivered by either the minister or one of the lay ministers, and a long formal prayer. At the conclusion of the formal ceremonies, announcements and daily offering amounts are read aloud. After this some deacons, lay ministers, and the pastor, along with a few wives, retire to the church hall for the to'ona'i. Other members return to their own or a family member's home for a large meal. At 3:00 P.M. one of the lay ministers leads a final worship service, this one specifically for older youth. Occasionally the deacons' or women's association meets on Sunday afternoons.

The balance of the week is no less busy. Monday evenings are often used for meetings and choir practice. Tuesday, Wednesday, Friday, and

Saturday are bingo nights. The games last from 7:30 to about 10:30 P.M. Choir practice is often held just before bingo on these nights, beginning at about 6:00 P.M. Saturday daytimes are often used for meetings of the women, youth, deacons, or the entire church membership, and Monday and Thursday evenings are often used for activities associated with traveling groups from Samoa.

Traveling groups, called *faigamalaga*, include youth groups touring California, church or village organizations conducting fund-raising for a specific purpose, and groups of villagers who are simply interested in taking a vacation. The traveling group is an important institution in Samoa, and a strict set of rules governs the exchange of oratory and gifts between hosts and guests. A four-part ceremonial is mandatory. The occasion is opened by the presentation of kava and a formal welcoming speech given by the hosts; second comes a presentation of gifts to the hosts by the visitors; third the visitors offer some form of entertainment; and last there is a farewell ceremony in which the hosts provide gifts for the visitors.

Church activities involve a significant expenditure of time and money. Though the church no longer requires regular family contributions to meet payments on mortgages or the upkeep of buildings, substantial amounts are still given to the minister and for church activities in Samoa. The average yearly contribution varies widely. It appears correlated to two things: the family's income, and the status of the family (household) or of significant family members within the church hierarchy. In my sample the median yearly offering to the church per household was $900, but the mean was over $1,200.

Those individuals who are most committed to church affairs generally contribute the most money. Correspondingly, positions in the hierarchy appear to go to those who can most afford them. But access to church status is not simply a product of economic status. Position in the church community derives from a number of factors, including not only generosity, but a range of personal attributes and actions Samoans admire. Individuals elected or appointed to church offices are generally perceived to be religious, knowledgeable about Samoan culture, and financially successful, with a good, prestigious job.

The church's ability to confer status and prestige has led to the formation of a core group of heavily contributing, intensely involved participants, holding by far most of the church positions. Other members of the congregation contribute comparatively fewer dollars and are less involved in day-to-day affairs. In the FSCC the important offices are held by migrants who have been in the area the longest, who have or are retired from well-paying jobs, and are comparatively better educated and better off financially than other members. However, some men with high status as matai and knowledge of Samoan custom may hold important positions regardless of their financial position. Since the church often hosts important cultural events, it is important that some leaders possess a detailed knowledge of how to handle such affairs.

One important source of church funds lies outside the public realm of attending church and contributing to its support: the bingo game. It is also a relatively new source, because until a few years ago bingo games for cash were not permitted by California law. Nearly all Samoan churches in the area, except for fundamentalists, who by doctrine do not believe in gambling, run bingo games. The FSCC, as noted, runs bingo games four nights a week; each night is for a different church organization. In contrast to church offerings, which are publicly given and announced, participation is purely a matter of personal choice. Some members do not like playing the game at all, and others come only to help organize and run the games. Several of the principal church leaders play frequently. At the FSCC bingo is an expensive activity. Playing with an average number of bingo cards, buying various "specials," and purchasing a snack means a nightly expenditure of at least $20. Some individuals say they play for the sake of the church, but most enjoy the game; Samoans are avid gamblers. On a good night the church will net $1,000. The average is probably $500 a night. The different organizations use their bingo earnings for a wide range of purposes. At the time of my fieldwork, much of the money was sent back to the main church in Samoa, then building a large seminary complex, and a large amount had just been used to buy and refurbish a home for the minister. Other uses include helping families in need, maintaining church buildings and property, and purchasing food for church events.

Interestingly, fewer than half the regular bingo players at the FSCC are church members. Many are non-Samoan, mostly residents of the immediate neighborhood. The church recognizes their importance to the game and does its best to entice them to continue coming by offering specials such as free food and drink.

The tremendous financial success of bingo has had an obvious impact on the involvement of church members in congregation affairs. Bingo has taken away some of the pressure on members to contribute on a regular basis. The FSCC leadership has tried to keep bingo income separate from the more socially important offerings, particularly the "*alofa*" (literally, "love"; "loving concern") offering to the minister. Some churches in the area, particularly those with younger and more pragmatic leaders, pay their ministers' salaries from bingo proceeds. But the FSCC's members object to bingo money as being "dirty" and prefer to make their own offerings to the minister in the conventional manner. The most important consequence of bingo has been the depersonalization of giving, and church members admit to a corresponding weakening of community bonds for this reason. Bingo has had other social effects. Time taken to conduct the games limits the time available for other activities. A few members said that the church used to be much more of a focus of family social life than it is now. With bingo adults come to play, leaving the children at home or to fend for themselves in the church parking lot. In earlier years the church organized more activities for youth and encouraged more contact between parents and children. Despite these worries, members recognize the value of bingo income for running the church.

The Social Role of the Church

Although costly in financial terms, church membership provides a number of benefits. Most important, the church is an arena of intense social activity that fosters the development of friendship networks; these in turn unite family groups. Young men and women have an opportunity to meet, develop relationships, and marry. Many families in a sense "grow up together" in the church and develop bonds that supplement those of kinship. To new migrants church networks provide a range of information and assistance of greater breadth and depth than is available within the immediate 'aiga. Deacons and other leaders, by virtue of their status as "successful" migrants, are important role models for new migrants and youth. They are valuable sources of advice, information, and aid. Next to family groups, religious networks are by far the most important referral sources for jobs and housing.

Church events are important to members because they are culturally meaningful. The FSCC's church service is virtually indistinguishable from the Samoan service. And the minister often uses the occasion to compare or contrast this or that element of Samoan culture with American ways, thereby drawing attention to the aspects of Samoan culture that are most meaningful to life on the mainland. Outside of religious services church members gather to participate in rituals and ceremonies that are similar to those enacted in Samoa. After funerals orators deliver formal speeches of thanks and recognition, fine mats are exchanged,* and Samoan foods

---

* These are woven from thin strips of *Pandanus* (screw-pine) and bordered with brightly colored cloth and feathers. Most mats are made in Samoa; however, a few women import dried *Pandanus* from Hawaii or Samoa and weave fine mats for special occasions. The quality of a mat is judged by the fineness of the weave. Fine mats are a highly valued medium of exchange in Samoa, and the giving of a fine mat confers prestige on both the giver and receiver. In California the giving of fine mats is still important, but much less so than in Samoa.

are provided for all. When traveling parties arrive, matai engage in a formal and stylized debate (*fa'atau*) to decide who should give the welcoming speech. Kava is presented, and a speech made in language and a format that are generations old. Village greetings (*fa'alupega*) are recited carefully, and old proverbs are pronounced and discussed with new elaboration and twists in meaning. In short, the church provides the only context for publicly enacting and revitalizing Samoan life as the migrants favorably remember it.

In this way the church provides an important, though incomplete, socializing function for youth who have never been to Samoa or were too young when they left to remember life there. The lesson is incomplete because the rituals youth see are removed from the sociocultural context in which they are most relevant. Nor are they sufficiently explained by those who possess a detailed knowledge of them and the ability to convey that knowledge in an articulate fashion. Yet youth do attend such events with interest and gain at least some idea of their unique history as Samoans. Significantly, one program recently initiated by a Samoan community organization in Los Angeles to address the problem of juvenile delinquency uses churches and networks of young "role models" to teach elements of Samoan history, language, and culture, and their importance in the urban American context.

Churches, although a force for cultural conservatism, also hold an intermediate position between Samoans and the larger urban society. This position serves to foster the development of an ethnic identity and to link families and helping institutions or programs. This intermediate role is most evident in the content of the discussions that go on routinely at church services and meetings. Individuals involved in church activities and networks do not simply exchange information about how to get jobs and other practical matters; they organize their thoughts about what it is to be Samoan in urban America. Practices and institutions they admire are discussed and occasionally adopted. Others they do not approve of are discussed and rejected. Throughout this process a consistent identity develops. Ministers also address the issue of what it is to be Samoan in a very different society, comparing and contrasting the Samoan way, fa'asamoa, to the American way (*fa'apalagi*). Using their usually superior education and experience they interpret for their parishioners the workings of the larger society with a distinctly Samoan moral message. In short, churches serve to draw boundaries between Samoans as a unique ethnic group, and other ethnic groups.

Churches also represent a point of interface between Samoans and American social-service institutions. Samoan community organizations realize that working through churches is an effective way to reach Samoans, and ministers often assist both Samoan and non-Samoan agencies or programs in contacting needy community members. For example, in 1982 there were two city-county programs for Samoans in San Francisco organized by Samoan community groups. The first was a community development program designed to provide language assistance, counseling, and referral services to people seeking aid from or needing aid to cope with some institution, such as the Juvenile Justice Department or the Immigration Department. The second was a vocational English-as-a-second-language program aimed at acquainting Samoans with skills needed to search for and find jobs, while simultaneously instructing them in the "culture" of the American workplace. Both programs filled a demonstrated need and were relatively successful. But without the churches, there would be no way of reaching the Samoan population in an effective way. Ministers, moderators, and other influential leaders act as referral sources that bring programs like these to the attention of the most needy. Both of these Samoan community organizations maintained close ties with ministers of all Samoan churches.

The churches themselves also try to provide some welfare services. Each congregation has its own policies on aiding needy families; most lend money to individuals who find themselves in need of emergency assistance. The FSCC has a policy of not lending money to church members, a regulation intended, so I was told, to prevent financial misdeeds in the handing out of church monies.* Even so, in some circumstances the minister may ask the church to bend the rules. A common instance is when a sudden death in a church member's immediate family necessitates a quick return to Samoa. In addition, the church always donates money toward a member family's funeral or wedding expenses. And sometimes toward an outsider's: when my brother died while I was working in the community, I was scolded for not letting the minister know right away and was then given a substantial contribution on behalf of the church "to help with the expenses."

Other Formal Organizations

Two other types of voluntary community organizations have made a relatively recent appearance in the Samoan community: advocacy groups that campaign for federal, state, and local funds or programs; and special-

* Accusations of irregularities and fraud are unfortunately common, particularly if factions develop among church members, and they can drive a congregation apart very rapidly. One church in Los Angeles was even forced to disband altogether when the minister discovered a prominent family was using bingo profits to support its members.

interest clubs. The first appear likely to stay in place for some time to come; the second tend to come and go.

The largest of the advocacy groups is the Office of Samoan Affairs (OSA), which has branches in Los Angeles and San Francisco. The board of directors consists of 24 of the leading ministers, chiefs, and community members. In the early 1980's, the group was active primarily on the federal level, lobbying not only on behalf of Samoans, but for other Pacific Island populations as well. OSA began in 1976 as an outgrowth of networks developed by concerned and educated community leaders and community-minded matai who saw a need for political action.

In the San Francisco area the oldest surviving civic organization of this type is Samoa mo Samoa (Samoa for Samoans). It was started by a Western Samoan woman and has since recruited several influential leaders and matai. In 1984 Samoa mo Samoa had two divisions: a club made up primarily of the original members and their associates; and a bilingual counseling office. Most club members are older women who live in a single housing project. Bimonthly meetings are held in the housing project's community center. The club conducts a number of fund-raising events and has occasionally run a bingo game. This money, plus dues, is pooled and used to help club members in need. In many ways the club functions as an informal rotating credit association.

Members of the club also volunteer to staff the bilingual counseling office, which provides bilingual services to Samoans needing emergency assistance. The staff has varied over the years as funds have fluctuated, but a core group of members has worked, both as paid staff and volunteers, since the beginning of the program.

Other organizations have been formed for a specific purpose, for example, to sponsor cricket, softball, or volleyball leagues. One or two families commonly provide the organizational impetus for such clubs. One sports club organized during my fieldwork was founded by a group of young, educated, and respected brothers from one of the area's largest 'aiga. Sports clubs are particularly important for youth, allowing them to interact with other young Samoans and do uniquely Samoan things. At one local park where Samoan cricket games are held weekly from spring through late summer, several hundred youth routinely congregate for socializing and participating in sporting events.

In summary, it can be said that Samoan voluntary organizations have arisen to provide services and activities not possible within the context of church or family. Political advocacy and social programs can more easily be provided by organizations claiming to speak for the community as a whole. As the needs of the Samoan community increase, particularly given the greater incidence of economic and social problems among the new migrants, it is likely that these organizations will increase in size, number, and importance.

Leadership Status and Prestige

One outcome of migration is a fundamental change of leadership at the local level. Many traditional leaders may choose not to migrate, particularly if they anticipate a loss of power under changed social circumstances. Leaders may have little authority if the skills that qualified them for leadership in the home society are obsolete or incidental to the demands of a different socioeconomic system (Scudder and Colson 1980). The extent to which migrants are able to develop a system of leadership is an indication both of how effectively they are able to maintain some sense of kin group and community integration and of what characteristics they perceive as having the most functional significance in the new setting. I have had occasion to discuss the changing qualifications for leadership and the role of the church as an alternative path to positions of status in the community. In this section I will discuss in greater detail the changing structure of Samoan leadership, its causes, and its consequences.

In Samoa matai possess and exercise authority in two distinct social domains: the localized 'aiga, where the chief is the sole authority over a group of households and their economic activities; and the community, the public domain where matai meet to settle village disputes, establish village rules, and hand down decisions affecting the entire village. This also involves representing one's 'aiga before the rest of the village and its council. As we have seen, chiefs are ranked vis-à-vis one another in two distinct categories: orators (*tulafale*) and "nobles" (*ali'i*). The two stand in a complementary relationship to each other, but it is the orator who possesses the most active dimension of power: oratorical skill and the responsibility for the giving and receiving of fine mats, food, and other items (Shore 1982). These two domains are where power is exercised and prestige gained; they remain an effective way to analyze leadership in the migrant community.

To an outsider the matai is the most visible evidence of cultural continuity between the islands and the mainland. This is because he retains his authority and function in public and ceremonial contexts. In terms of the daily exercise of authority and power over an 'aiga group, however, a matai is in a much more tenuous position. The land resources on which his power is based are in Samoa. Moreover, it is difficult to exercise control over wage-earning 'aiga members. Indeed, where the matai is dependent on employed nontitled household members, he may have to accede to their desires regarding the disposal of income, even for ceremonial purposes.

Yet the position of leadership within an 'aiga is still an important one. Even when the title has little meaning in terms of land control and status in the village of origin, many heads of household clusters, especially a senior brother or well-established elder, have assumed a matai name. In networks where no one holds a matai title, members may designate one person to look after stateside 'aiga affairs and represent them among the kindred when the occasion warrants it. For each 'aiga group I was able to identify, one individual was given this authority, either by the local 'aiga group or by the senior matai in Samoa. These individuals organize 'aiga meetings, contact relatives living elsewhere in the case of a death or other event, and coordinate contributions. But people acting in this capacity are not called matai, and on occasions where other matai are present they cannot speak on their or their kin group's behalf unless absolutely no one else present can do so.

Of the 57 men in my sample, two were ali'i, eighteen were tulafale, and two held both titles. One woman also possessed a title, but it was only honorary and did not involve any 'aiga or community responsibilities. These figures are taken on trust: the 22 men simply stated that they possessed these titles. I have been told that some Samoans who call themselves matai have not taken the formal steps necessary to accept a title. This involves returning to Samoa, being accorded a formal title-acceptance ceremony (*saofa'i*), and registering the title with the appropriate legal agency in either American or Western Samoa. In California it is usually impossible to determine who has taken these steps. Many public occasions arise where matai argue vehemently over their own and others' rights to speak. Rolff (1978) reports a case in Los Angeles where a saofa'i was terminated when, after an hour's debate between the several matai present, there was no agreement on who was entitled to speak for the various branches of the kindred in attendance.

The preponderance of orator titles in the sample is interesting. This is not an accident of sampling but reflects a preference for the privileges that the tulafale title brings. Samoans appreciate that a greater public role is given orators, and that they function more directly as representatives of the 'aiga group in the migrant context. Additionally, orators have greater access to fine mats, cash, and food on ceremonial occasions. Ali'i in traditional Samoa represent a passive or latent dimension of public power that is relatively unimportant to leadership in the urban context. As one man told me, "I have made my title an orator title because I have to speak for the family and I like getting all those fine mats." He made this change by simply asserting his rights as an orator, which in his case usually goes uncontested. If he were to return to his village, his claims of tulafale status would not be recognized.

Not all individuals identifying themselves as matai lead a household cluster. In two households of brothers, both men held titles, but one was decidedly senior. The junior matai in these households performed a number of public functions, particularly in the conduct of cultural events within the church, but within the 'aiga they exercised little authority. In one of the families the brothers had divided up responsibilities to appear at public events so as to share expenses.

Matai titles do not involve any authority over the affairs of the constituent households beyond organizing and managing contributions and presentations. Matai may occasionally attempt to assert authority over an 'aiga group, but I was told this invariably leads to considerable conflict between those willing to recognize his authority and those not. Recently migrating matai are regarded with a greater degree of suspicion than established migrants who have been given matai titles; the latter are perceived as having "earned" their position by proving themselves capable as providers in a cash economy.

The role of the provider is an extremely important one in the migrant context. For most daily household activities, authority is constituted in an older male provider (if there is one). But the situation can become complicated when younger men and women provide most of the household income, yet cannot overrule the decisions of an older man or woman resident. There is likely to be some tension if the elder chooses to take a heavy hand in controlling household finances.

Since matai leadership on the mainland is primarily titular and ceremonial, several men who had access to titles said that they would have little reason to accept them unless they intended to return to Samoa. Some of these men had no desire to participate in public ceremonials, others were pursuing status in different ways, and still others were simply pragmatic about the day-to-day relevance of the matai institution:

Three nights they tried to get me to take a title, but I turned them down. I turned them down because I don't have anything for becoming a *matai*. I appreciated their asking and knew they were thanking me for what I have done for my wife's family. But what *pule* [authority, power] do you have anyway? I've got seven children, these are *pule* enough; seven *pule* running around the house. And in the Bible the *matai* is nothing. The only thing in the Bible that is like gold are the children God gives us to care for.

Beyond the local 'aiga network, where a matai holds power in a few circumscribed, well-defined areas, lies the community sphere. Here the matai occupies a much different status, a public position in which he represents a kin group, gives and receives honors, and validates and works to widen his and his 'aiga's status and prestige in the eyes of the community. It is this role that makes the prospect of a title attractive to some, and it is in this arena where the distinction between titled and untitled men is most pronounced.

Originally, as Ablon (1971a) reports, few matai migrated to California, so senior 'aiga members possessing good oratorical skills were often appointed to this position. This state of affairs has gradually shifted over the years. More matai have migrated, and senior matai in Samoa have appointed a number of men to represent them in stateside affairs. It is much less common now to see nontitled men rising to speak on public occasions unless they can appeal to some other basis of leadership, such as church position.

Though migrant matai are unlikely to hold a title of sufficient rank to exchange formal oratory with a senior ranking chief in a Samoan village, visiting matai will often permit them to speak, recognizing that no one else can do it. Elder deacons, lay ministers, and even on some occasions ministers may also use their status in the church to exchange oratory with a visiting senior matai, even if their matai titles in the secular sphere are insignificant. Most of the titled men in San Francisco I spoke with agree that only three to four titles in the entire area would be considered "high" in Samoa.

This pattern of moving from the secular to the religious sphere to assert one's status indicates that the Samoan system of leadership has opened up considerably in the migrant community. There has been a blending of secular political rank with rank defined by position within church organizations. By offering alternative avenues to positions of community leadership, this process has made ranking a complex matter, particularly in relation to a village system. Consequently, when traveling groups arrive from the islands, it may be tricky to establish rank relationships between the host matai and church leaders, and the visiting ali'i and tulafale (who may themselves hold positions in a church back home).

It thus takes someone with a detailed knowledge of rank throughout the islands to determine just who should speak and how that person should be introduced. Samoan men told me that visiting matai will often take advantage of what they assume to be the migrants' lack of knowledge of formal ceremonial comportment and poor oratorical skills. In one case I observed, a very high-ranking chief of a traveling group stopped the welcoming speech of a man representing a host church because the man's title made him an inappropriate choice as speaker. I was told that in the formal debate between orators for rights to speak this man emphasized his rights on the ground of fa'asamoa rather than on the ground of his church position—which would have been quite appropriate in this case. On another occasion, a funeral, a talking chief of high rank explic-

itly told the assembled crowd that he wanted no one to stand up and answer him, because he knew there was no one in attendance of sufficient
rank to do so. Undeterred, an untitled but knowledgeable man, and an
excellent speaker, stood up and addressed the chief as a representative
of the church. Though the visitor repeatedly attempted to humiliate the
speaker by calling attention to his untitled status (using his informal or
"young man's" name), the local man's oratorical ability sustained him,
and in the migrants' eyes he won a great victory.

The blending of religious and secular dimensions of leadership in the
migrant community represents a creative development of an effective system of urban leadership that takes advantage of the position of the church
as urban village. As I noted earlier in the chapter, churches have developed in a number of ways to organize 'aiga dispersed throughout a city
into a village-like social institution. Consequently, they provide a context
for enacting a number of formerly secular Samoan activities and thus for
pursuing status and prestige. Matai become deacons as they do in Samoa,
but so do untitled men, and through their efforts they can rise in the
church hierarchy.

Deacons are elected by the congregation in some churches and appointed by ministers or councils in others. Although nearly all adult men
who serve the church by attending and contributing regularly can become
deacons, only a few represent the active leadership of the church. They sit
on committees, organize and run bingo, oversee special offerings for certain church purposes, and make the bulk of the decisions on church
affairs. It is from the ranks of this core group that officers are routinely
elected to positions in the congregation or in the administration of the
local district to which most of the Congregational churches belong. Together these individuals represent what Samoans call the dignity (*mamalu*)
of the church membership (*'ekalesia*). Access to this prestigious group appears to be through a synthesis of the traits that are valued in Samoa and
admired in "successful migrants": religiosity, speaking ability, intelligence, knowledge of Samoan custom, demonstrated generosity, past service to the church, observance of Christian morals, education, a prestigious and/or well-paying job, willingness to spend a great deal of time
and effort in church affairs, and a knowledge of and experience with
American culture and social institutions. The last represents a very important value for stateside migrants. Familiarity with the host country
has also been found to be an important prerequisite for leadership among
Samoan migrants to New Zealand (Pitt and Macpherson 1974).

Samoans show a good deal of respect for those of their fellows who
have lived in California or Hawaii for a number of years, speak good English, are perceived to know many Americans, and are generally familiar

with the somewhat mysterious workings of the American economy: buying homes, procuring bank loans, applying for welfare, setting up bank accounts, and so forth. Wealth, skill in making money, and education are also highly valued traits. Interesting in this respect is the degree to which some women have been able to gain community-wide status and prestige by possessing the same set of traits that qualify men for leadership positions. The two chief community organizations in the Bay Area at the time of my research were headed by women.

Holland (1989) suggests that emerging leadership positions for women are an urban outgrowth of Samoan gender-status patterns. In Samoa the relationship between husband and wife, like the relationship between men and women in general, is complementary. Men assume responsibility for the public sphere, and women for the domestic sphere. Parallel rankings in these distinct spheres are evident in Samoan villages and also, as noted here, in the church congregation. In the urban context, given the need for the community to represent itself where domestic responsibilities and American human services institutions intersect, namely, in the domains of education, health care, and family welfare, Samoan women are acceding to positions of public status vis-à-vis American society. But these positions, though respected by the Samoans, do not confer on women the kind of esteem and prestige within the community accorded to men of status.

The importance of the emerging leadership system cannot be underestimated: the men and women most likely to achieve these positions are those who can act as effective culture-brokers. They serve the community directly by transmitting information on desired services in American society and indirectly by pushing the community's interests to government agencies whose programs affect, or are intended to affect, Samoans. Another important characteristic of the emerging leadership system is that it is accessible to young migrants whose orientation is clearly to urban California rather than the Samoan village. Although most church organizations are headed by older men and women, in the churches I am familiar with there is a growing group of young and gifted leaders who represent a positive force for effective future leadership.

SIX

Formal and Informal
Networks of Exchange

I have had frequent occasion to refer to the special life-crisis events that activate Samoan kindred networks. These are events for which nearly every Samoan contributes money, food, fine mats, and other goods, and which together work to preserve the matai system. To an outsider the patterns of exchange evident in major life-crisis events are the most striking of Samoan social behaviors. The degree to which 'aiga members, even quite distant bilateral kin, continue to coalesce around the people affected and their immediate family in the urban setting suggests that this institution serves to foster a profound sense of social solidarity. Yet it is also clear from listening to Samoans speak of the amount of money they contribute and the strong community pressures for conforming to the ideal of generosity in these circumstances, that the institution places a considerable financial burden on them and their households. The stress of contributing to kindred members in order to maintain one's reputation is particularly great for those whose very economic survival is at stake.

Life-crisis exchange networks as they have been elaborated in the urban society embody an apparent contradiction. On the one hand they serve to provide a pool of resources for occasions that demand large outlays of cash. In so doing, they increase the solidarity and cohesiveness of the 'aiga. On the other hand, for individuals experiencing financial difficulties, the perception of constant demands to give is a significant stressor. This paradox is understandable if we look at the structure and function of stateside patterns of economic exchange. The most public and remarkable exchanges occur around life-crisis events, or what the Samoans call *fa'alavelave*.

The Fa'alavelave

The term fa'alavelave literally means "difficulty," "problem," or "trouble," but in practice it refers to any event that upsets the normal course of daily activities. These events range from the funeral, which is by far the most important, to helping a relative campaign for political office. In short, any activity occurring in a kindred that necessitates or attracts the attention of others, or requires their involvement, is a fa'alavelave. The events I observed and upon which this discussion is based were several funerals (*maliu*), a wedding (*fa'aipoipoga*), and the visit to San Francisco of several traveling groups from the islands (*faigamalaga*).

In Samoa fa'alavelave involve the competitive but reciprocal exchange of food, fine mats, cloth, and other hand-made objects. Weddings appear to be the only occasion where exchange is largely complementary. The groom's side contributes trade goods (*oloa*), and the bride's side fine mats (*'ie toga*) and tapa cloth (*siapo*). Funerals and other life-crisis events are characterized by a symmetrical, and by virtue of the actors involved, competitive exchange of items. As Shore (1982: 206) notes,

> Direct symmetrical exchanges operate in Samoa on a number of levels. . . . Individuals or groups who contribute money, mats or food to a family during a funeral . . . or other life crises expect their gifts to be reciprocated, largely in kind. Prestige accrues both though the ostentatious presentation of one's gifts and also through the equally public receipt of the return gift.

This system of exchange is not simply an economic act, but a social transaction where status is validated, and the sanctity or importance of an event is celebrated. The goods contributed for such events are redistributed to participating households and used to support visitors or supply the needs of the fa'alavelave ritual. In general the contribution and redistribution of these goods does not seriously affect members of this subsistence economy.

By contrast, urban, stateside fa'alavelave primarily involve the exchange of cash. Collected funds are used to satisfy financial needs associated with the life-crisis event. The pattern of redistribution has become asymmetrical, with money and goods flowing in only one direction. Ablon (1970) suggests that the emphasis on money arose as a mutual-aid tradition to meet a practical need for immediate resources, as in the case of buying a funeral plot and casket. Individuals give with little expectation of immediate return, though most recognize the expenditure as a long-term investment that will at some point be returned. Cash has been infused into the basic competitive structure of the fa'alavelave and has been emphasized to a far greater extent than the food and fine mats that are the typically exchanged items in Samoa. The amount of money given on any one occasion is likely to exceed what is needed to meet immediate expenses. Ablon (1970: 219) writes: "The 'overgive' serves to emphasize the cultural value placed on generosity of the greatest extent that a family can manage in this country, where living costs are high. . . . A conspicuous display of money is more impressive than a conspicuous display of food."

In her analysis of 'aiga exchange networks among a small community of Samoans in Southern California, Rolff (1978) suggests that the Samoan conceptualization of redistribution in times of fa'alavelave has shifted to fit characteristic Samoan kinship "provider-dependent" relationships to a market economy. I have described how household size and structure depend on the financial situation of individual members. There are those with resources, and they fund those temporarily without. It is, as Rolff argues, an asymmetrical pattern of exchange where money flows from one source to another but not immediately back again. 'Aiga networks function in this sense "as very flexible kinds of rotating credit associations" (p. 159).

Ostentatious giving, aside from functioning to meet cash needs associated with the event, serves to confer prestige on the giver and his or her household. Matai and those aspiring to such leadership positions often use fa'alavelave to increase or publicly validate their status. On some occasions, particularly where 'aiga leaders formally present a contribution (*sua*), the display of wealth is calculated to create the greatest impact. During the visit of a traveling group from a major village of Tutuila, one matai presented a series of gifts donated by his extended family. These gifts were given to the group's senior orator on behalf of the group members to whom the matai and his family were related. After a lengthy oratory in which the local matai traced out the genealogical connection between givers and receivers, he made a ritual presentation of food, drink, and fine mats. Then, very deliberately, he brought out $1,500 in crisp one-hundred dollar bills, counting them out aloud as he arranged them in a long row on the mat in front of him. This was done to the delight and approval of the assembled participants.

It is important to note that, though generosity reflects well on the whole presenting group, the household head or matai is the one who reaps the greatest rewards in terms of prestige, not only because of the size of the gift but also because this gives him a chance to show off his oratorical skills. The other contributors' part tends to get lost. An individual contributor's reputation for generosity is developed within the household and 'aiga, not within the community (or kindred). But many occasions arise in which individuals give not for prestige purposes or out of feelings of generosity toward the eventual recipients, but because it is expected of them. At this level many people express some dissatisfaction with the whole system and the powerful forces for conformity that undergird it. To illustrate this point, let me describe how people were contacted and became involved in one very large fa'alavelave, a Samoan funeral.

A Samoan Funeral

Leova died quite suddenly on Friday evening. Within hours of his death, his older brother placed calls to members of the kindred living in Samoa, Hawaii, and California. Important relatives made arrangements to fly in from the islands, and in order to accommodate these travelers, Leova's 'aiga decided to hold the burial service a week from the coming Monday. A titled cousin of the deceased was assigned by the 'aiga's senior matai, also living in the San Francisco area, to make arrangements with the funeral home, take care of buying food and supplies, and keep a detailed account of incoming contributions.

A meeting of the local 'aiga was hastily called. This group consisted of Leova's oldest brother, the matai, the other surviving siblings in the area, several cousins on the father's side, and all the spouses. After some discussion each of the couples in this core 'aiga group was assigned a contribution of $500, 20 fine mats, and food and lodging for the soon-to-be arriving guests. Members were also assigned such tasks as remaining at the home of the deceased to greet mourners, answer phone calls, and ensure that the widow and her children were well cared for.

As the matai of related 'aiga learned of the death, they called 'aiga meetings. In each of these meetings 'aiga members discussed and decided on the size of the individual contributions and the total amount they wished to give as a group to Leova's 'aiga. One large 'aiga network headed by a prominent elder matai who was related to the dead man's mother soon gathered and presented a contribution of $500 and 50 fine mats. Similar presentations were made by individual households or 'aiga groups on the father's side and on the affinal side of the kindred. Arriving relatives from Samoa brought contributions, though smaller, collected from kindred back home. In addition, church members, friends, migrants from the same village as the deceased, and the deceased's church contributed money, fine mats, and often food. When the figures were added up after the burial, $18,000 had been collected in cash alone.

Out of this money, about $8,000 went for expenses directly related to the burial: the cost of a very elaborate coffin, mortuary services, and a burial plot. A large sum was used to purchase food for the final feast:

mountains of chicken, fish, taro, bananas, "chop suey," and canned soft drinks. At this feast five senior clergy and four lay ministers were present. Each received fine mats, food, and cash from the family. So did other important church officers: elder deacons, moderators, and so forth. Visiting matai representing different branches of the kindred received fine mats and food (*sua*), honoring both their presence and the contributions they brought from their own 'aiga. The remaining cash was given to the widow. Reports varied on how much was left over; most informants thought that it was about $2,000.

The most impressive aspect of this funeral was the extremely far-flung networks activated by the death. Probably every single adult who could trace a relationship through consanguineal or affinal links was asked or volunteered to contribute, either individually or as part of an 'aiga. People linked to the deceased through friendship and church membership were also involved. One man I interviewed gave two separate contributions: one, a fine mat plus $50, was given to the deceased's oldest brother, an old and dear friend; the other, a fine mat plus $40, was given through the matai of an 'aiga that was related affinally to the deceased. In another case a woman and her husband contributed $50, two fine mats, and a keg of salt-cured beef through the same matai, whom the wife recognized as the California head of her mother's side of her kindred. Several others I knew contributed through this matai. The total of contributions made through this one man was well over $1,000. Few of the people who made them, including the matai, had had very much contact with the deceased, but all knew of a relationship between their 'aiga and his or knew one of his close bilateral kin.

Attitudes Toward Fa'alavelave Exchange

When questioned about contributing to distant kin, nearly all the distant relatives of Leova approved of the collection process because they approved of the deceased and his 'aiga. They saw their contribution as a way to show love and respect. When this question was extended to include all fa'alavelave, attitudes appeared to vary by age. Older men and women, regardless of their cohort of migration, saw the system as a drain on resources, but a necessary one that they did not mind. These individuals often offered an example of how they became aware of the importance and function of the fa'alavelave institution through a death or some other crisis in their own immediate household or 'aiga network. Many younger people, on the other hand, announced that contributing to the fa'alavelave of distantly related kin was taking a good thing much too far. Said one, "I don't mind giving for things in the close family, but I can't give to everyone I'm related to. I got three kids to feed." Though this change in attitude may be related to acculturation, generational differences in access to prestige offered by the institution is also a factor. Younger people are rarely directly involved in the planning and staging of redistributive feasts. It is not until they grow older, probably well into middle age, that Samoans, both men and women, become established in the church and 'aiga. Several people agreed that they had not liked the fa'alavelave system until they became older and realized how useful it was. They then began to participate with greater interest.

Comments made by young and old alike illustrate a significant degree of variation in attitudes toward the institution, and some uncertainty about whether or not it should be maintained outside Samoa. When probed about their experiences with past fa'alavelave, only a small minority indicated that they approved of the institution without question. Most people indicated that they had serious reservations at times when continual demands on scarce income stressed household resources. Most also emphasized the distinction between close kin and distant kin. Yet despite variation in attitude, there was significantly less variation in behavior. As can be seen in Table 6.1, presenting the range in yearly contributions for men and women in the sample, very few people refuse to contribute something when asked. (Because married couples usually contribute as a unit to affairs in either spouse's kindred, the figures shown represent the total contribution for married informants.) Though older men and women with grown children are not expected to contribute much of their own income, they may in fact do so if they have the resources. Some will represent the 'aiga if they have sufficient status.

Since the mean of more than $2,000 reflects the contributions of a few

TABLE 6.1

Yearly Contributions to Fa'alavelave

(*1983 dollars*)

Amount	Men		Women	
	Number[a]	Percent	Number[a]	Percent
$0–200	4	7.1%	5	11.4%
$201–500	7	12.5	3	6.8
$501–1,000	15	26.8	12	27.3
$1,001–2,000	15	26.8	13	29.5
$2,001–3,000	4	7.1	3	6.8
$3,001+	11	19.6	8	18.2
Mean	$2,082		$2,085	
Median	$1,200		$1,350	

NOTE: The amounts shown are for the couple in the case of married informants.
[a]Four informants, one man and three women, did not know or could not remember how much they contributed.

wealthy individuals whose positions and greater resources involved substantially larger donations than was typical of most, the median of about $1,300 is a more meaningful figure in this case. But even so, considering the relatively poor economic position of most Samoans, the figure is quite high. Accordingly, let us return again to the question of whether these expenditures directly constitute a stressor for the individual or indirectly lead to stress from the pressure for conformity to community values. There are two sides to this question: the first is the simple economic question of who gives, how much, and to what effect; the second is the social and cultural question of how giving functions to affect the participants' status in the family and community.

Rolff (1978) argues that the intensification of fa'alavelave networks in the community she studied occurred in response to conditions of poverty, as a system of mutual aid, but also served to perpetuate that poverty by leveling the income of participating households. She discovered a significant amount of variation in the participation of households in 'aiga networks and a correlation between poverty and participation in networks of exchange. In general Rolff believes that two forces for cultural differentiation and change are evident in the migrant community. She calls these "individuation" and "consolidation." Individuation results from increased affluence, which permits Samoans to withdraw from mutual-aid and prestige networks. Consolidation is an intensification of involvement in these networks, and a response to and continuation of conditions of poverty under the American socioeconomic system. In Rolff's words (pp. 237–38):

For poor Samoans, survival and a modicum of economic security are the most compelling considerations. They have fewer viable options in cultural orientation open to them. . . . But as income increases, migrants do have the choice between enhancing their prestige within the Samoan community or maintaining and possibly enhancing their affluence. The problem is then one of which alternative to trade off for the other or of how to compromise between the two. Hence the emergence of [different] cultural orientations in Shoretown, orientations which differ in their degree of consolidation, as well as in the values, attitudes, and behavior patterns that reinforce a particular level of involvement in Samoan affairs.

Since Rolff's analysis is based on research in a small and relatively poor community in Southern California, many of her findings differ from mine. The San Francisco community grew much faster than the "Shoretown" group and was thus "consolidated" more rapidly. The population of Shoretown did not exceed 500, and many of the households had no close kinship ties to others in the community. Some families had been moved into the area by the military, and this may have contributed to their comparative isolation from established 'aiga networks. Community and migration differences notwithstanding, Rolff's argument bears closer examination, since the main issue she addresses is whether Samoan kinship networks are adaptive, and if so, to what degree.

The first and most important dimension of Rolff's thesis pertains to the nature of economic activity within the 'aiga. Though she is cognizant of formal and informal spheres of exchange, she does not draw a strict line between them in her analysis. In the course of my research I questioned my informants about the regular exchange of money, goods, and services in which they engaged with relatives of friends. Their responses made it clear that informal and formal exchange not only differed in amount and frequency, but involved a different group of people and a different conceptualization of generalized reciprocity. The transactions themselves, therefore, have different meanings for those involved.

Formal and Informal Spheres of Exchange

The formal sphere of exchange has already been discussed: the collection of money and goods for a life-crisis event or other purpose involving the kindred. Although there is always a certain degree of "overgive" in these circumstances, the donations do not circulate to any substantial degree within a kindred network. Any money left after expenses are covered is given to ministers and a few titled individuals. Only in two cases did I note any significant redistribution of goods collected in the course of a fa'alavelave. In the first a traveling group presented the host church with several dozen cases of canned tuna and corned beef, 200 fine mats, and 30 sleeping mats. At the conclusion of the formal welcoming ceremony, one of the orators divided up the mats and food, giving a share to a representative of the main church 'aiga in attendance. In the other case, a wedding, a small amount of cash was given to some of the titled representatives of the 'aiga groups in attendance, plus church officers, to "honor" their contributions to the wedding itself. These presentations, or sua, did not total more than $50 in cash. At Leova's funeral only ministers and lay ministers received cash; titled representatives received fine mats. The bulk of the money donated on these formal occasions goes for a specific purpose and does not reenter 'aiga networks in any substantial amount. Fa'alavelave involve a system of contribution and collection throughout the 'aiga networks for occasional and unique expenses quite beyond the exigencies of day-to-day living.

Moreover, the large kindred networks activated in times of a fa'alavelave hold together only for that occasion and purpose, subsiding until another life crisis in the kindred draws attention. Among my informants the average was between six and twelve times a year. The big fa'alavelave, the weddings and funerals of very close bilateral kin, rarely occur more than once a year. Outside the core 'aiga network, a person's relationship to the kindred members involved is likely to be highly formal. In many cases a person will give his or her contribution to the recognized head of the household group, who will in turn present it to the appropriate person. The relationship between individual givers and receivers may thus be indirect and even impersonal.

Informal patterns of exchange and mutual aid are very different. They involve smaller amounts of cash and greater amounts of goods and services exchanged among a close personal group of relatives and friends. These transactions are far more socially meaningful. This kind of giving is likely to be motivated not so much by formal obligation or community pressure as by feelings of generosity and respect (though one's reputation as a giver is also important within this close group). As in other settings and cultural contexts, the process of daily exchange in Samoan networks joins individuals in personal relationships (see, e.g., Stack 1974). One man described this pattern of exchange as follows:

Samoans are different from Americans. Americans like the equal way; I know that from where I work. You buy your drink, I'll buy my drink. Samoans are different. If we go somewhere to eat and I have money, I'll pay for the whole dinner. And if I don't have money, well, you'll probably just buy me dinner yourself. This is the Samoan way in all things, especially among friends and relatives. It's like my insurance payment when I help someone out. The Samoan way is also the Christian way. Just cast bread on the water, it'll come back sooner or later.

This statement is a good illustration of the attitudes Samoans have about the regular sharing and helping relationships in which they are frequently involved. It includes not only making small loans, but buying gas for a friend's car, providing transportation, babysitting, sewing a dress for a relative, or providing food for visitors.

Informal exchange networks often develop out of the provider-dependent relationships that arise in the process of chain migration. Most migrants found initial sustenance and support within a household occupied by close bilateral kin, and as we saw, many in my sample lived with their relatives for as much as five years (Table 3.3). The relationships created and strengthened by this initial experience form the basis for a continued reciprocity. The strength of these ties is illustrated in Table 6.2. It shows that in times of economic need people regularly turn to members of their immediate family.

Involvement in informal exchange is much more a matter of need, and results, as Rolff describes, in a rapid circulation of surplus wealth from providers to dependents. I have no hard data on which to evaluate her argument that such circulation is greatest among poorer segments of the

TABLE 6.2

Primary Source of Economic Aid in Past Times of Need

Source	Men		Women	
	Number[a]	Percent	Number[a]	Percent
Bank or credit card	5	8.9%	5	11.6%
Sibling	21	39.5	12	27.9
Parents or children	13	23.2	15	34.9
Affine	5	8.9	6	14.0
Other relative	5	8.9	3	7.0
Friend	1	1.8	1	2.3
Never happened	6	10.7	1	2.3

[a]No response from one man and four women.

population, because it is difficult to assess what items are exchanged with whom on a daily basis. Based on my observations and conversations with informants, I believe that Rolff may have oversimplified what is actually a more complex process. 'Aiga network ties in my sample often cut across economic boundaries, and though it is certainly true that both informal and formal patterns of exchange tend to level income somewhat, this hardly means that everyone is kept poor. However, I would agree with Rolff's conclusion that for the poorer households informal and formal exchange is more necessary; they are dependent on the rapid circulation of wealth in times of need. Economic security is not so immediate a concern for more affluent households.

The relationship between formal and informal spheres of exchange is not a direct one. Although individuals may be involved in one kind of exchange to the exclusion of the other, my observations suggest that this is not usually the case. I met only one woman who had little informal-network involvement but contributed to several family fa'alavelave each year. The reverse is probably more often the case; people may participate in mutual-aid networks within their immediate kin group and circle of friends to the exclusion of heavy fa'alavelave involvement. The reasons for this are based on the nature of the exchange and the purposes individuals perceive for it. Informal networks function, as indicated above, to provide a minimum of economic security, while fa'alavelave—the large feasts—are where status is validated and prestige increased. Such status and prestige are purchased at a high price; for some the price is simply too high.

Hence, as I have discussed here, many individuals exhibit considerable ambivalence about fa'alavelave involvement. Samoans recognize that fa'alavelave place tremendous demands on them and can mean chronic financial difficulties for some households. More important than financial considerations here, however, are strong values for conforming to family obligations. One's identity as a Samoan and dedication to the fa'asamoa as it exists on the mainland rest on one's reputation as a giver when things affecting the 'aiga require it. For those who can ill-afford to contribute in the first place, the maintenance of this institution represents a considerable psychological stressor. The alternative to participating is not greater poverty, but marginalization and isolation from the Samoan community and from one's 'aiga. Many individuals in the lower-income brackets expressed how "trapped" they felt between the need to provide for their household and the need to maintain their standing in the family. One man expressed this position well: "It really makes people suffer to bring all the Samoan ways over here. . . . It's so expensive and there are too many bills to pay. . . . When they bring over all this *fa'asamoa* the families suffer. Many people learn to hate their culture because it makes them poor."

Individuals appear to follow two paths to ease the economic and psychological strain that fa'alavelave contributions produce. First, they pursue a "minimax" strategy, making large contributions to those events "close" in the kindred and limiting or eliminating their participation in the affairs of distant kin. One's contributions within a closer circle of 'aiga are not only more visible to those involved but more likely to be based on personal ties. These relationships often entail a greater frequency of contact and thus in the long run a greater degree of reciprocity.

The second strategy is to maintain one's standing in the informal sphere, so that when a big event comes up, one can turn to friends and kin in this network for help. Since most of the relatives a person is closest to will be involved in the same fa'alavelave, this often means pooling resources to make one contribution. For individuals not involved in such informal-exchange networks, the pressure on household income is much greater. Therefore, the informal network acts as a support group in normal affairs, but becomes doubly effective for fa'alavelave, allowing members to pool their resources or draw on informal loans and contributions. The potential stressfulness of the fa'alavelave institution can be buffered to a certain extent by a person's ability to participate in a core network where mutual cooperation and aid are common.

Rolff (1978: 165–67) recognizes the importance of this core support group, though not explicitly differentiated as such, when she comments:

The trend to intensify network involvement in Shoretown appears to be based on the following principle: the greater the frequency of financial cooperation within a mutual aid network the smaller the participating people's contribution to the eventual donation; or if people intend to make an especially good showing, the larger the donation of the eventual contributor. . . .

The trend toward decreased network involvement . . . is based on the following principle: the less frequent the financial cooperation within mutual aid networks, and the smaller the networks, the larger is the financial drain on a given household if contribution standards are to be met.

A final point to make here concerns the options to intensive network involvement. Rolff argues that affluent people or households possess the opportunity to "opt out" of Samoan networks altogether and pursue the economic and status rewards available to Americans. There is no simple cause-and-effect relationship between economic status and social behavior, however. To exercise this option means perceiving the rewards of American society as superior to those offered within the migrant community. Opting out is thus less a product of affluence than a matter of acculturation—though the two may go hand in hand. Individuals must first know enough about American society to want what it provides, and then have the means to pursue it. One would therefore expect those most prone to changing values, particularly the young or those who marry non-Samoans, to fall into this category. That appears to be the case among the Samoans I know, though I met very few who believed that American society offered them anything of greater personal value than the prestige and status offered in the Samoan context.

In sum, affluent individuals who perceive no use for prestige as defined in Samoan terms can opt out of both formal and informal networks, recognizing that their economic security does not depend on their involvement. For those in the very poorest category, informal networks may provide a modicum of economic security, but the amount required to compete for status in the formal sphere may be too great. So the affluent have a choice, whereas the poor may be forced out of the running altogether.

It is interesting in this regard to examine the relationship of per capita income to the percentage spent on fa'alavelave. The data in Table 6.3 sug-

TABLE 6.3

Percent of Income Donated to Fa'alavelave

Per capita income	Men			Women		
	Number[a]	Mean	Standard deviation	Number[a]	Mean	Standard deviation
<$1,500	6	6.6	6.6	6	8.5	4.9
$1,501–2,000	9	12.1	8.3	7	15.8	7.3
$2,001–2,900	13	11.9	8.2	17	13.5	12.9
$2,901–4,000	14	8.6	6.7	5	3.7	2.3
$4,001+	14	8.6	6.7	5	3.7	2.3

NOTE: Since contributions for such events are often made on a household basis, percentages were calculated as total contribution/total household × 100. Each individual was thus assigned a percentage. Individuals are grouped by per capita income, or household income/number in household. The data are for the previous year's income and contributions.
[a] Incomplete information on eight respondents, one man and seven women.

gest a general tendency among those in both the lowest and the highest income categories to contribute proportionately the least. However, as the standard deviation statistic illustrates, there is considerable variation within each income group.

In a material sense it can be argued that the money people spend on their relatives and church reduces their ability to buy property, automobiles, and other consumer goods. In the long run this may become a problem, since it renders Samoans as a group more vulnerable to the capriciousness of the economy than they would be if they saved and invested their money in what Americans consider to be appropriate ways. On the other hand it can be argued, as many Samoans do, that they *are* investing, and in a much more fragile and valuable commodity: their 'aiga and kindred groups. In the final analysis, which is the more valuable and represents the least cost in human terms? For Samoans the answer remains elusive. They do not like being poor, but they highly value their culture, are proud of their kin groups, and enjoy the public displays of wealth that bring them together and provide a sense of shared history, tradition, and identity. The solution for Samoans is therefore not to reduce the degree of their involvement but to increase their access to the resources needed for that involvement—to keep their communities alive, integrated, and distinctive.

tradictions arising in social status and role expectations. Culture change, particularly in the context of intercultural migration, introduces new statuses and roles and produces greater variability in social expectations held by community members; social expectations are not completely shared. Stress occurs when the expectations that define appropriate behavior are unclear (see Cassel 1974, 1975) or when individuals are unable to live up to status and role expectations or aspirations. Dressler (1982, 1988), for example, has shown that material acquisition is an expectation associated with prestige and high status in a variety of cultures marked by rapid change. Individuals who do not have the resources necessary to acquire the prized goods, but try to do so anyway, will be under stress because of the conflict between available resources and the expectations associated with their desired social position. Similarly, what have been termed "stressful life events" are often associated with rites of passage or role changes, in which individuals are placed in situations where social expectations are unclear (see Mestrovic and Glassner, 1983).

The socioenvironmental processes that produce conflicts in social expectations may be termed *social stressors*. Stressors are factors that create in the individual a state of emotional arousal, feelings of struggling against the environment, or to use Selye's (1956) terminology, a "general adaptation" reaction. Dressler (1982: 7–8) provides the following synopsis. The individual is assumed to seek a psychological steady-state. When changes in the social environment upset this state, he or she will seek to restore it. Changes that are culturally meaningful and cause an upset to internal homeostasis are termed stressors. If the corrective actions taken by the individual fail to restore homeostasis, the individual will be under stress. Thus, stress can be seen as arising when an individual's adaptive capacities fail. The purpose of this study has been to elucidate those social and cultural changes arising out of the migration experience that are social stressors, and correspondingly, those resources that increase the individual's adaptive capacities.

Let me emphasize the "culturally meaningful" part of the above definition. A significant body of research on stress has failed to consider crosscultural variation in the process of stress, and perhaps more astoundingly, how stress is differentially experienced by men and women. Furthermore, one of the dominant ways in which stress is operationalized—as an outcome of "life changes"—fails to differentiate between structural stressors, which are chronic (e.g., poverty), and acute, transitory stressors (e.g., running short of money at the end of the month). Finally, in analyzing health outcomes, it is essential to recall Cassel's basic premise (1976) that stress leads to a state of "generalized susceptibility," which may in turn result in differential health outcomes depending on the individual's constitution, age, and powers of resistance. Not only may stress, generally conceived, have alternative effects, but specific kinds of stressors may have quite specific sequelae. Thus acute life changes may be manifested immediately as psychosomatic complaints (tiredness, loss of appetite, headaches, and so forth), while chronic stressors may be more predictive of degenerative conditions, such as high blood pressure and cardiovascular disease. There is a substantial literature in psychiatry and anthropology (e.g., Kleinman 1980) suggesting that cultural factors determine or underlie the somatization of sensations of psychological distress. So not only should stress be considered in its specific social, historical cultural, and gender contexts; it should also be examined, where possible, in light of multiple health outcomes.

Three strategies were used to measure health. First, blood pressure measurements were taken very carefully on each individual in the study, both before and after the interview. The lowest of these measures was recorded for use in the analysis discussed here. I took all the measurements myself, using a high-quality mercury sphygmomanometer with appropriate-sized cuffs. As a measure of health, blood pressure has the advantage of being objective and, if taken carefully, reliable. It is not prone to the same kinds of interpretations and translation problems that affect self-report questionnaires. Blood pressure is also a major public health problem for Samoans, and when elevated carries significant risk for cardiovascular difficulties, as well as overall health.

Although self-report measures are prey to problems of interpretation and bias, they are ways of getting at what might be called "feelings" or "sensations" of healthiness and thus provide another, though indirect measure, of overall health. Shortly after beginning the epidemiologic phase of the study, I added a substantial set of health questions to the interview schedule. These questions were of two kinds. The first set consisted of questions about overall health, cardiovascular health, presence or absence of diabetes, and so forth. Included in this set of questions was a query concerning the person's history of hypertension. For purposes of analysis, I added to this question my own diagnosis of hypertension based on the person's blood pressure during the interview. The second set of questions was derived, in part, from the Health Opinion Survey instrument (Leighton et al. 1963); this survey was later translated into Samoan by the Graves in their study of migration and health among Pacific Islanders in New Zealand (1985).* The questions will be familiar to those with experience in psychosocial or psychiatric epidemiology and largely reflect

---

* A word of caution on the interpretation of the self-report-based measures. First, statements about ill-health, aches and pains, and so forth, may be ways of expressing complaints about life in somatic terms. In other words a high complaint score may be another measure of stress and thus confounded with it to some degree. However, this is properly an empirical question that I did not examine in this study. Second, and related to the problem of confounding, self-reported statements of ill-health or discomforts may reflect personality fac-

a concern with psychosomatic complaints. The interested reader may refer to the Appendix for the exact wording of these health questions.*

The Physical Health History index measured closed-ended responses
to seven questions: the frequency of chills and fevers in the past year; the
frequency of colds in the past year; the frequency of stiffness or soreness
of the joints in the past year; the respondent's appraisal of his or her life-
time health; a diagnosis of hypertension by a physician (ever); a diagnosis
of heart disease by a physician (ever); and a diagnosis of diabetes by
a physician (ever). The scores on this index ranged from 0 to 16, with a
mean of 6.5 and a standard deviation of 3.81.

In the Psychosomatic Complaint index, individuals were asked to respond to fifteen closed-ended questions on how frequently they had experienced the following problems in the past year: pain in arms and/or legs;
back pain; stomach pain; upset stomach or nausea; loss of appetite;
asthma; chest pains; heart palpitations or beating hard enough to be
bothersome; numbness of extremities; dizziness or faintness; trembling
hands; headaches; migraines; feelings of exhaustion; and difficulty sleeping. The scores on this index ranged from 0 to 39, with a mean of 13.8
and a standard deviation of 9.1.

As noted in Chapter 1, the causes and consequences of Samoan obesity
have been the subject of much research. The data gathered so far suggest
that Samoan obesity varies with degree of modernization, either *in situ* or
as an outcome of migration, and that this obesity is related to some health
measures, in particular blood pressure (McGarvey and Schendel 1986).
Given the consistency of the findings and the significance of obesity as a
consequence of Samoan modernization, it is important to consider the
particular relationship of this problem and age to the health measures
used in this study.

Table 7.1 presents the cross-tabulation of health measures by age,

---

tors instead of, or in addition to, actual health status. Samoans are known for their physical
stoicism; those with high complaint scores may simply be less stoic or more self-revealing in
interviews than others (see Howard 1986). McGarvey and Schendel (1986) used complaint
scores based on a different set of items as a measure of "emotional coping" in Samoans (the
measure was unrelated to blood pressure). Third, self-report measures are dependent on
good interviewer-respondent rapport. The data presented here are of very high quality, and
I have a great deal of faith in them, but it is possible that a high complaint score may be a
function of one of the many intangibles that affect the personal interview, particularly when
the participants are products of markedly different cultural worlds. In any case the resulting
measures, however psychologically driven, represent an individual's subjective assessment
of his or her well-being, and this is in itself a valuable measure.

* The following statistical procedures were used. All health variables were recoded to
reflect an ordinal range of possible values ranging from least to most severe. Items were then
intercorrelated using non-parametric correlation procedures. The resulting matrix was then
analyzed using standard factor analysis procedures with a varimax rotation. A two-factor
solution was selected because it was theoretically meaningful and accounted for an appre-
ciable amount of the item variance. Items that loaded above the .40 level on each of the two
factors were summed to derive the health measure.

TABLE 7.1
Health Measures by Age Group

Measures	<40 years	40–54 years	55+ years	All ages
MEN				
Systolic blood pressure				
Number	12	26	19	57
Mean	129.3	139.3	141.6	138.0
Standard deviation	15.7	16.3	27.8	20.9
Diastolic blood pressure				
Number	12	26	19	57
Mean	86.3	94.4	87.8	90.5
Standard deviation	9.3	12.7	14.0	12.9
Physical health				
Number	12	21	12	45
Mean	4.8	7.2	7.8	6.7
Standard deviation	3.1	3.8	3.3	3.6
Complaints				
Number	12	21	12	45
Mean	11.0	16.3	12.8	14.0
Standard deviation	9.3	11.2	6.3	9.7
WOMEN				
Systolic blood pressure				
Number	15	16	16	47
Mean	125.9	136.3	152.6	138.6
Standard deviation	13.1	13.5	22.9	20.1
Diastolic blood pressure				
Number	15	16	16	47
Mean	83.3	87.0	92.1	87.5
Standard deviation	10.0	10.7	16.0	12.8
Physical health				
Number	12	15	9	36
Mean	4.9	5.5	9.4	6.3
Standard deviation	3.1	3.7	4.4	4.1
Complaints				
Number	12	15	9	36
Mean	13.9	13.3	13.6	13.6
Standard deviation	8.6	9.4	7.8	8.5
TOTAL				
Systolic blood pressure				
Number	27	42	35	104
Mean	127.4	138.2	146.6	138.2
Standard deviation	14.1	15.2	25.9	20.5
Diastolic blood pressure				
Number	27	42	35	104
Mean	84.6	91.6	89.7	89.2
Standard deviation	9.6	12.4	14.9	12.9
Physical health				
Number	24	36	21	81
Mean	4.8	6.5	8.5	6.5
Standard deviation	3.0	3.8	3.8	3.8
Complaints				
Number	24	36	21	81
Mean	12.5	15.1	13.1	13.8
Standard deviation	8.9	10.4	6.8	9.1

TABLE 7.2

Correlation of Age and Body Mass with Health Measures

Measure	Number	Age	Body-mass index
Men			
Systolic blood pressure	57	.19	.28*
Diastolic blood pressure	57	−.08	.17
Physical health	45	.31*	.02
Complaints	45	.02	−.17
Women			
Systolic blood pressure	47	.53**	.10
Diastolic blood pressure	47	.29*	.14
Physical health	36	.48**	−.03
Complaints	36	−.05	.26
Total			
Systolic blood pressure	104	.35**	.17*
Diastolic blood pressure	104	.10	.10
Physical health	81	.40**	−.02
Complaints	81	−.01	.04

NOTE: Body-mass index = weight/height × 100. Significance: *p < .05; **p < .01.

and Table 7.2 shows the statistical association of a measure of body mass (weight/height×100) and age with health. In Table 7.1 one can discern a somewhat curvilinear association between age and health for the men. This is especially noticeable for the diastolic blood pressure and psychosocial complaint scores, which show the highest mean levels at ages 40–54, decreasing thereafter. This is suggestive of many social explanations, most important, that men of this age group are, in Samoan society, at, striving for, or nearing the apex of positions of prestige and leadership. Such a pattern of leadership acquisition with middle to late-middle age, while present, is clearly not as marked for Samoan women. Table 7.1 thus shows a well-defined linear relationship for women except for the psychosocial complaint score. Table 7.2 confirms these age-health associations, with age showing a significant relationship with health in men only in the case of the physical health score, while in women age is strongly and significantly associated with blood pressure and physical health. The relationship between age and physical health is a logical one, given that the items used to construct the scale are weighted somewhat toward the chronic, degenerative diseases that tend to affect people in the older age groups.

Body mass, on the other hand, is not nearly so good a predictor of health, being significantly associated only with systolic blood pressure in men. The striking correlation of age (a factor clearly associated with a range of psychosomatic processes) with the various health measures, and the lack of a strong correlation of body mass with most of the health measures belies the importance of looking at social and cultural factors. Unless specifically noted, the effects of age and body mass are statistically controlled in the analyses that follow.

Stressors in Samoan Migration and Adaptation

While in Samoa in 1982 I had the good fortune to meet and discuss my research topic with a high titled ali'i who also held a graduate degree from an American university. He was deeply interested in discussing some of the theories then prominent in social science on why migrants typically experience an increase in chronic diseases. In particular we discussed Marmot and Syme's now-classic study (1976) on heart-disease among Japanese-Americans. Their basic finding was that Japanese acculturation was associated with a significantly higher rate of coronary heart disease. The authors, as well as a generation of sociologists and anthropologists, believed this demonstrated the sometimes pernicious consequences of culture change, which (1) results in a loss of traditional supportive institutions; and (2) places individuals in social situations in which they have no guide for behavior (they do not share expectations with non-Japanese in the same situation on role performance) and cannot predict the behaviors of non-Japanese. After listening with much interest to my discussion of the scientific literature, this perceptive chief indicated disagreement with the basic assumption that culture change was bad:

In my case, and for the people in my extended family whom I know well, there is nothing very difficult about learning how to live in America. It just takes a little time, that's all. . . . If you are good at your own culture, you will be good at any other. You learn very quickly how to switch back and forth whenever you need to.

In addition, he continued, most stateside Samoans live in a virtual Samoan world and have not yet become as integrated into American society as have the Japanese. No, he said, it was economic change that was the most stressful: suddenly having to pay for things, running out of money, being evicted, and so forth, and trying in the midst of all this to meet family obligations and responsibilities in the context of the Samoan community.

Now, of course, anthropologists often find that members of a culture are not in the best position to evaluate the conflicts within it, or even its basic principles, but I mention these comments because in a profound way they presaged the findings of my research. Coming back to the mainland for an intensive study of the migrant community, I was constantly reminded of the chief's comments as I undertook to understand urban Samoan culture. As I shall point out, it is not culture change as such, although some problems involving children and health care do bring Samoans into what they find confusing and stressful contact with Americans, so much as the particular socioeconomic situations in which they find themselves striving to satisfy Samoan needs in Samoan terms that cause people the most stress in their day-to-day lives.

As I have had frequent opportunity to point out in the preceding chapters, poverty has become a significant problem for many individuals, especially those migrating after 1970. Although some Samoans, particularly those who arrived while the American economy was still strong, live quite well by our standards, a growing number do not. For Samoans poverty entails a number of things that they find particularly objectionable: low-quality and crowded housing; living in undesirable neighborhoods; limited access to status and prestige in both the church and the 'aiga; and a constant tension created by worrying when the next family fa'alavelave might demand another contribution. In general poverty also restricts people's choice on the degree to which they wish to affiliate with kindred. As discussed in Chapter 6, the poor realize that heavy involvement in family affairs is a way to ensure help when they need it, yet involvement at this level keeps them poor.

Samoans who were having financial difficulties often reported that poor housing and neighborhood conditions caused them substantial worry and anxiety. With the average rent for a three-bedroom apartment or house in the San Francisco area running well above $600 a month in 1983, many migrants have been forced to move into public housing. This is especially true for more recent migrants. In San Francisco most have chosen to live in public-housing tracts or nearby private apartments in the southern part of the city: Visitacion Valley and Hunters Point. The vast majority of this housing consists of two- and three-bedroom townhouse-style apartments, which though of adequate design, are of generally poor construction and often unmaintained. In parts of Visitacion Valley, for example, I visited apartments that had not had windows for months and where water poured in through a hole in the roof when it rained. Samoans found these conditions objectionable, yet often failed to complain to authorities for fear of losing the apartment. Many had more people living with them than was legally permitted and did not want to bring problems to the attention of anyone who might report them. Others simply did not know that they had a right either to complain or to request better housing.

In addition to these difficulties, Samoans reported that they found it worrisome to live in neighborhoods where crime and violence were all too common. Excessive noise was also mentioned as an objectional feature. Some racial problems have also appeared in the poorer neighborhoods. When speaking of what they did not like about their living situations, Samoans often objected to living in close proximity with some ethnic and racial groups they feared or disliked.

Many of the objections regarding neighbors and neighborhood conditions may begin to disappear as more and more Samoans move into and congregate in the same housing projects—something that is occurring in several locations. This process would lend some familiarity to the cultural landscape. In 1983, however, problems with housing, neighbors, and neighborhoods were the most frequently mentioned difficulties among the poorer group.

Socioeconomic disadvantage, therefore, is not restricted to causing worry over economic survival but can be seen to make life on the whole more difficult. For those living at or below the poverty line, simple life changes take on the weight of uncertainty. When troubles arise at work, a new baby is born, or a child gets in a fight at school, when a relative dies or a child has marital problems, the attention demanded of the individual is attention already burdened with a multiplicity of other worries. Samoans speak of two kinds of life events that cause them concern: those that upset the normal routines of life, demand some kind of extraordinary attention, and usually involve economic expense directly or indirectly, such as losing a job or moving to a new home; and those that affect relationships within the immediate or extended family, for example, arguments with relatives or a death in the 'aiga. Both kinds of life events are seen as particularly troublesome by individuals who lack economic resources.

In Samoan cultural terms, being poor also entails problems meeting familial obligations, and paradoxically, makes it that much more important to meet them. People know that in order to be able to call on family members in the future, they must maintain a reputation as generous givers in their own right. And this means not only giving a helping hand to close relatives and friends, but also vigorously maintaining their reputation as participants in fa'asamoa. For this reason people in the poorer categories reported a considerable degree of constant worry over the occurrence of fa'alavelave. The worry over maintaining and attaining Samoan status is a culturally specific brand of social inconsistency (see Dressler 1985, 1988). We will return to this point in due course.

By way of general summary, then, Samoan migrants are subject to two kinds of stressors. One kind is the stressor of social inconsistency discussed above. In the other category fall what I call structural and/or situational stressors. Structural stressors are broadly associated with the conditions that accompany poverty, such as insufficient housing, crime, or racial conflict. Poverty creates not only money-related stressors, as I have noted, but also acts in a synergistic way, and this is certainly how Samoans perceive it, to make life changes and situations more worrisome and problematic. Situational stressors are problems that arise in the family—arguments with kin, problems with children, fa'alavelave, and the like.*

Social Inconsistency

Since the mid-1940's many studies of the social determinants of chronic disease and symptoms of mental disorder have focused on the theoretically stressful nature of the lack of consistency among different measures of social status. The specific theoretical language varies from scholar to scholar, but the basic argument is that a person occupying different ranks on different status dimensions will have conflicting expectations about others' behavior and be uncertain about his or her own behavior (Dressler 1988; Hughes 1944; Lenski 1954). Although a still much-debated idea in medical social science, the concept of social consistency is a useful one for linking the macrostructural aspects of social change with individual experience. Dressler, a leading researcher in this area, has pointed out that modernization or acculturation, which includes most importantly the penetration of world market forces into local economies, leads to the association of status with material acquisition. In this view attempts to attain or maintain a high standard of living without adequate financial resources are particularly stressful.

In my analysis of migrant Samoan culture I suggest that life on the mainland aggravates a social-structural paradox, in which to maintain one's status as a contributing member of the community, an individual must have access to the American economy (see Chapter 6). To remain a part of the church, to achieve status in the family, to be, in fact, a Samoan, takes money. Although many people are able to sustain their social involvement at a desired level, particularly those in the first-migrant cohort who were able to find good jobs and affordable housing, a great number of the people I met, both in my interviews and in less formal settings, struggle for that delicate balance between family subsistence and participation in Samoan affairs. Often they do not find it.

In the Samoan context, then, social inconsistency describes the tension between individual and household needs and social status demands and

* In previous publications I employed one summary stressor score covering "situational stress" (e.g., Janes 1986). In preparing this book I endeavored to use more detailed measures of stress in order, first, to look at the differential effects of stressors on men and women, and second, to reflect more closely the significant facets of the migration and adaptation experience.

aspirations.* Social status in this sense refers to both leadership status, which Samoans, especially Samoan men, pursue with avid interest, and status as a contributing member of a kinship group. In other modernizing contexts, researchers have found that the pursuit of status, particularly as evidenced by the acquisition of material goods, is what places individuals in inconsistent positions (e.g., Beiser et al. 1976; Dressler 1982, 1985; Graves 1967).† For the most part, however, Samoans aspire not to an American lifestyle, but to distinctly Samoan rewards. An older woman, holding an important role in her extended family, articulated her experience with social inconsistency in the following way:

Sometimes I just lie in bed all night and can't sleep. I'm just thinking about the family problems. I worry that a relative might pass away, and then I'll have to get involved. I worry a lot about being short when it comes time for the *fa'alavelave*. It's always these worries which cause the stomach problems and the headaches too.

Those who do possess financial resources but because of age, sex, personality, or lack of other prerequisites for status have little access to positions of leadership or prestige may experience a similar but somewhat more subtle sense of inconsistency, depending on their goals and motivations. A younger, well-educated, and relatively affluent man expressed this frustration as follows:

I try to help them get things done the right way in church; you know, set up a careful accounting system for bingo, for maintaining the buildings, and so on. But those old guys won't listen to me. I don't have the speaking ability in Samoan to persuade them—you know how Samoans value speaking ability. They are also too much involved in the *fa'asamoa*. I can't be; I recognize the different ways of doing things. But I'm crazy I guess, I just keep trying.

Because my purpose was to examine general social and cultural aspects of adaptation, I did not collect the psychological data on individual status aspirations that would permit a direct test of the social-inconsistency hypothesis. However, there are two indirect means for measuring and assessing social inconsistency on a structural level. Operationally, we can define social inconsistency as consisting of a significant difference between any two salient pairs of status dimensions (Dressler 1982, 1988).

---

* Mestrovic and Glassner (1983) apply the Durkheimian notion of "homo duplex" to this conflict between individual desires and social demands, and they argue that it is a universal characteristic of most stressful situations.
† Dressler refers to this kind of inconsistency as "lifestyle stress," operationalized as the signed difference between material style of life and economic resources. I prefer the term social inconsistency because my concern is the absolute value of the difference between economic resources and social status, which is closer to what medical sociologists conventionally mean by social or status inconsistency.

I have found that for Samoans two interrelated status dimensions are primary within the community: economic status and involvement/leadership status in the church or 'aiga. The hypothesis here is that those who are of relatively high status in the community but have limited access to the resources necessary for maintaining that status will experience stress. The opposite might also be true: those with resources but little status or few opportunities for attaining positions of leadership might experience stress at having their social aspirations frustrated. This "low status" inconsistency might also be an indirect measure of acculturation, or at least, low levels of social support (as Samoans define it; see Chapter 8).

To test the social-inconsistency hypotheses two status scales were constructed. The first consisted of rank of per capita income, felt to be an adequate measure of available economic resources. The second was a leadership scale. For men this was a composite measure of four variables: chiefly status; leadership position in the church; leadership role in the kindred or household regardless of matai or church-related status; and kindred "service," as represented by the percentage of annual income invested in fa'alavelave, or life-crisis events. For women the scale consisted of all but the variable of chiefly status (although women do occasionally hold such a position). Each of the variables had three possible values: no status, minor or limited status, and high status. The sum of these ranks was taken as the Intracommunity Status score. The absolute value of the difference between the two scales was taken as a measure of intracommunity social inconsistency.

An effort was also made to determine the salience of extracommunity social inconsistency, defined as holding a status in American society, with few educational or vocational skills that would make the social expectations attached to such status familiar. This is the usual method of assessing social inconsistency in socioepidemiological studies undertaken on U.S. populations (e.g., Syme et al. 1964), and was the method employed by McGarvey and Schendel (1986) in their study of Samoan men and women living in the urbanized Pago Pago area of American Samoa. Although I use the term "extracommunity" to refer to social inconsistency defined in terms of American rather than Samoan characteristics, as noted in Chapter 5 such inconsistency has clear salience in Samoan terms. Especially for men, prestige in the community is increasingly provided by status outside it. Thus, in many ways extracommunity social inconsistency may be something of a double-edged sword, not only exacting costs in Samoan terms, but also exposing men to unfamiliar status expectations accorded them by non-Samoans. Conversely, having the skills but not being able to procure a high-status job may have similar costs by reducing the proba-

TABLE 7.3
Correlation of Social Inconsistency with Health Measures

	Extracommunity status		Intracommunity status	
	Consistent	Inconsistent	Consistent	Inconsistent
Measure	Mean (N)	Mean (N)	Mean (N)	Mean (N)
Men				
Systolic blood pressure	133.8* (36)	146.6* (20)	133.3* (28)	142.5* (29)
Diastolic blood pressure	89.2 (36)	93.4 (20)	88.1 (28)	92.8 (29)
Physical health	5.8* (27)	8.2* (18)	6.6 (22)	6.9 (23)
Complaints	12.1* (27)	16.8* (18)	15.5 (22)	12.4 (23)
Women				
Systolic blood pressure	133.8 (20)	140.7 (25)	135.7 (32)	144.7 (15)
Diastolic blood pressure	85.4 (20)	89.3 (25)	86.1 (32)	90.5 (15)
Physical health	5.5 (17)	7.1 (19)	6.6 (24)	5.7 (12)
Complaints	10.1* (17)	16.7* (19)	13.4 (24)	13.9 (12)
Total				
Systolic blood pressure	134.7* (58)	143.3* (45)	134.6* (60)	143.2* (44)
Diastolic blood pressure	87.8 (58)	91.1 (45)	87.1* (60)	92.0* (44)
Physical health	5.7* (44)	7.6* (37)	6.6 (46)	6.5 (35)
Complaints	11.3* (44)	16.7* (37)	14.4 (46)	13.0 (35)

NOTE: Significance in difference between consistent/inconsistent categories: * p < .05; one-tailed t-test.

bility of access to Samoan status. For men extracommunity status was defined as holding a white-collar position and/or a job that required supervisory authority. Skills necessary for performing such positions were defined as having (1) at least a high school education; and/or (2) U.S. military experience. For women status was likewise defined on the basis of employment but also considered was their role in extrafamilial affairs or leadership, such as in Samoan community organizations, that demanded significant contact with non-Samoans. Skills were defined in the same way as for men. The absolute value of the difference between skills (present or absent) and work status (high or low) was then calculated.

Health measures were cross-tabulated by categories of intra- and extra-community social inconsistency; the results can be found in Table 7.3. For the purposes of this table, the intracommunity scales were dichotomized and the difference then calculated, resulting in a simple comparison of inconsistent and consistent categories. The extracommunity measure is, by the nature of its construction, dichotomous. In the regression and correlation analyses that follow, the standardized, absolute value of the difference between the status scales is used.

Extracommunity social inconsistency is significantly associated with systolic blood pressure, physical health, and psychosomatic complaints in men; intracommunity social inconsistency is related only to systolic blood

TABLE 7.4

Regression of Health Measures on Social Inconsistency

Category	Men MAP[a]	Men Physical health	Men Complaints	Women MAP[a]	Women Physical health	Women Complaints
Age	.02	.27	.00	.42**	.45**	.02
Body mass[b]	.30*	.11	−.18	.20*	.03	.26
Intracommunity social inconsistency	.30*	.08	−.17	.13	−.15	.00
Extracommunity social inconsistency	.27*	.29*	.25	.14	.08	.11
Multiple R	.45*	.43	.35	.50*	.50*	.27*
Multiple R²	.20	.19	.13	.25	.25	.07
Adjusted R²[c]	.14	.10	.04	.18	.16	.00

NOTE: Betas (standardized coefficients) are shown. Betas were estimated from a full, nonhierarchical regression model where all variables were forced into the equation at once. Significance: *p < .05; **p < .01.
[a]"Mean arterial pressure" (Dressler 1985), a summary measure of systolic and diastolic blood pressure calculated as [(systolic pressure) + 2 (diastolic pressure)]/3. This abbreviation is used routinely in the subsequent tables, as is the definition of body mass.
[b]Weight/height² × 100.
[c]Adjusted R² is a conservative estimate of variance explained by a regression model when the sample size is small and the number of variables comparatively large.

pressure. In women neither of the social-inconsistency measures shows a statistically significant relationship to health, although the data do show predicted differences between inconsistent and consistent categories.

To assess the relationship between social inconsistency and the health measures while controlling for body mass and age, a regression model was constructed.* Table 7.4 presents the results. In men both intra- and extra-community social inconsistency is significantly associated with blood pressure, etic status inconsistency is associated with physical health, and neither measure is associated with psychosomatic complaints. In women both measures of social inconsistency fail to correlate significantly with any of the health measures.

Tables 7.3 and 7.4 generally confirm the hypothesis that social inconsistency as I have defined it is a significant stressor for men, but not for women, although the gross differences between gender groups was not found to be statistically significant (as measured by the t-ratio). The dif-

* As recommended by Hope (1975), the sum of the status measures used in constructing the social inconsistency scores was analyzed as covariates with the difference (social inconsistency) scores in a regression model. The average effects of status did not significantly affect the relationship between the difference scores and the dependent variables. Because of the large number of variables considered and the relatively small size of the sample, and because the summary status measures did not affect the relationship of social inconsistency and health, they are not shown in the regression analyses of this and the following chapters.

ferent pattern of gender-health relationships, is, however, provocative. For men intracommunity status through intense involvement in kindred affairs, public performance in such affairs, and holding a desirable job provides a variety of psychological rewards. Those men in the consistent categories, who have the skills and resources to attain and maintain leadership status, accrue the benefits of symbolically powerful and culturally sanctioned public recognition (see Leighton 1978). But access to such leadership status may be blocked by a lack of skills or resources, or very difficult to maintain under circumstances of economic scarcity. The very characteristics that make Samoan leadership status a goal that men pursue avidly are those that render its attainment a powerful stressor. Seen in this way, social inconsistency is probably as much a feature of traditional Samoan society as it is of the stateside community. However, where wage labor and status in the wage economy become added prerequisites to the attainment of leadership status, the potential for inconsistency likely increases.

Structural and Situational Stressors

The factors that contribute to Samoan stress can be further determined by examining the relationship between health and exposure to chronic difficulties entailed by urban life. In the literature these troublesome events are generally called life-events stress, and a sophisticated methodology has arisen to measure both the occurrence of a specific "stressful" situation and the meaning it has for the individual concerned (Dohrenwend and Dohrenwend 1974; Rahe 1974; Theorell 1976). This line of research suffers on two logical grounds: it emphasizes the relationship of acute, ahistorical factors to chronic diseases or disorders; and it is based on assumptions about the nature of psychological stress that are probably closer to white, middle-class models than any "objective reality." Because of these fallacies, research that depends on the *a priori* and acultural identification of stressful life events has been soundly criticized (A. Young 1980). These are legitimate criticisms, and ones that led me to search for culturally meaningful stressors and to attempt to measure them by means of a survey. Did Samoans themselves tacitly distinguish different kinds of stressors in their responses to survey questions?

In previous publications I employed a simple, culturally grounded stress scale, which I termed "situational stress" (Janes 1986; Janes and Pawson 1986). This scale was fashioned in an *a priori* manner to represent the major chronic, structural, or situational processes clearly articulated by Samoans to be problematic. Because of apparent gender differences in the health effects of this measure, I wanted to go further in this study, to see if one could speak of different kinds of stressors and if so, whether these had different effects. Using factor analysis, three distinct categories of stressors emerged. Scores on individual items making up these categories were summed to create a simple index. The categories and the interview items are as follows:*

1. *Structural stressors:* chronic economic problems or situations stemming from economic problems, measured as consisting of housing problems, difficulties with non-Samoan neighbors, living in a poor, rundown, and crime-ridden neighborhood, and lack of money. Scores on this measure ranged from 0 to 12, with a mean of 5 and a standard deviation of 3.6.

2. *Family stressors:* events in the household or extended family that command extraordinary attention, measured as consisting of problems with children, death in the extended family, death in the immediate family, birth of a child, disagreements with relatives or church members, and unexpected expenses typically demanded by kindred events. Scores on this measure ranged from 1 to 17, with a mean of 6.4 and a standard deviation of 3.6.

3. *Acute stressors:* unanticipated life changes or events, measured as consisting of a child leaving home or getting married, running out of money, losing or changing a job, an accident or sickness in the household, and moving to a new home. Scores on this measure ranged from 0 to 12, with a mean of 4.3 and a standard deviation of 2.8.

There is some overlap in the acute and family stressors index items. However, in general the family-stressors index measures problems that are more disruptive, and therefore demand a greater degree of psychological adjustment, than the "occasional hassles" with family members measured in the acute-stressors index. Furthermore, the family-stressors measure represents more chronic, long-term disruptions than the acute-stressors measure. When considered in light of the foregoing chapters, the family-stressors score is an index of problems specific to urban living. Problems with children often involve interaction with school or legal authorities, and thus encompass potential cultural conflicts. Deaths in the extended family involve expense, time off from work, possible conflicts

---

* The basic procedures used in constructing the factor analysis were generally as follows. All stressor items were recoded into a standard four-point ordinal scale, with 0 representing, hypothetically, the lowest stressor responses, and 3 the highest. Some theoretical weighting was undertaken based on knowledge of the community; for example, any death in the immediate family in the past year was scored a 3. A matrix of correlation coefficients was then generated, using non-parametric rank-order correlation techniques. This matrix was then analyzed using factor analysis techniques with a varimax rotation. A three-factor solution was accepted because it accounted for the majority of the variance, and it made good cultural sense. Items loading at the .40 level or above on the three factors were then summed.

TABLE 7.5

Second-Order Partial Correlations of Stressors with Health Measures

Stressor	Systolic blood pressure	Diastolic blood pressure	Physical health	Complaints
Men				
Structural	.19	.19	−.08	−.10
Family	−.03	.06	.08	.23
Acute	.06	.08	.20	.35**
Women				
Structural	.24	.20	.29*	.32*
Family	.47**	.46**	.53**	.36*
Acute	−.14	−.05	.24	.38*
Total				
Structural	.19*	.17*	.07	.07
Family	.16	.22*	.27**	.25*
Acute	−.04	.01	.20*	.38**

NOTE: Controlled for effects of body mass and age. Significance: *p < .05; **p < .01.

with relatives over contributions, and the disruption of normal family routines. Deaths in the immediate family, in addition to all the above, may involve grief and role change, as well as a more intense participation in funeral activities. The birth of a child may mean an added drain on household resources and bring a temporary and potentially disruptive co-alescence of female kin. Disagreements with relatives or church members is a measure of the often-divisive and potentially stressful conflicts that arise in the community, conflicts that may go on for some time and be tremendously disruptive to the core 'aiga group. Finally, fa'alavelave expenses, though nearly continuous, cannot be anticipated and often demand such extensive resources and participation that the family may not recover for some time and be unable to meet regular household expenses.

The partial correlations of the stressor scales with health measures are presented in Table 7.5. Here we see considerable gender differences. In men the only relationship is between the acute-stressors score and psychosomatic complaints. But for women family stressors are correlated at a highly significant level with all the health measures, and the other stressor scores are correlated at a significant level with complaints.

These results imply significant gender differences in the perceptions and/or effects of stress. The significance of structural, family, and to a certain extent acute stressors in women suggest that difficulties in the private, domestic domain are experienced most directly by women and are events to which they must make the most active response. Conversely, as discussed in the previous section, the stressors that affect Samoan men are largely those of the public sphere, where the pursuit of and maintenance of leadership status are the primary goals. The logic of such gender differences becomes more apparent if we consider the nature of Samoan gender relationships in general and how they change after migration.

Holland (1989) notes that differential responsibility in such areas as social life, contributions to subsistence, childrearing, and education as reflected in the Samoan division of labor both on the mainland and in the islands is such that neither sex could be effective alone. Gender roles are thus conceived of as matched pairs and involve an acknowledged notion of teamwork or complementarity unfamiliar in Western society. The demands of migration and urban adaptation have required that many women take a more active public role than in Samoa, particularly in interaction with formal U.S. institutions of education, social services, and health care. As noted in Chapter 5, some women have come to act increasingly as public spokespersons for the community. Although men continue to reap the primary psychological benefits attached to public statuses, such as matai, president of a church congregation, or elder deacon, women's contribution to social welfare has come to be recognized and valued. Where men remain predominant in the public Samoan domain, women are increasingly active in the public American domain— though, to be sure, their numbers are still small.

The responsibilities of such public status, combined with the expectation that women should serve as primary custodians of the domestic sphere—especially in supporting their husband's status aspirations—and often that they will work outside the home as well, may place enormous stress on them. If things are not going well in the family and if money is short, that stress may be particularly pernicious. It is interesting in this regard to note that spirit possession in the migrant society, termed *ma'i aitu,* seems to affect primarily women and has been hypothesized to be an outcome of "role stress" (I. Lazar 1985). This stress occurs because of stringent prescriptions on the appropriate behavior of women in both the public and the private domain; spirit possession suspends such role expectations for a time. Thus while stress for men arises in the public sphere, stress for women arises in the domestic sphere, and though still to a limited extent, in the public sphere as well.

Stressors and Health: Combined Effects

Although bivariate analyses are useful in examining specific hypotheses, it is important to assess the overall and combined effects of stressors, demographic, and physiological variables on health. Such analyses allow us to make some general statements on how well known social and cultural risk factors, for example, might predict a given health outcome

TABLE 7.6

Correlation Matrix of Demographic, Morphologic, and Stressor Variables

Variable	(1)	(2)	(3)	(4)	(5)	(6)	(7)
			MEN				
(1) Age	1.0						
(2) Body mass	−.15	1.0					
(3) Intracommunity social inconsistency	.06	−.18	1.0				
(4) Extracommunity social inconsistency	.19	−.03	−.13	1.0			
(5) Structural stressors	−.13	−.16	.13	−.09	1.0		
(6) Family stressors	.07	−.01	.13	−.04	−.02	1.0	
(7) Acute stressors	−.06	−.23	.06	.14	.24	.05	1.0
			WOMEN				
(1) Age	1.0						
(2) Body mass	−.14	1.0					
(3) Intracommunity social inconsistency	−.12	−.02	1.0				
(4) Extracommunity social inconsistency	.30	−.08	.17	1.0			
(5) Structural stressors	−.07	−.12	.25	.09	1.0		
(6) Family stressors	.25	−.28	.04	.22	.11	1.0	
(7) Acute stressors	−.19	.01	.03	.15	.28	.05	1.0

both singly and in concert. Employing a multiple regression model, I assessed the general linear relationship between health and all the stressors discussed above. Table 7.6 presents a correlation matrix of the independent variables. Table 7.7 shows the regression of the health measures on stressors, body mass, and age.

The results generally confirm the bivariate results already discussed, though in this case it is possible to evaluate the amount of variance explained by the social versus the demographic and physiologic variables. In men social inconsistency and body mass account for most of the variance in blood pressure. Age is the best predictor of physical health, and acute stressors are the only significant predictor of psychosomatic complaints. Generally, the effects of the stressors on men, except for the social inconsistency scores, are not significant. Again, the pattern is remarkably different for women. Family stressors are significantly correlated with all the health measures, accounting for between 10 percent and 23 percent of the total variance. The difference between men and women on this parameter is statistically significant. Acute stressors are associated at a significant level with complaints. Overall, the regression model for women predicts between 39 percent and 54 percent of the total variance in the health measures. The regression analysis thus confirms the conclusions

TABLE 7.7

Regression of Health Measures on Stressors

Measure	Men			Women		
	MAP	Physical health	Complaints	MAP	Physical health	Complaints
Age	.04	.27	.01	.30*	.41**	.08
Body mass	.33*	.13	−.13	.33*	.18	.37*
Structural stressors	.19	−.11	−.12	.19	.24	.22
Family stressors*a*	.01	.07	.23	.44**	.48**	.32*
Acute stressors	−.02	.17	.30*	−.20	.11	.36*
Intracommunity social inconsistency	.28*	.07	−.21	.06	−.21	−.05
Extracommunity social inconsistency	.28*	.26*	.20	.11	−.03	−.04
Multiple R	.48	.47	.52	.68**	.74**	.62*
Multiple R^2	.23	.22	.27	.47	.54	.39
Adjusted R^2	.11	.07	.13	.35	.43	.23

NOTE: See Table 7.4.

[a]The significance of the difference between men and women in the parameter of family stressors was calculated by taking the difference of unstandardized coefficients for each dependent variable and dividing by the average of the standard errors to yield a t-ratio. The differences were as follows: MAP = 1.88, t = 2.98, p < .01; physical health = .51, t = 3.74, p < .01; complaints = .30, t = .670, n.s.

drawn from the bivariate analyses and illustrates the profound nature of family stressors on women discussed above.

The data show quite clearly that family problems, acute life "hassles," and economic difficulties, particularly when they result in social status inconsistencies, are differentially related to ill-health in Samoan men and women. The patterns of stressor-health relationships by sex reflect Samoan gender relationships and the division of labor as transformed by migration and urban adaptation.

Stressful life circumstances or social inconsistency are certainly not unique to Samoans. But their predicament is exacerbated by the adaptive process. Moving from a descent group–based agricultural economy to a capitalist economy is not without problems. For Samoans these problems are compounded by the monetization of status and prestige; they accrue most directly from demonstrated generosity and conspicuous giving. Principles of monetary economics have been incorporated into Samoan rituals, and with it a shift from a symmetrical system of competitive but immediately reciprocal exchange to an asymmetrical system that is equally competitive but only indirectly reciprocal. If Samoans are to engage in the important rituals that foster a sense of social solidarity and cultural continuity, they must have access to considerable economic surplus. It is in circumstances of chronic social inconsistency, or slippage between one's need for social involvement and one's economic resources, that stress and ill-health may result. It is also under circumstances of fulfilling domestic responsibilities in a context of social engagement that women are placed under enormous stress, stress that is expressed in higher levels of ill-health.

Table 7.7 not only points to gender differences but also suggests that different stressors are related to specific health outcomes. It is possible that acute stressors, and to some extent family stressors—which are in a sense acute—are more predictive of complaints than of other health problems because this is the principal avenue by which Samoans express acute stress. In any case studies of biological mechanisms underlying the stress process indicate differential effects of chronic and acute stressors (see Kasl 1984; Rose 1980). It is tempting to hypothesize that acute stressors are manifested immediately in the kind of general malaise that the complaint score measures, and if continued over a period of time, take a more pathological course. However, such causal relationships are impossible to construct given the cross-sectional design of this study. Still, it seems reasonable to suppose that transitory but problematic life events would be immediately expressed in the language of general ailments or complaints, particularly if such language is culturally meaningful, whereas relatively long-term and structural conditions, such as social inconsistency, would be most predictive of the chronic conditions of high blood pressure and heart disease. This line of reasoning underlines the need for further psychophysiological research on the phenomenon of stress.

The one factor that may serve to ameliorate stress is the existence of a supportive group of relatives and friends. Not only does this group buffer the effects of an event by providing funds and psychological support, but a person's knowledge that such a group exists and can be called on in times of need is, in the long run, likely to be a powerful emotional, as well as instrumental, boost. As we will see in the next chapter, the potential for support is as significant as the actual provision of support.

EIGHT

Social Support, Resistance Resources, and Health

The degree to which social and cultural stressors affect health is ultimately dependent on the psychological and social resources available to individuals. Following Antonovsky (1979) and others (e.g., Cassel 1976), I call these "resistance resources." From an ecological perspective resistance resources consist of those factors or processes that facilitate the "fit" of humans to their environment, or in a more psychological sense, facilitate "tension management." Antonovsky, for example, argues that resistance resources foster a "sense of coherence." By this he means an orientation that expresses the extent to which an individual has a feeling of confidence that events and environments are predictable, and that "things will work out as can reasonably be expected" (1979: 123). A sense of coherence develops from external environmental cues and information—social support and cultural continuity—and internal "confidence," or what psychologists might refer to as "locus of control."

In the preceding chapters I argued that some Samoans are placed in circumstances in which they are forced to struggle to achieve a modicum of economic security and social recognition, and that those who find themselves in such tenuous circumstances exhibit greater levels of ill-health than others. In this chapter we shall see how social resources not only buffer stressors, but are, in general, directly health-enhancing.

The Kin Group and the Church

A corollary of the social-inconsistency hypothesis that has been applied specifically to migrants is that of "cultural incongruity." It proposes that people who find themselves in foreign social situations where behavior is unpredictable experience stress. This postulate has been invoked to explain the higher rates of cardiovascular disease generally found among migrants from rural to urban areas (e.g. Cassel 1975; Scotch 1963). The problem is, migrants themselves are rarely examined to determine whether they actually feel they are in "incongruous" situations; the fact of migration is taken as prima facie evidence of cultural incongruity. The emphasis is usually on the degree to which areas of origin and destination differ: the greater the difference, the greater the hypothesized stress (e.g. Hackenberg et al. 1983; McGarvey and Baker 1979).

This argument has a certain degree of intuitive appeal and has been supported, though indirectly, by descriptive epidemiologic research. However, two assumptions implicit in the cultural-incongruity hypothesis are suspect. First, migration is assumed to involve moving to a social environment for which one is by upbringing unprepared (Cassel 1975). Yet data on migrants suggest that at least some are self-selected for traits that would make the destination less foreign or threatening. For example, migrants may possess considerable educational or employment experience and may have lived for a time in urban areas—such as port towns or small cities. This experience would serve to prepare them for life in their new milieu. Many Samoans, particularly early migrants, had considerable experience working with Americans in or around the urban port complex of Pago Pago. Others had training as teachers or nurses. These people were prepared in many ways to enter American society and economic institutions without experiencing any fundamental incongruity.

A second assumption is that migrants inevitably find themselves in social situations with which they are unfamiliar. A quick survey of the anthropological literature on migration, however, shows that migrants reconstruct familiar institutions for themselves that function to provide informal socialization to new urban roles (e.g., Banton 1965; Epstein 1961; Gutkind 1969; Little 1965). Samoans have their families, churches, and civic organizations. These institutions provide a familiar social world that is instrumental in helping them cope with the demands of urban life. Those who commit themselves to pursuing goals that lie outside the Samoan social and cultural sphere would find themselves in more foreign social situations than those who remain committed to goals that are culturally familiar. Consequently, Samoans pursuing an American lifestyle would be those most likely to experience cultural incongruity and to be seriously affected by setbacks in their aspirations.

Samoans have adapted two familiar institutions to urban American society that provide them with a familiar and predictable sociocultural environment: the core 'aiga and the church congregation. The church and 'aiga also enable individuals, from the comfort of a secure social environment, to learn about Americans, American society and institutions, and appropriate modes of urban behavior.

The 'aiga, under whose auspices a person migrates, functions to provide, minimally, initial economic assistance; socializes the individual to such activities as finding jobs and housing; and provides a significant measure of psychological security. This process is not unique to Samoan migrants to San Francisco or even California. Of the migrants to New Zealand, for example, Pitt and Macpherson (1974: 24) write:

Although the individual's economic dependence on his family may decrease, his emotional dependence may increase. The family provides a secure setting in which a migrant can interact adequately because he shares its set of values and its language and has a similar set of definitions of situations. . . . The family provides social situations which he fully understands and which bring some predictability into his life.

The church is a similar social environment. Mainland congregations have grown to encompass many activities that were formerly village affairs, for example, systems of leadership and prestige. Listen to the Samoan clergyman Bert Tofaeono (1978: 40–41) on the church-as-urban-village:

To be recognized as a Samoan you had to belong to a church. Instead of the villages of Leone, Fagatogo, and so on, you were of the First Samoan Church of Los Angeles, the First Samoan Church in Culver City [or the] Samoan Church of Long Beach. . . . As far as the culture is concerned, the framework of the community sets the chief as pastor and the ranking chiefs as deacons. . . . To have a position of prestige you had to be either a deacon, or a deacon with a matai title.

Church activities also reinforce and maintain aspects of Samoan culture that migrants value. The church is a place where one can meet and develop a network of friends. Most important, the church community provides an important reference point, a sense of belonging to an integrated and cohesive human group. Together, the church and 'aiga function to instill the "sense of coherence" described above. We might expect therefore that feelings of cultural incongruity would be limited by the degree to which individuals become involved in and committed to those institutions.

Networks of Social Support

The term social support, which has gained great currency in the field of social epidemiology, is commonly used to describe the degree and nature of help available to an individual within his or her social network. Researchers have argued consistently, and based on reasonably consistent empirical evidence, that social support promotes health, especially in buffering stressors (Berkman 1985; Broadhead et al. 1983; Cobb 1976; Cohen and Syme 1985). Despite its empirical validity, however, social support remains a problematic concept; the meaning of social support, its operationalization, and its measurement vary considerably across studies. Social support has been variously defined in emotional, cognitive, and instrumental terms (e.g., House and Kahn 1985; Kahn and Antonucci 1980). As a consequence, there have been calls for a grounding of the meaning of social support in its cultural context (see Jacobson 1987). In addition, as the anthropologist Jacobson argues (1987: 58), the study of social support opens up a " 'window' into the 'structures of meaning' that constitute a culture."

In Western industrialized cultures social support has often been confused with social integration; that is, social involvement of any kind inevitably implies social support. However, it is important to distinguish in kinship-based societies between social support and formal social involvement in which kinship status expectations involve considerable obligation. Samoans recognize kinship at a great distance from the nuclear family, so each Samoan may be potentially integrated into a very large network of kin that he or she may use from time to time as a source of information on jobs and housing, for a place to stay in an emergency, or as a source of money when family events require it. But in order to rely on kin support, one must expect to be used as well: to attend family ceremonies and provide money and goods for such functions; to honor and respect the position of family chiefs and elders; to provide housing if asked; and in general to behave properly to such kin so as to maintain one's reputation as properly fulfilling kin obligations with aplomb and loving concern (*alofa*). As described in Chapter 6, most migrants are proud of the degree to which they continue to honor such obligations, but the emotional and material costs of doing so result in a great deal of ambivalence about the good of such obligations in the mainland society. In New Zealand Graves and Graves (1985) found that Samoan migrants who were most reliant on kin actually reported more health problems than others. They suggest the excessive obligations involved in maintaining kinship relations in the urban setting as one plausible explanation for this finding (see also Howard 1986).

Kaplan et al. (1977) and Pilisuk and Froland (1978) argue that the culturally specific context of social support cannot be understood without analyzing the structure and content of individual networks. This is especially important when considering the Samoan material. Examining the organization of Samoan networks and identifying the supportive elements within them not only provides a picture of how they are health-enhancing, but gives us a glimpse, in Jacobson's words, of the "structures of meaning" that underlie the organization of Samoan social relations.

Social-network analyses have been conducted on many levels, with different goals and methodologies. On the most formal level, network analysis involves a systematic exploration of individuals' social encounters or of the relations associated with a specific behavior or event. Political factionalism, patterns of communication, voting behavior, and the adoption of new behaviors, norms, or morals are examples of research problems successfully subjected to network analysis (Mitchell 1969). The kind of detailed and exhaustive fieldwork involved in applying the rigorous methods of conventional network analysis, however, permits examining only a few individuals or situations. These methods were clearly beyond the scope and intent of this research. Although I have collected a large body of data on the social contacts each individual in my sample reported, these are what network theorists term "first-order" observations; that is, only how the network looks from the perspective of the person questioned, not how each of the other people in the network is connected to the others. I therefore use the term social network in a narrower and somewhat more theoretical sense than it is used in most network studies as more suitable to my primary purpose here: to detail the general structural and interactional features of migrant Samoan social networks in order to determine where support lies and how it functions.

Samoans are a very social people: they conceive of themselves in terms of their relationships with others; define appropriate behavior in terms of the social actors present; and are judged by their ability to fulfill roles according to the norms and values of Samoan culture. One is not simply a "good" person in an absolute sense, but good in a particular social relationship or role: a "good" mother, matai, brother, or 'aiga member (Shore 1982). Samoan children are taught from an early age to be sensitive to social cues, to those characteristics that circumscribe and define appropriate behavior. As they grow older they are reminded to tend carefully to their social relationships (*teu le va*).

It is therefore not surprising that by the cultural standards of white, middle-class Americans, and despite difficulties imposed by the demands of jobs and living in dispersed "private" households, Samoans spend an extraordinary amount of time involved in social interaction. As we have seen, the most important relationships are those with other household members, with the primary cooperating household group (core 'aiga network), and with friends and other relatives in the kindred with whom one shares common interests. These constitute a core group. Radiating outward from this core are less intense, less frequently reinforced ties to distant relatives, church members, and acquaintances. Farthest from one symbolically and affectively are those people with whom one engages in transitory, formal, or impersonal interactions. These may be workmates, community leaders, or non-Samoan neighbors. Unmet members of one's 'aiga may also fall into this category, though psychologically Samoans conceive of unknown relatives as a latent social network that is structured by theoretical kinship rights and obligations and thus symbolically closer than, say, a circle of acquaintances at work. The three parts to a Samoan's social network, then, represent a gradually increasing distance. This distance, usually articulated by Samoans as falling into simple close/not close categories, actually represents a continuum along which important relationship characteristics change.

Individuals maintain by far their most intense relationships in the core 'aiga network. As is typical of such networks, everyone in the group knows everyone else and is involved equally intensely with each member. If one conceives of the members of the core 'aiga network as points, and lines connecting points as social relationships, then nearly every point would be joined to every other point. These networks are based on a set of just a few but very important ties between siblings, or where there are no siblings in the area, one or two other close bilateral kin, and in rare cases, friends. These relationships not only are important in Samoan cultural terms, but have been emphasized and strengthened by migration. The relationships created by the initial economic bond between established migrants and the siblings and close relatives that followed them tend to persist and in many cases continue to involve a good deal of economic reciprocity.

Of these very close relationships, those with siblings remain the most emotionally and economically critical. Every person I spoke to in my sample who had siblings in the area visited them regularly—at least once a month. Even those who had had disagreements or arguments with their brothers or sisters continued to visit and occasionally provide for their needs. There are good social and cultural reasons for the strength of these bonds. First, siblings share the same kindred obligations and thus cooperate in contributing to the same set of kindred events. Even in the case of a person's obligations to his or her affines, siblings may share responsibilities. Second, the sibling bond carries considerable symbolic weight in Samoan thought and, indeed, in all of Polynesia (Marshall 1981; Shore 1982).

Shore (1982), who has examined the basis of social action in Samoa in depth, provides a fascinating analysis of same-sex and cross-sex sibling relationships. He suggests that in many ways sibling relations constitute in microcosm the basis of all relationships in Samoan society. Brother-sister bonds, like male-female relationships in general, are complementary in terms of role expectations and charged with considerable psychological and cultural importance. The behavior of brothers to sisters, and vice-versa, is "sacred" and strictly prescribed:

> The sister is *mamalu* (dignified) in relation to her brother, who shows her *alofa* (loving concern) and *fa'aaloalo* (respect) through positive concern for her welfare. . . . In relation to his sisters, a boy's status is primarily utilitarian. He "moves about" and "works" for the good of his sister. . . . Through spending his own energy he nourishes her (Shore 1982: 233–34).

By contrast the relationship between same-sex siblings (*uso*) is symmetrical and consequently competitive, subject to fewer cultural constraints, and intimate. This intimacy, while representing a certain amount of cooperation, also involves a spirit of competitive aggression, a spirit that can lead to conflict, strain, and jealousy. This is especially true when brothers must compete for titles and political status within the 'aiga. Village upheavals, the splitting of titles, and long-term 'aiga feuds can often be traced to conflicts between brothers. Sisters share a similarly competitive relationship, but it is less intertwined with political ambition. It is also likely to be more intimate and is not directly affected by political concerns. Moreover, marriage often separates sisters, and married women usually become involved in the political affairs of their husband's 'aiga and are not affected to the same degree as their brothers by the immediate affairs of their own 'aiga.

The economic and political contexts in which sibling roles take on the most social and cultural meaning are much different on the mainland. The most important difference is that brothers are no longer under the same pressure to attain titled status within the 'aiga. There are alternate paths to leadership and prestige that do not depend on matai status, and these do not tend to exacerbate sibling rivalry to the same degree as in Samoa. Hence, there has been some lessening of tension between brothers, though the spirit of competitiveness is still quite evident. One older man made an interesting comment in this regard:

> I have lots of trouble running short on money. . . . Sometimes I have to go to my family to ask. My brothers, they usually get mad at me for asking, they just "blast" my ear, but I just put up with it because I need the money. They will always give it to me if they have it. My sister, though, she always gives me more than I need. . . . Sometimes she gives me money without [my] asking. I prefer to go to my sister for this reason.

This comment speaks volumes about the competitive/aggressive spirit of the brother-brother relationship in contrast to the more formal and constrained relationship of brother and sister. Indeed, the giving of advice and free stating of opinions are a common element in uso relationships.

Another man, in speaking of a mild heart attack he had suffered, reported the following sequence of events:

I was on the phone talking to my brother about a problem in the family. We got into an argument over it; I tried to get him to see my point, but he just wouldn't do it. I go so mad at him I could hardly breathe. I put the phone down and sat in a chair trying to catch my breath. My wife came in, took one look at me, and called the doctor. . . . This brother, I always argue with him, but we understand each other. I don't know what I would do without him. You have to take the bitter with the sweet.

None of the women I interviewed reported negative experiences with their sisters; most indicated that they were very close. Women also demonstrated more concern for the welfare of their sisters' families, and it was common for sisters to share babysitting chores, shopping, and taking children back and forth to school, and to buy things for each other's children and households. In one large core 'aiga network, composed of four sisters and two brothers and their families, the women constitute a very intimate and interdependent subgroup. They all live within a five-minute walk of each other, and they and their children spend much of their free time visiting back and forth. The eldest sister, also the first migrant of the group, is by virtue of considerable education and job experience the head of the family. She not only provides financial assistance for the others but acts as their representative in dealing with housing, welfare, and health-care institutions.

Though cross-sex and same-sex sibling relationships are qualitatively distinct, both involve a significant amount of potential support. Brothers and sisters recognize a fundamental and sacred kinship bond, termed *feagaiga*, which binds them in a helping relationship. Individuals know that should serious difficulties arise, their brother or sister (*tuagane* or *tuafafine*) will be there to support them, to take care of family if needed, and to deal with the rest of the kin group on their behalf. It is a fundamental and culturally important relationship that will likely persist over several generations in the migrant community. Same-sex, or *uso*, relations are perhaps the more important in an immediate psychological sense, though they may also entail significant economic reciprocity. *Uso* are those in whom one can confide and find help in times of trouble.

Beyond the day-to-day psychological and material support provided by siblings, this group also stands as a cooperative group in times of fa'alavelave. Since siblings possess the same set of consanguineal kin, they often share the burden of 'aiga contributions, thereby lessening the potential stress of such life-crisis events. The more brothers and sisters one has in the area, the less the economic burden on one household.

Other close and supportive bilateral kin belong to the core network and are in many cases as important as siblings. These are parents, children, spouses, and other relatives with whom one has developed a close relationship. For older people grown children are an important source of economic support. Parents are also important to adult children, but not quite to the same degree. Their relations with parents are often formal and asymmetrical in the sense that the parents expect a great deal of economic support from them, but not vice versa. Spouses are also very important sources of support, though my research goals did not permit me to direct much attention to the nature of the conjugal bond.

In addition to relatives, close friends can be considered part of the core network. Friends are commonly made in two important social contexts: within the church and within the kindred. The latter may appear somewhat contradictory, since kindred members are relatives. However, outside the core 'aiga group kindred members are not seen frequently, and relationships are more often based on obligation than on intimacy or friendship. Yet Samoans do establish friendships with some of their kindred; this is perhaps inevitable, given the amount of time adults spend on fa'alavelave affairs. Close friendship is highly valued by Samoans. In times of need, many informants admit, "friends are more important than relatives." Indeed, a measure of friendship may be whether that person becomes involved in your family affairs and vice versa. Said one woman, "I would do anything for my close friends. We help each other with the fa'alavelave, with babysitting, and with rides." In some cases friendship may also importantly supplement or replace sibling relationships where these are few or nonexistent. Like sibling relations, friendship involves considerable psychological support and often significant economic assistance. The reader will recall that friends are part of the informal-exchange network whereby people help each other in day-to-day affairs (Chap. 6).

In sum, for Samoans the core network, really *the* social support network, consisted of the following personnel: siblings in area, number of other relatives one visited with regularly or was close friends with, and number of friends. I have added together these different categories, and Table 8.1 presents the totals. One can see a substantial variation in the size of these networks, and hence the availability of social support.

The determinants of this variation were found to consist of a combination of three important factors. First, variability in the migration process, combined with demographic factors, resulted in some people migrating with little help from relatives, having few relatives in the area, or having these relatives pass away or move elsewhere. Second, some people have chosen to pursue a more self-reliant strategy of adaptation and have purposely not developed close mutual-aid relationships with relatives and

TABLE 8.1

Core Social Networks

Number of people	Men Number[a]	Men Percent	Women Number[a]	Women Percent
<3	3	5.7%	9	21.4%
3–5	15	28.8	11	26.2
6–8	18	34.6	13	31.0
9+	16	30.8	9	21.4
TOTAL	52	100.0%	42	100.0%

[a]Information on five men and five women missing or incomplete.

TABLE 8.2

Correlation of Core Social Networks with Health Measures

Measure	Men (N = 52)	Women (N = 42)	Total (N = 94)
Systolic blood pressure	−.29*	−.26*	−.22*
Diastolic blood pressure	−.34*	−.15	−.17*
Physical health	.07	−.03	.03
Complaints	.19	−.15	.01

NOTE: Controlled for effects of age and body mass. Significance: *$p < .05$.

friends (Graves and Graves 1980, 1985). Finally, there are generational differences in the degree to which people become involved with relatives to the exclusion of friends, or vice versa. Younger people (aged 30–40) in my sample, particularly those who had been in California for many years, were more concerned with maintaining friendships and were involved to a greater extent in informal mutual-aid networks of friends. This pattern corresponds to the "peer reliance" that the Graves (1980, 1985) observed among younger Polynesian migrants to urban New Zealand. Older people were comparatively more committed to relatives and had fewer friends. Friendship also differed by sex: men reported both having more friends and visiting with them more often; women reported more of a reliance on kin, especially sisters. And, then, personality factors undoubtedly play a role in the size of a person's networks. As in all cultures, there are some people who are not adept at social relationships or prefer to remain unencumbered by social responsibilities.

To assess the effects of the size of these groups on health, I present in Table 8.2 a correlation of the size of core social networks with the health measures. Social network size is negatively and significantly associated with systolic blood pressure in both men and women, and with diastolic blood pressure in men. It is not correlated with any of the other health measures, and even shows a slight positive correlation with complaints in men. As in the relationship between church involvement and blood pressure, the social network measure is long-term and structural, indicating a general degree of latent social support (and knowledge that support exists if needed). One would thus expect that it would be most closely related to chronic conditions such as blood pressure. And, as suggested previously, there is bound to be a level of acute stress embodied in close, supportive social relationships, which have been correlated specifically with higher complaint scores. One need only consider the comments of the Samoan man who suffered a heart attack after arguing with his brother to understand the volatile nature of *uso* relationships.

Another strategy for assessing the degree of social support is to focus on the actual support exchanged. Individuals were asked in the interview to indicate how frequently they had received various sorts of assistance from friends or kin. These ranged from child care to gifts of food. There was little variation on several items, particularly those that nearly all Samoans engage in to some degree: gifts of food, providing transportation, helping out around the house or yard, and the like. All three of the items that did exhibit significant variation fall into the category of essential instrumental support: help minding children, help finding a job or housing, and help with an external authority (e.g., social worker, housing official). A fourth item was found through factor analysis to be correlated with these three: how long people lived with relatives before finding housing for themselves and their family. As noted in Chapter 6, informal-exchange networks often develop out of dependent-provider relationships established just after migration. The provision of housing is the most fundamental of these initial relationships and often initiates lifelong reciprocal exchanges between provider and dependent.

Two dimensions of social support were thus identified: social support that derives from a person's involvement in a meaningful network of kin and friends, which might be thought of as representing *potential* resources; and support of a more instrumental kind that stems from the exchange of important assistance and services. Because church involvement was related to network size, and may in fact represent an alternative source of support for those with few kin in the area, I chose to include it with the overall social-resource measure. The two social-support measures and their components are as follows: *

---

* All the items were subject to confirmatory factor analysis. Initially, a three-factor solution was chosen that encompassed three kinds of social support: sibling-specific support,

1. *Social resources:* A five-item scale consisting of ranked responses (five possible ranks per item) to the following questions. (a) About how often do you attend church services? (b) How many close friends do you have in the area? (c) How many friends do you visit more than once per month? (d) How often do you visit with relatives (except siblings) who live in the area? (e) How many siblings do you have in the area that you visit more than once per month? The scores on this measure range from 0 to 23, with a mean of 12 and a standard deviation of 4.5.

2. *Instrumental support:* A four-item scale consisting of ranked responses (three possible ranks per item) to the following questions. (a) How many times in the past year have friends or relatives helped you with child minding? (b) How many times in the past year have friends or relatives helped you find a job or housing? (c) How many times in the past year has a friend or relative gone with you to see a person in authority (non-Samoan)? (d) How long did you live with relatives before getting your own place? The scores on this measure range from 0 to 8, with a mean of 3.3 and a standard deviation of 1.9.

The relationship of the social-support measures to health is presented in Table 8.3. For men social resources are inversely and significantly correlated with systolic and diastolic blood pressure, but instrumental support is not correlated significantly with any of the health measures. A much different pattern is seen in women: whereas social resources show a modest but statistically insignificant relationship with blood pressure, instrumental support is highly and significantly associated with blood pressure. Neither of the support measures is significantly associated with physical health or psychosomatic complaints.

The differential pattern of support-health relationships by gender is striking and further exemplifies the importance of considering gender-specific experiences in migration and adaptation. Based on the stress data presented in the previous chapter, I suggest that women's position in the social fabric, and the particular constellation of developing cultural expectations that attach to that position, render them comparatively more vulnerable to economic and family stressors. It is in the context of such stressors that active, instrumental support becomes most effective. On the other hand men's competition for leadership status and commitment to kindred involvement, while also depending to some extent on instrumental support, are dependent on social-network resources.

---

nonsibling social resources (including church participation), and material support. Because the relationship between the sibling and nonsibling support score was not completely orthogonal and showed similar effects with regard to health, I combined the two scores into a single measure. (See also Janes 1986; Janes and Pawson 1986.)

TABLE 8.3

Second-Order Partial Correlations of Social Support with Health Measures

Measure	Men (N = 52)		Women (N = 42)		Total (N = 94)	
	Social resources	Instrumental support	Social resources	Instrumental support	Social resources	Instrumental support
Systolic blood pressure	−.39**	−.09	−.24	−.34*	−.24*	−.20*
Diastolic blood pressure	−.40**	−.13	−.14	−.30*	−.17*	−.21*
Physical health	.02	.02	−.04	.02	.01	.02
Complaints	.16	−.01	−.15	−.13	−.02	−.06

NOTE: Controlled for effects of age and body mass. Significance: *p < .05; **p < .01.

Other Relationships

Outside their core networks, Samoans typically maintain a large number of relationships to individuals with whom they share kinship or some social activity. The most important of these relationships are defined by kinship and characterized by interaction that involves formal rights and obligations. The outstanding example is seen in the ubiquitous fa'alavelave, where there is an economic exchange between kin who may have no other occasion for interacting. A life-crisis event like a funeral causes a large but temporary network of 'aiga members to form for the purposes of providing funds, prestige items, and food to the affected subgroup of the kindred. But this network lapses afterward, and the people who came together for the services and feasting may not see one another for a year or more.

These formal kindred networks also include a large number of asymmetrical relationships. One engages in an interaction or exchange with the appointed head of the family, or matai, who holds the ceremonial authority (*pule*) to assemble and present contributions. Conversely, a matai may have certain obligations to the family he makes this presentation to, or to other, more senior matai present at the affair. Such relationships do not necessarily involve immediate reciprocity. One gives to a relative's funeral knowing that this contribution will eventually be returned when a fa'alavelave occurs closer to home. But the reciprocity involved is highly generalized, more theoretical than actual. As one Samoan said, "You give, give, give and try to remember that some day it will come back to you, even if it's for your own funeral!"

These obligations carry considerable moral force in the migrant community. One's reputation as a community member, not to mention within one's household and 'aiga, is usually based on generosity in all things. Consequently, these more formal relationships not only involve less immediate material or psychological support, but can prove to be a considerable burden. Thus, as I have noted, stress may arise from the status inconsistency experienced from trying to maintain extended family obligations with few economic means or little substantial core-network support.

At the greatest symbolic and affective distance from the individual are those people with whom he or she maintains impersonal relationships: other Samoans with whom one has little contact, such as in the case of community-wide activities, and non-Samoans with whom one has developed "acquaintance" relationships at work or in other contexts. Samoans sometimes establish what they call friendships with non-Samoan workmates, but these relationships are kept carefully separate from the more important and all-encompassing social world of church and kin group. Only younger men and women reported any close involvement with non-Samoans. Little more needs to be said of these relationships, because for the most part they bear little on day-to-day life.

Although formal kindred involvement varies, even the people with the least amount of interest in extended family or church remain involved in a primarily Samoan social world. Those who dislike extensive kindred involvement spend time with Samoan friends instead. Very few Samoans, even among the younger and more educated circles, are predominantly involved in non-Samoan social networks. One of the most striking characteristics of the Samoan population is the degree to which it has maintained an exclusive community within the complex heterogeneity of urban Northern California. Samoans remain "incapsulated" in their own networks to the exclusion of others, in much the same way that Mayer's "Red" migrants in East London, South Africa are: "The Red syndrome, which has been termed incapsulation, has one feature, a 'tribal' type of moral conformism, stressing the superiority of the original undiversified institutions; such institutions make for multiplex relations and a close-knit type of network; and this again makes for consistent moral pressure and conservatism" (Mayer 1961: 292).

Also like Red migrants, Samoans typically evince the attitude that Samoan institutions are by and large superior to American institutions. The close-knit networks they maintain within the large and far-flung kindred and within the important institution of the 'aiga tend to embody strong forces for conformity and conservatism. This appears to have been a consistent response to forces for social change throughout their history. Shankman (1976) has noted that increased conservatism has been the

Samoans' predominant reaction to colonialism, economic development, and urbanization. This conservatism leads to a consolidation of Samoan networks and institutions, that is, a stronger commitment to those areas of life that are the most secure and familiar: the family and the church (Rolff 1978).

Samoans also see their lifestyle as morally superior to the Americans', and more satisfying. Though many American traits are prized, particularly education and technical or professional job skills, Americans themselves are often stereotyped as being selfish, anti-family, ignorant of religion, and ungraceful in social situations. Samoans may learn quite effectively how to live in the world of "Americans," to be "more North American than the North Americans" (Mackenzie 1977), but their commitment in terms of personal energy and the pursuit of satisfaction is decidedly to their personal networks of relatives and friends. Adopting a more individualized or self-reliant strategy does not necessarily involve opting out of Samoan society, only deemphasizing some classes of relationships. Like other immigrant groups (see, e.g., Cronin 1970; Gluckman 1961; Mitchell 1966), Samoans move easily between the public sector of jobs and school, where they interact with non-Samoans, to the private world of family and church, where beliefs, values, and behavior are shifted to fit the rural Samoan norm. As the next generation comes of age and some come to perceive this private and conservative world as less than optimal, the boundaries between Samoan and non-Samoan worlds will blur. But at this writing the migrant Samoan community remains integrated and exclusive.

Another factor besides generational difference needs to be considered here: the degree to which economic problems may overburden 'aiga networks. Franco (1978), for example, has suggested that in Hawaii the mutual-aid functions of the extended family network are reaching their limit. This may be true of the San Francisco community too, especially in the case of fa'alavelave exchange, but it is doubtful whether the close core networks will be affected to any large degree. For the moment, anyway, as in the case reported by Stack (1974), networks of informal exchange are more important than ever among people with limited means. However, the system could well begin to break down when the second generation comes of age, a group that may not possess as strong a set of positive values on the need for mutual aid and cooperation within the household cluster as their parents now hold. This would have particularly disastrous consequences in a situation of severe poverty. In short, we may begin to see manifested some of the aspects of social disorganization thought to deleteriously affect health (Antonovsky 1979; James and Kleinbaum 1976; Leighton 1978).

Stress and Resistance Resources: Combined Effects

Although each of the stressor and social-resource measures discussed is of substantive interest in its own right, it is perhaps of greater importance to examine how these independent variables combine and interact in explaining variance in the health measures. This is especially true of social support, for it has been suggested that support functions in two ways: directly, to promote health by maintaining a sense of coherence and indirectly, to buffer the effects of stressors (Cohen and Syme 1985).

Three analytic questions are important in this regard. First, how do the stressor and social-support variables intercorrelate? Second, are there synergistic effects or interdependencies between pairs of independent variables that shed light on how sociocultural factors affect blood pressure? And third, what is the combined power of the independent variables in predicting health? To answer these questions, a series of multiple regression models were constructed to find the best "fitting" model for each

TABLE 8.4

Correlation Matrix of Demographic, Morphologic, Stressor, and Social-Support Variables

Variable	(1)	(2)	(3)	(4)	(5)	(6)	(7)	(8)	(9)
			MEN						
(1) Age	1.0								
(2) Body mass	−.15	1.0							
(3) Intracommunity social inconsistency	.06	−.18	1.0						
(4) Extracommunity social inconsistency	.19	−.03	−.13	1.0					
(5) Structural stressors	−.13	−.16	.13	−.09	1.0				
(6) Family stressors	.07	−.01	.13	−.04	−.02	1.0			
(7) Acute stressors	−.06	−.23	.06	.14	.24	.05	1.0		
(8) Social resources	.06	.30	−.03	−.08	−.05	.33	.02	1.0	
(9) Instrumental support	−.21	−.15	−.27	−.08	.40	−.40	.01	−.30	1.0
			WOMEN						
(1) Age	1.0								
(2) Body mass	−.14	1.0							
(3) Intracommunity social inconsistency	−.12	−.02	1.0						
(4) Extracommunity social inconsistency	.30	−.08	.17	1.0					
(5) Structural stressors	−.07	−.12	.25	.09	1.0				
(6) Family stressors	.25	−.28	.04	.22	.11	1.0			
(7) Acute stressors	−.19	.01	.03	.15	.28	.05	1.0		
(8) Social resources	.07	.06	−.02	−.05	−.41	−.08	.05	1.0	
(9) Instrumental support	−.22	−.19	−.25	−.14	.08	−.37	.08	.03	1.0

TABLE 8.5

Regression of Health Measures on Selected Social Variables

Category	MAP[a]	Physical health	Complaints
MEN (N)	57	44	44
Age	.07	.30	.03
Body-mass index	.44**	.12	.11
Structural stressors	.29*		
Family stressors			.26
Acute stressors		.14	.25
Intracommunity social inconsistency	.20		
Extracommunity social inconsistency	.22*	.21	.25
Social resources	−.48**	.03	.08
Instrumental support	−.26*	.05	.21
Multiple R	.65**	.43	.49
Multiple R²	.43	.18	.24
Adujsted R²	.34	.05	.09
WOMEN (N)	47	36	36
Age	.36**	.38**	.05
Body-mass index	.26*	.19	.39*
Structural stressors	.17	.32*	.25
Family stressors	.35*	.53**	.37*
Acute stressors			.34*
Intracommunity social inconsistency	.07		
Extracommunity social inconsistency			
Social resources	−.05	.13	.02
Instrumental support	−.18	.09	.06
Multiple R	.67**	.73**	.64*
Multiple R²	.44	.53	.41
Adjusted R²	.36	.43	.26

gender group, and then to examine variable interactions. Using stepwise regression procedures, the most predictive set of stressor variables was isolated for men and women. Next, the direct effects of the support measures were assessed and included where they added significantly to the variance explained by the model. Table 8.4 is a correlation matrix of independent variables; Table 8.5 shows the regression of the health measures on selected stressor and social-support variables.

In men body mass, structural stressors, extracommunity social inconsistency, and both support measures predict a significant amount of the variance in blood pressure. Only age is significantly predictive of physical health, and the overall model for main effects does not reach a statis-

TABLE 8.5 *(continued)*

Category	MAP[a]	Physical health	Complaints
TOTAL (N)	104	80	80
Sex	−.20*	−.05	.00
Age	.18*	.38**	.05
Body-mass index	.28**	.12	.15
Structural stressors	.19*	.08	.02
Family stressors	.14	.28*	.28*
Acute stressors	−.09	.16	.35**
Intracommunity social inconsistency	.10	−.05	−.09
Extracommunity social inconsistency	.19*	.09	.11
Social resources	−.22*	−.01	−.04
Instrumental support	−.16	.06	.07
Multiple R	.55**	.53**	.48*
Multiple R²	.30	.28	.23
Adjusted R²	.23	.17	.12

NOTE: Betas (standardized coefficients) are presented in this table and Table 8.6. Betas were estimated from a hierarchical regression model in which age and body mass were entered first, followed by the significant stress variables and then the two support variables. The adjusted R^2 measure, given the small sample size and large number of independent variables, is a more conservative indicator of variance explained by the model. For the gender subgroups a "best fit" model was derived using a variety of stepwise procedures, thereby limiting the number of independent variables in the equation. Coefficients are, however, estimated from the model described above. Betas for the full sample are provided for the reader's reference. Significance: *p < .05; **p < .01.

[a]Because of the large number of independent variables and the small number of missing values for the support measures, missing values on independent variables were recoded to the mean. This conservative strategy avoided a problem with the listwise deletion of cases where any variable is missing.

tically significant level. In women age, body mass, and family stressors are the best predictors of blood pressure, but surprisingly, the main effects of the instrumental support score disappear because of its interrelationship with the two stressor scores entered into the equation first. For women, unlike men, structural stressors and family stressors are significantly predictive of physical health. Age is too, as it is for men. Nearly half of the overall variance in the score can be predicted by the four variables in the model. The same variables also predict a fair degree of the variance in the complaint score.

To summarize the data in Table 8.5, general, acute, family, and structural stressors are the social variables most predictive of health in women, and the two social support measures, status inconsistency and structural stressors are predictive of blood pressure in men. But only one social variable shows a relationship with the self-report health measures: acute stressors. The significant main effect of social support on blood pressure is especially striking. A surprise was the disappearance of the strength of the instrumental-support relationship in women after considering the effects of the stressor measures. It is possible that instrumental support's primary effect is to buffer the effects of family or structural stressors, so that when the effects of those stressors were considered in the main model, the main effects disappeared. To assess the interactive or synergistic effects of the social-support measures, it is necessary to consider what statisticians refer to as "interaction effects."

The multiple-general-linear hypothesis assumes that the effects of the independent variables are additive. However, where the relationship between an independent and dependent variable, for example, instrumental support and blood pressure, varies as a function of a third variable, for example, family stressors, it is necessary to consider the variance explained by the product of two independent variables after the main effects have been considered (Cohen and Cohen 1975). Any significant amount of variation explained by the interaction term is thought to reflect an interdependent relationship between the independent variables and the dependent variable.

To test this relationship, twelve interaction terms were constructed, encompassing all possible interactions between stressors, including the physiological stressor of obesity, and the social-support measures. The interaction scores were then standardized to a mean of 0 and a standard deviation of 1. After the main effects were entered hierarchically into the regression model, each interaction effect was evaluated singly. Where the interaction term reached a significance level of .10 or more, it was retained. Table 8.6 shows a full model of the main effects and significant interaction effects for men and women.

It is notable that in men the relationship between body mass and blood pressure varies as a function of social support. As hypothesized, instrumental support is related to blood pressure in women as a function of family stressors. Thus in women the instrumental-support measure, while not exhibiting significant main effects, does in fact interact with family stressors to influence blood pressure. Further analysis of the shape of this interaction suggests that where family stressors are prevalent, instrumental support has a striking direct effect on blood pressure. Where they are less prevalent, instrumental support is not directly related to blood pressure. The finding that social support has both direct and buffering effects is consistent with most recent research (e.g., Cohen and Wills 1985; Reis 1984), as is the finding that men and women experience support in different ways and with different outcomes (Berkman 1984).

TABLE 8.6

Regression of Health Measures on Selected Social Variables with Interaction Effects

Category	Men			Women		
	MAP	Physical health	Complaints	MAP	Physical health	Complaints
Age	.11	.30	.03	.35**	.38**	.05
Body mass	.92**	.12	−.11	.23	.19	.39*
Structural stressors	.34**			.18	.32*	.25
Family stressors			.26	.62**	.53**	.37*
Acute stressors		.14	.25			.34*
Intracommunity social inconsistency	.20					
Extracommunity social inconsistency	.14	.21	.25			
Social resources	.43	.03	.08	−.04	.13	.02
Instrumental support	−.26*	.05	.21	.12	.09	.06
Social resources × body mass	−1.17*					
Instrumental support × family stressors				−.41*		
Multiple R	.68**	.43	.49	.70**	.73**	.64*
Multiple R²	.47	.18	.24	.49	.53	.41
Adjusted R²	.38	.05	.09	.40	.43	.26

NOTE: Interaction effects were examined singly. Effects explaining significant additional variation were then incorporated into a regression model, in which main effects were entered as a block and then the interaction effects were added as a block. See also note to Table 8.5.

Of special note is the interaction of body mass with social support. In men the interaction between the two explains 3 percent additional variance in blood pressure. Further analysis of the shape of this interaction suggests that at the upper levels of body mass, social resources have an especially strong buffering effect. At the lower levels social resources have little direct effect on blood pressure. Surprisingly, and perhaps given the mind-body dualism that implicitly structures research in the health sciences, physiological and sociocultural stressors are not usually considered in concert (but see Dressler 1983 for a similar finding). In particular the data suggest, though tentatively, that it may not be body mass per se that is the risk, but the interrelationship of body mass and social support.

In adapting to a complex urban system, with the potential for cultural conflict and economic stress, social resources are a valuable commodity. They provide a dynamic kind of information to the individual that proclaims, in effect, "help is here if and when you need it." In the face of serious stressors, tacit or explicit awareness that resources exist may prevent the kind of disequilibrium that leads to psychophysiological break-down. In the Samoan community such "salutogenic" resources are located in at least two institutional settings—the church and the family—and are represented in the active exchange of culturally valuable commodities and services within the core social network. Social resources were found to have a profound and positive influence on the health of Samoan men and women, both directly and in interaction with some of the measured stressors.

The gender-patterning of salient stressors and social resources reflects the general sexual division of labor in Samoan society as altered to fit the urban life. Men, striving for recognition in the public Samoan domain and pressing to fulfill kindred obligations, are subject to the stressors em-bodied in poverty and status inconsistency, and in this context powerfully benefitted by social resources. Women, though part of the family and community-leadership system, in a complementary-status relationship with their husbands, are also affected by poverty but most seriously by problems arising in the private, domestic domain for which they are pri-marily responsible. And in this context of vulnerability to economic and domestic stressors, women are benefitted by access to fundamental, ac-tive, and instrumental support in the informal-exchange sphere.

The social-resource measure is also interrelated with body weight in men. The data suggest a synergistic relationship between the physiologi-cal state of obesity and the social and cultural factors analyzed here, thus supporting Caudill's (1958) oft-cited but rarely examined argument that stress occurs in "linked systems."

The logic of the relationships between social support and health has been provided in the chapters assessing the social consequences of migra-tion. Samoans restructure kinship groups to fit the exigencies of urban living. The household becomes the primary cooperative unit, but inten-sive exchange is fostered between households of closely related kin. This group, together with close friends who participate in the exchange, con-stitutes the core social network and represents the "bank" of potential so-cial support. The urban church congregation has replaced the village as a sociopolitical institution and a setting for promoting cultural continuity, pursuing leadership status, articulating cultural distinctiveness, and main-taining interfamily integration. The church keeps Samoans enmeshed in an urban brand of fa'asamoa.

Thus while certain patterns of economic adaptation, in particular the development of the fa'alavelave institution within the cash economy, may exacerbate, for some, economic, familial, and life difficulties, the commu-nity provides powerful buffering institutions. The challenge for Samoans as individuals and as a viable community is to find that crucial balance between maintaining their culture and coming up with the resources needed to do so. Samoans have met this challenge in the past through cultural "consolidation" and conservatism (Rolff 1978; Shankman 1976); one hopes the rapidly maturing second generation will be able to marshal an equally effective response as it adapts to life in urban America.

NINE

Health-Care Utilization

The availability and quality of health services are important determinants of health and disease in populations undergoing rapid change. Paradoxically, acculturation has been associated with both a decline in overall health from exposure to new ills in a new environment and an improvement in overall health from better protection against common infectious ailments (see, e.g., Dennett and Connell 1988; Wirsing 1984). However, once infectious diseases cease to be a significant cause of mortality, cosmopolitan biomedicine appears to decline as a determinant of community health, being much less effective in treating chronic diseases and psychosocial disorders (Kunitz 1983). Moreover, whether a host society's health services have an influence, either positive or deleterious, on migrants' health is an iffy question (Kasl and Berkman 1983). An obviously central issue is the availability and acceptability of health services to the migrant community.

Someone who is sick or has a sick family member must make decisions about how the sickness is to be treated. These decisions are based on prior experience with healers, the individual's own understandings of the cause of diseases and expectations about treatment, and economic and social factors that affect access to health-care institutions. By virtue of many years of experience with American hospitals and doctors, Samoans hold definite attitudes toward American medicine, and these attitudes significantly influence their participation in the health-care system, including the treatment of some of the serious conditions discussed in this book.

As noted in Chapter 1, the rate of high blood pressure in Samoans is quite high, somewhat higher than the American rate (Table 1.1). In addition, Samoans manifest an increase in body mass across the migration gradient. The overall increase in body mass is associated with other risks, including coronary heart disease and diabetes. A study of fasting blood-glucose levels in California Samoans revealed that 18 percent of the men and 9 percent of the people tested had plasma glucose levels that exceeded the 95th percentile for fasting plasma glucose in the U.S. population (Janes and Pawson 1986). These figures are suggestive of an adult-onset diabetes rate several times the U.S. rate and similar to the rate found in modernizing populations in the United States and the Pacific (Zimmet and Whitehouse 1980; Zimmet et al. 1981). Baker and Crews (1986) report that diabetes-related mortality has increased in American Samoa.

Hypertension and diabetes are treatable conditions, provided that follow-up is good, medicines are taken regularly, and diets are adhered to. If unmanaged, both expose an individual to an increased risk of heart disease, stroke, and renal damage, to name but a few dangerous sequelae. It is therefore important to consider the degree to which Samoans seek health care for these conditions, their experiences with the care they receive, and the possible impact this has on the community's overall health.

When Pawson and I asked the possible diabetics in our study whether they had sought medical attention, nearly all said they had not, or if they had, had not continued seeking care. Health-care providers serving Samoan communities report that Samoans underutilize available services, do not return for follow-up appointments, and routinely seek care only in situations of acute illnesses (Janes and Pawson 1986). In 1981 I reviewed the medical records of a local clinic with a large Samoan clientele. Cardiovascular conditions and diabetes were the most common diagnoses in adult Samoan patients; diseases of the upper respiratory system ran a close second. Obesity and referrals to the clinic dietician were noted in a large percentage of the medical charts. Once the original symptoms had been ameliorated, compliance with treatment regimes was generally poor. Cook (1983) has found a similar pattern in Hawaii Samoans.

Stateside Samoan Medicine

Samoans hold a dual view of disease etiology that affects their health-care-seeking behavior. Only certain conditions are considered treatable by health-care personnel in hospitals and clinics. Many are considered refractory to American medicine and treatable only by Samoan healers. Much of the Samoans' slowness to use American facilities until conditions reach an acute stage is due to their preference for their own healers, of which there are several kinds.

Samoans are reluctant to talk about their medical system, especially the elements that involve supernatural causes and spirit possession. Although I knew of several practicing "herbalists" (*foma'i*) in the San

Francisco area and had the opportunity to interview one of them, only late in my research did I learn about a separate class of "Samoan sicknesses" regarded as untreatable by American, or *palagi*, medicine. These sicknesses, seen as supernaturally caused and as retribution for some moral delict on the individual's part, were typically taken to one of many well-established Samoan general practitioners (*taulasea*), or more rarely to Filipino healers, whose explanatory models and healing procedures appeal to Samoans as similar to their own.

In a detailed account of stateside Samoan medical practices, Thomas Lazar (1985) notes that the system of disease etiology involves levels of explanation that range from what Foster (1976) terms naturalistic notions to personalistic ones. Often a condition is ascribed to a combination of both. Cook (1983), for example, has found that one child's illness was attributed at once to the parents' actions, God, and germs. There is also a separate class of diseases held to be specifically "Samoan sicknesses" (*ma'i Samoa*). As Romanucci-Ross (1969) reports in her insightful analysis of medical pluralism in Manus, Papua New Guinea, many Samoans evince a cultural pride in "their" unique sicknesses. These sicknesses are generally attributed to the actions of malevolent ghosts (*aitu*), which typically represent embodiments of dead relatives who take action against the living out of anger over violations of cultural or moral prescriptions. The most common mechanism of action is possession (see T. Lazar 1985). I once heard even young, U.S.-born Samoans identify a relative's medical problem (something wrong with his legs) as a "Samoan illness" and therefore refractory to treatment by Western-trained personnel.

Thomas Lazar (1985) identifies four principal types of Samoan healers: the *foma'i*, or herbalist; the *taulasea* or "general practitioner"; power healers, who specialize in the manipulation of supernatural power in curing spirit possession; and diviners (what Lazar calls the "man who knows"), who specialize in determining the cause of illness. And these healers generally treat illnesses, including spirit possession, in one of three ways: massage (*fofo*), internal or external treatment with herbal concoctions, and communication with malevolent spirits.

Massage is considered essential for restoring the individual's life force, or *to'ala*, to its appropriate place in the abdomen (T. Lazar 1985). Herbal remedies are manufactured from a variety of plant leaves, roots, and barks that are brought in from Hawaii or Samoa by visitors. In fact there is considerable traffic in medicinal plants between the islands and the mainland, and because Samoans are such a highly mobile population, healers are often able to "order" plants through their own or their patient's traveling relatives. Massage and herbal remedies are used in tandem in treating internal conditions such as stomach ailments and headaches, as well as in cases of injury or chronic pain. Herbal concoctions are used for external conditions such as rashes, sores, and burns. Most Samoans I talked to are convinced that Samoan medicines are more effective in relieving symptoms and curing skin problems than Western medicines. Communication with a possessing aitu, according to T. Lazar (1985), is initiated by the healer (taulasea), who using massage, external herbal medicines, and a dose of "Devil's weed" (*ava'ava aitu*), persuades the spirit to speak through the patient and reveal the cause of the possession (usually taboo violation, a moral infraction, or some violation of Samoan custom).

In choosing what kind of medical resources to use, Samoans follow a pattern similar to that reported by Colson (1970) in Malaysia. Acute conditions are often taken to American hospitals or doctors (assuming that the individual has access to them; see below). Samoans expect symptoms to be relieved within a short time, and if they are not, seek healing alternatives (T. Lazar 1985). Thus chronic, long-term conditions that cause discomfort tend to be taken to Samoan healers, or Samoan healers are used in conjunction with Western practitioners. Spirit possession, which may result in the patient's hospitalization in the acute phases (it seems to resemble an acute psychotic episode; see ibid., pp. 298–99), is thought to be treatable only by Samoan healers experienced in communicating with aitu. Finally, common ailments like headaches, constipation, flu, colds, sore throats, and indigestion are typically treated initially and often solely by someone in the family; if the problem persists, a foma'i or taulasea is usually consulted. As noted, many Samoans consider herbal medicines and massage superior to Western biomedicine in treating these ailments.

Conflicts in Therapeutic Roles

Samoans encounter problems in seeking care from Western-trained practitioners that stem from conflicts in therapeutic roles. These conflicts take two forms: those stemming from the cultural differences between Samoan and American explanatory models of illness; and those stemming from differing expectations of appropriate role behavior in the therapeutic encounter.

Although migrant Samoans should not be considered a homogeneous lot in terms of medical beliefs, most are wont to symbolize and express their psychobiological sensations in a way that is quite foreign to practitioners trained in American biomedicine. It is not merely a problem of conflicting etiologic beliefs—for Samoans with their "layered," multicausal etiological system and long experience with Western medicine in Samoa are accustomed to entertaining different theories about illness—

but a matter of a different focus on time and symptoms that leads to con-flicting notions of appropriate clinical care. Samoans' purpose in the therapeutic encounter is, as one might expect, to have their symptoms relieved. The success of the treatment is evaluated shortly thereafter, and if the symptoms persist, alternative resources are sought (T. Lazar 1985). American health professionals focus instead on underlying causes, and especially in the case of chronic diseases, view treatment as long-term management rather than short-term relief. Furthermore, American heal-ers carry a set of assumptions and not a small number of moralistic beliefs about the interrelationship of lifestyle and disease that may not only con-flict with Samoan beliefs but even lead to the stigmatization of Samoan patients, compromising in a profound way the delivery of appropriate health services. Differing ideas about body size and its antecedents and biological sequelae are the more profound of these explanatory model conflicts.

To Samoans body size as a symbol of lifestyle conveys little moral in-formation. In Samoa large body size is a visible correlate of high social status: being a chief or a minister, having a well-paying government job or position, having many children, or even just being of advancing age in general. As a visual cue conveying socially important information, it is less important than other aspects of bearing and comportment. This is especially true among migrants, where a large body size is the statisti-cal norm. Body size is also not seen as a condition that affects health in any fundamental way, although Samoans are aware that Americans and the American health-care system perceive obesity as a problem. To Samoans obesity is perceived negatively only when it becomes uncom-fortable or makes moving about or accomplishing one's tasks difficult (Mackenzie n.d.).

American views of body size could not be more different. To Americans body size is a culturally salient visual marker. Fatness is disdained as an unattractive physical trait and is a visual contradiction of several basic and powerful white American cultural values: self-control, restraint, in-dustriousness, self-denial, and so on (Mackenzie n.d.). What Americans define as obesity, which would clearly include most Samoans, is a sign of a person's failure to uphold these values, a failure to pursue the proper path of restraint and moderation in all things. The obese in America are morally suspect. Labeling a person obese is tantamount to denoting his or her moral failure (ibid.).

When Samoans seek to enter American society and participate in American institutions—institutions controlled by the upper and middle white classes that have the greatest fear of fat—they confront these values head on. In the context of health care, obesity has become symbolic of a "chronic disease-prone" lifestyle and is thus a clinical sign of medical deviance. In seeking care, Samoans are often amazed, confused, and taken aback by the degree to which their body size becomes the overriding issue in the clinical encounter. The single-minded focus by health-care providers on obesity as an indication of the individual's health and social worth causes many Samoans to avoid clinical encounters as much as possible, or to search for physicians who do not make their body size the major issue in their provision of care.

The degree to which physicians' preoccupations with Samoan obesity interfere with the provision of care became apparent when I began the research for this book. I had contacted the head of a hypertension clinic in the area and asked him if I could make arrangements to refer Samoans I found to be hypertensive. His reply was as follows:

Sure, send all the Samoans you want, but it won't do any good. [Why do you say this?] Because they won't take their medication and they won't lose weight. How can we be expected to help them if they won't lose weight? Their weight is the real problem, and if they won't comply with the diets we give them, there is really little else we can do.

When treating a Samoan who is overweight by their standards, especially for chronic diseases, physicians tend to see the person's obesity as nearly the sole determinant of the condition, or at least as the major risk factor for later disability. Health messages about obesity are conveyed in a negative, accusatory way. Consider this example. A woman, now sixty and with the body size reflective of her age, status, and ten children, went to see her doctor for what she described as an "annual checkup." Her regular physician, a kind fellow with a large Samoan clientele, was sick that day, so she was seen by his younger associate. This doctor not only scolded her about her body size in a negative, condescending, and patronizing manner, but finally told her that unless she lost at least 50 pounds she would die soon. Said this woman, "I just went for a checkup. It was none of his business how much I weighed. And he treated me like a child; he made me feel ashamed."

This is not to suggest that obesity is not a risk factor for chronic disease and death, for the bulk of epidemiologic evidence suggests that it is related to many cardiovascular and metabolic diseases and even to some cancers. The problem is that (1) from an epidemiologic standpoint, obesity is always just one of many factors related to a condition and may not even be the most important one; (2) American health professionals, as integral members of their culture, have a difficult time conveying health information about the risks involved in obesity without shrouding it in strong, moralistic language or mannerisms; and (3) Samoans do not believe body size is a relevant medical issue at all, and given the way such information is given, are not likely to change their minds. The consequence of clinical encounters where obesity is an issue is that Samoans and providers alike negatively stereotype each other's behavior. In a vicious circle, each incident tends to further reify the stereotypes. To clinicians Samoans remain intractable, reluctant to follow clinical advice and to return for proper follow-up. To Samoans professionals remain rude, inappropriately focused on irrelevant personal characteristics, and altogether unpleasant to deal with. And so the professional health-care sector is underutilized, perhaps even dangerously so.

The conflict in ideas about appropriate professional/client interaction, although exacerbated by the medical establishment's stigmatization of obesity, is not limited to encounters where body size becomes an issue. Samoans in general perceive health professionals as reluctant to treat them with the dignity and status they feel they deserve. In other words Samoans and professionals possess a set of conflicting expectations about how the other party should behave. My experience as a consultant in health settings involving Samoans reveals that professionals have little idea about what makes Samoans unique, aside from their body size, and tend to lump them with all the other non-white, "uneducated" minority groups they see in their practices. They thus take an authoritative role that involves little exchange of information: why bother if the patient will not understand it anyway? This kind of authoritative role is especially problematic for older Samoan men and women, who expect some deference from professionals in these encounters, especially when they are younger than their patients (which they often are in public, low-cost hospitals and clinics; Cook 1983). Again, faced with the prospect of an uncomfortable encounter, Samoans tend to avoid seeking care unless it is absolutely necessary.

Access to Care

A point often overlooked in studies of medical pluralism has to do with the political economy of the Western health-care delivery system. Though it is well beyond the scope of this book to engage in a detailed criticism of American medicine, two points must be made. First, Samoans, and this is especially true for new migrants, are poor. Few have the ability to pay for health services. They must therefore rely on welfare, private insurance, Workmen's Compensation benefits, or "medically indigent" care services provided by county health departments. Second, American medicine is a centralized, highly bureaucratic, and socially stratified institution. For those who must rely on public services, seeking medical care demands a

well-developed facility for gaining entry to and manipulating bureaucratic structures. Linguistic barriers aside, the complexities of the medical
bureaucracy, particularly as it functions to restrict the access of people of
lower socioeconomic status, can be taxing to even the most savvy and
culturally adept American. For Samoans the cultural and linguistic barriers are immense. As a consequence, the Samoan community organizations often function in patient-advocate roles, as do anthropologists,
who, like myself, encounter individuals in great need of care. And even
with such representation, access to care is extraordinarily difficult if the
individual cannot pay for services.

Given the availability of good Samoan medical resources, conflicting
explanations of illness and risks for illness between American clinicians
and Samoans, conflicting role expectations, and structural and economic
restrictions on access to medical resources, it is really of little surprise
that Samoans underutilize American health-care institutions. Indeed, in
our review of medical charts at a local low-income clinic (Janes and
Pawson 1986), the two frequently encountered notes "patient is non-
compliant" and "patient lost to follow-up" are not only entirely understandable, but from the Samoans' perspective, laudable evidence of their
attempts to maintain their dignity in a setting that affords them far too
little.

Mortality Patterns

Obesity, diabetes, stress, the underutilization of American health-care
resources, and high rates of hypertension would all seem to point to increased mortality from chronic and degenerative diseases. A considera-
tion of Samoan mortality patterns suggests, however, that the cause-and-
effect relationship is not so simple as that.

After 1950 there was such a marked decline in infectious-disease mortality in American Samoa that by 1980 its survivorship rates were indistinguishable from U.S. rates except for a higher rate of trauma deaths in
men and a higher male infant mortality rate (Baker and Crews 1986).
The shift was to deaths from cardiovascular, neoplastic, degenerative,
and chronic diseases. The epidemiologic transition to the ills of modern
society, typical of developing countries, thus appears to have been completed in American Samoa. Patterns of mortality by cause suggest a pattern comparable with the urban United States in most cases. One unusual
finding, however, has been that despite increasing obesity in the American Samoan population, there has been no overall trend toward increasing cardiovascular disease mortality. The age-adjusted death rate from
CVD for 1970–74 was 242.5 per 100,000, substantially lower than the

rate in the United States, though higher than the rates in several other developed countries (Baker and Crews 1986: 109). Still, the lack of a trend toward increasing CVD deaths is surprising in view of the degree of modernization experienced in American Samoa since the Second World War, and especially since 1960.*

Samoan mortality data from Hawaii and California are perhaps of greater interest, since they would reflect in a general way the consequences of exposure to modernizing forces at the extreme end of the continuum. Recent analyses of Hawaiian data show that the mortality rates for CVD in 1974–78 were comparable to those found in American Samoa in the 1976–78 period (Baker and Crews 1986).

In 1982 and 1986 my co-researcher Ivan Pawson and I reported on what our analysis of death records in California said about the mortality experience of the Samoan subpopulation (Pawson and Janes 1982; Janes and Pawson 1986). Because Samoan deaths were not recorded separately in the state's death registry, we were forced to use a computer algorithm that took advantage of the Samoan language to extract records. Assuming that most Samoans, particularly in the older age groups, had Samoan first or last names, we had the computer select from the "Other" ethnic category everyone whose first or last name fit Samoan linguistic characteristics. From this list we manually selected Samoan names. A total of 255 Samoan death records was retrieved for the years 1978–82. Though we almost certainly missed several deaths in our search because some Samoans, particularly in the younger age ranges, have American names, this error is probably offset by the 20 percent undercount in the 1980 U.S. census of Samoans (Chap. 3). Table 9.1 lists mortality rates for California Samoans, all Californians, and American Samoans in the older age groups. Although Baker and Crews (1986) employ a slightly different age and disease classification in reporting mortality rates for American Samoa, it is possible to see, in a general way, how mortality compares across the subpopulations and with the California population as a whole.

The data presented in Table 9.1 show that mortality rates for cardiovascular disease are similar in the 45–64 age group for American Samoa and California Samoans. The morality rate from CVD is much higher for California Samoans over the age of 65, although the small numbers of deaths recorded in this age group in California make this mortality rate unstable. Perhaps of greater interest is the close similarity of heart disease mortality rates for California Samoans and all Californians, suggesting that Samoans are now subject to the same risks for chronic and degen-

---

* The few available data for Western Samoa suggest that though it is behind American Samoa in the overall transition from infectious to noninfectious-disease mortality, infectious-disease mortality is now declining significantly (Baker and Crews 1986).

TABLE 9.1

*Estimated Age-Specific Mortality Rates from Selected Causes for American
Samoans, California Samoans, and All Californians*

(*Deaths per 100,000 population*)

Age group	Cardiovascular disease	Heart disease	Malignant neoplasms	Cerebrovascular disease
64 and under				
American Samoans[a]	375.1	–	268.0	–
California Samoans[b]	335.9	274.8	325.7	61.1
All Californians[b]	–	277.0	289.6	38.2
65 and over				
American Samoans	1,983.0	–	409.2	–
California Samoans	2,516.8	2,202.2	809.0	314.6
All Californians	–	2,157.1	1,019.3	604.6

SOURCES: American Samoa, Paul T. Baker and Douglas E. Crews, "Mortality Patterns and Some Biological Predictors," in Paul T. Baker, Joel M. Hanna, and Thelma S. Baker, eds., *The Changing Samoans:
Behavior and Health in Transition* (New York: Oxford University Press, 1986). California, Craig R.
Janes and Ivan G. Pawson, "Migration and Biocultural Adaptation: Samoans in California," *Social Science and Medicine* 22 (1986): 821–34.

NOTE: Three-year centered rates for American Samoans, and five-year centered rates for California
Samoans.
[a] 50–64.
[b] 45–64.

erative diseases as the general population. Yet because migrant Samoans
as a group have been shown to be subject to greater risks for cardiovascular and heart diseases than the U.S. population (see Baker et al.
1986), above all because of diminished physical fitness, a high rate of
hypertension, and obesity, one might expect mortality rates from these
diseases to be higher than Table 9.1 generally shows them to be. As discussed by Janes and Pawson (1986) in detailed analyses of these data, it
is conceivable that factors in the social and cultural environment may
buffer such risks. It may also be hypothesized that those risk factors may
be exacerbated by social and cultural stressors or lessened by social support, as discussed in Chapter 8. Methodological problems have perhaps
also affected the mortality rates for California Samoans. Given the problems of record retrieval, combined with the relatively young migrant
population (and therefore a small population of at-risk older adults), the
mortality rates in Table 9.1 are only estimates.

Thus the role that the Samoans' underutilization of American health-
care resources plays in the overall mortality picture can only be conjec-
tured. Given, for example, the high rate of hypertension in the middle-age
group plus the likelihood that such hypertension is uncared for, and thus
uncontrolled, one would hypothesize a higher incidence of deaths from
cardiovascular and cerebrovascular diseases. Indeed, the data in Table 9.1

suggest that the cerebrovascular disease (i.e., stroke) rate for California Samoans in the under-65 age group is twice that of the general California population. However, health-care utilization is but a single component of a community's health; in the Samoan case it is just one piece in a complex ecological picture that includes the many variables addressed in this book: urbanization, migration, social change, stress, patterns of social affiliation, and obesity.

TEN

Conclusion

In the preceding pages we have seen how Samoan migrants, faced with the need to adapt to the demands of an urban, capitalist society, have responded with a creative kind of cultural "consolidation" (Rolff 1978), in which the forms of institutions have been changed to meet new circumstances, but the functions have remained largely unaltered. Churches have become urban villages, providing the community a public social arena where new kinds of leadership, though based on the same political patterns, might emerge. The structure of cognatic descent groups, the 'aiga, has remained largely intact, although now the constituent families live in independent households linked through economic and ritual cooperation. Although matai no longer exert control over the economic activities of independent households, they and their 'aiga members remain oriented to the important life-cycle rituals that bring together far-flung kindred in celebration of their kinship and distinctiveness as Samoans. On the face of it, these institutions appear marvelously adapted to an impersonal, urban environment that could hardly be more different from the one left behind (see Ablon 1971a).

Yet as the number of migrants increased and the availability of employment declined, some Samoans began to find themselves trapped in a structural paradox, a tension between the cultural push to participate in Samoan affairs and the economic pull to fulfill household and immediate family needs. The source of this paradox lies not in the structure and content of Samoan social networks, or in the demands of Samoan cultural institutions, but in a changing urban environment that is leaving growing numbers of Samoans in a state of dire poverty. In a sense newly arriving Samoans face a problem of "double adaptation," of adapting to new Samoan institutions and to a new environment at the same time.

The worsening economic conditions have introduced significant economic heterogeneity into the stateside Samoan society that threatens existing communally based institutions. A growing population of economically disadvantaged is a burden on existing Samoan resources. Established relatives must provide housing and sustenance. Although this system, supplemented where necessary by welfare and subsidized housing, still functions to provide most Samoans with a modicum of economic security, it is taxing to all involved. Those who have sufficient resources resent providing for those who do not, and yet their position within the church and kin group depends on demonstrated generosity. On the other side of the issue, those with sparse resources have fewer avenues to prestige, which in the stateside society requires expensive participation in church and kindred activities. In addition, for those with little money, life is simply more difficult.

The degree to which Samoan institutions have become monetized is one of the most important aspects of their development on the mainland. The most visible and remarkable of these institutions is the fa'alavelave, or life-crisis event. In Samoa these events are occasions for competitive exchange, feasting, and oration. But the goods exchanged are not needed to defray the expenses of the event and are redistributed to those in attendance. The exchange itself is a mechanism for showing generosity, demonstrating oratorical skill, and accruing prestige. In the United States life-crisis events involve considerable direct expense: burial plots, caskets, the rental of a hall for a wedding, and food for the feast. Cash has thus become the item of greatest importance in ceremonial exchange. Moreover, the status and prestige functions of the exchange have persisted. The infusion of cash into what was by nature a competitive institution has resulted in a tradition of overgive, of ostentatious presentation not unlike the potlatch (Rolff 1978). Prestige in the migrant community has come to represent a person's ability to amass cash.

The same pattern can be seen in the Samoan church. Churches have held a central role in Samoan society since the nineteenth century, and their development in migrant society has followed the island pattern. Like everything else in the American context, a church is an expensive institution to maintain: land and buildings are needed, bills must be paid, and the minister and his family must be housed and fed. To be a member in good standing of one's community—the Samoan church—one must be active in giving to the church and participating in its affairs. The church represents, perhaps, an even greater pressure for conformity in giving, for unlike economic exchange within the kin group, church giving is an individual affair. For kin group events one can often give as a member of a group, a branch of a kindred. There is always the possibility that one can go to others for help in making a contribution. But in the eyes of the community, one gives to the church for oneself and one's immediate family only. The pressure on the individual to give is therefore much greater and is increased by values that support religious activities. For those with few resources who decide that immediate family needs must come first, marginalization or alienation from the church community may result.

For these unfortunates, the economic-related stressors are aggravated by the fact that the church and kin group function within the urban setting to meet a number of important needs. The 'aiga provides one with at least short-term economic support, and if an important life-crisis event comes up in the immediate family, one can count on substantial assistance. Within the kindred, small clusters of cooperating households, often based on sibling or close bilateral kin ties actualized in the migration process, share a number of important activities. This group is potentially a secure "haven" for veteran and recent migrants alike. The church, usually comprising a few primary kindred groups, has arisen as a focus of community interaction, cultural revitalization, and Samoan identity. The church has become the urban Samoan village. Persons locate themselves in the framework of Samoan culture by identifying their 'aiga history and the church congregation to which they belong. As a center for social and cultural activity, the church permits the continuation of a Samoan political system, but blends this with the more functional need for leaders who are knowledgeable about American ways. Socially, the church binds together members of dispersed households into a functioning village-like social structure. Culturally, the church unites members into a single moral community possessing a unified system of beliefs and practices. Together people can enjoy the events, rituals, and feasts that represent what they like about fa'asamoa—the Samoan way. Psychologically, participation in church affairs offers members a sense of belonging and a strong sense of personal identity, value, and importance.

Stressor-Health Relationships

The tension between status or community involvement and economic resources has been found to be a common consequence of social change cross-culturally. Dressler (1982) suggests that the monetization of social status that accompanies social change, particularly when it results in a concentration of resources in the hands of a few, creates situations where people are caught between the desire for a new and apparently superior way of life and their ability to pay for it. In the Samoan case individuals have not come to internalize American economic or social goals, even though, paradoxically, pathways to Samoan status within the urban community have become, to a certain extent, Americanized. Thus for Samoans social inconsistency describes the aggravation of contradictions within Samoan social structure as it changes in response to capitalist economics.

Positions of leadership and prestige in family and community, linked to both participation in kindred feasts and, in a more circumscribed sense, to occupational and wage-earning status, present the opportunity for the greatest degree of social inconsistency. Men striving to gain or maintain positions of leadership or intense kindred involvement without the skills or resources to do so effectively exhibit the highest levels of blood pressure and physical ill-health. Social inconsistency is not so obviously a risk factor for women. This gender difference is understandable in light of the Samoan political system, in which the rewards of community-wide prestige are accrued primarily by men. Women, though occupying positions of extra-community leadership—primarily cultural brokerage positions—obtain fewer personal and intracommunity benefits at greater potential cost, given their added responsibilities for maintaining the domestic sphere.

Problems encountered as a consequence of participating in a market economy and the exigencies of urban living also determine the level and intensity of "hassles," or what have often been termed "stressful life events." My research revealed the cultural importance of three distinct dimensions of life-events stressors: structural stressors resulting from economic deprivation; family stressors stemming from problems and/or status changes within the extended family; and acute stressors, a series of short-term problems or one-time events. All three measures were found to be associated with ill-health, though relationships were differentially patterned across gender and dependent variable groups. Structural stressors were significantly associated with blood pressure in men and with physical health and psychosomatic complaints in women. Family stressors were correlated at a high level with all the health measures in women, corresponding to the burden of responsibility they bear for managing family relationships and domestic affairs. Acute stressors were associated with psychosomatic complaints in men.

The differential patterning of stressor-health relationships was striking. The gender differences, although commonsensical, have not to my knowledge been analyzed systematically across any set of cultures. The striking relationship of family stressors to health in women in the multiple-regression model not only demonstrates the importance of family issues for women, but suggests the necessity for further research to address gender issues in detail. The differential between acute and chronic stressors is also provocative. In general the data show a significant correspondence between chronic stress and chronic health conditions, particularly in men.

Thus the structural-stressors measure, as well as the social-inconsistency measure, is more predictive of blood pressure and overall physical health. The acute-stressors measure, on the other hand, is most predictive of psychosomatic complaints.

The differing health outcomes of chronic and acute stressors have been noted by others (e.g., Kasl 1984), although the meaning of "chronic" and "acute" varies from study to study. The biological mechanisms associated with the different kinds of stress have yet to be identified, but studies of endocrine response have shown systematic differences between laboratory-imposed chronic and acute stressors (Rose 1980). Failing a full understanding of the physiology of stress, one cannot with any certainty explain the data presented here. However, several possible and plausible explanations can be proposed. The complaint score most directly measures the degree to which individuals express physical discomfort or admit to regular ailments. It may be that Samoans are wont to express stress partially in terms of somatic sensations (e.g., headaches, heart palpitations, indigestion, lack of sleep). The independent and dependent variables may, to a certain degree, be confounded. An alternative explanation may be that acute stress is first experienced as a set of interrelated somatic sensations, and that given a continuation of the stimuli (or a series of stimuli), and depending on the psychobiological constitution of the individual, it will then go on to develop into a chronic condition. In any case physical discomfort may be a precursor of more permanent neurogenic changes.

The degree to which social and cultural stressors affect health is ultimately dependent on the psychological and social resources individuals possess that enable them to cope. If impoverished individuals, for example, have a large group of close relatives and friends to whom they can turn in times of need, a modicum of economic security is assured. The psychological dimensions of social support are more difficult to measure but are at least equally important. This kind of support is believed to provide individuals information that their psychological needs are being met—information that a person is esteemed and loved, for example (Cobb 1976).

I have not differentiated in my analysis between emotional and instrumental support, but I did distinguish between active instrumental support, as evidenced by the intensity of the exchange of goods and services, and social resources, a measure of at least potential or perhaps even latent support in a person's social network. In the social-resources measure I endeavored to distinguish relationships that are of sociological significance. This is where an ethnographic approach is most useful (see Jacobson 1987). For Samoans the most supportive relationships are those found within the close bilateral circle and with certain close friends. People have a number of other relatives outside this group with whom they will interact from time to time, but these are not truly supportive in the sense used here. Such kin are simply those with whom one is bound by mutual obligation. As I have noted, church participation and kin-group involvement may offer support, though in a more subtle way: providing a sense of identity or social solidarity, a setting to interact with others and perhaps make friends, and a place where one can observe and participate in important rituals.

Both measures of social support were significantly correlated with health. In men social resources and instrumental support were inversely correlated with blood pressure at highly significant levels. Instrumental support also correlated with physical health in interaction with acute stressors. In women instrumental support clearly buffered the effects of family stress in predicting blood pressure. Thus while adapting to an urban economic system involves its share of stressors, Samoan society provides ample buffering mechanisms. These lie at the heart of the core 'aiga network, in the patterns of informal (as distinct from formal fa'alavelave) exchange, and within the cultural institution of the Samoan church.

If one looks at processes favoring health, rather than disease, or "salutogenesis" as Antonovsky (1979) calls it, it is clear that Samoan society does provide individuals with ways to meet their basic social and psychological needs. The structural contradictions and the weight of kindred responsibilities do not emerge as serious stressors until one looks at those individuals under serious structural and family pressure, and without adequate social resources. Given, in particular, the significant salutogenic effects of social support in this cultural context, regardless of age and body mass, it is now clear why Samoan mortality rates have generally not exceeded those of the society in which they now live, for all their higher levels of physiological risks (Chap. 9). It should also be clear that avenues toward reducing levels of stress in the Samoan community lie not in "removing" structural contradictions or "limiting" family involvement— for the institutions of support are embedded in the Samoan social structure—but in significantly increasing the resource base on which the community depends. Salutogenesis for Samoans, then, involves maintaining their unique urban social institutions, and their sense of cultural distinctiveness, while at the same time learning how to exploit and manipulate the American political-economic environment.*

---

* In 1984 a local Samoan community organization was awarded a grant from the National Institute of Mental Health to undertake a "preventive intervention" project to reduce stress levels in the community. Among other things, the project was designed to give Samoans the skills to exploit available economic and social service resources more effectively, and at the same time strengthen their sense of identity and their social supports. Unfortunately, squabbling between the project director and the community organization resulted in the withdrawal of funds before the project got off the ground.

Stress: Individual Lifestyle or Sociocultural Process?

A review of the stress literature reveals an intellectual tension between theoretical orientations that locate stress in the psyche of the individual and those that emphasize environmental origins. Although such a tension reflects disciplinary differences—psychologists focusing on cognition, and social scientists on structural inconsistencies—there are tacit cultural values that empower knowledge of individual stress: stress is the individual's responsibility; it does not stem from the environment. Hence "life events," to which all humans are at some point subject, rise, unpredicted, in the environment. If the individual appraises them as threatening and has few adequate "coping skills," stress results. The question of what environmental factors determine why one person can cope with a certain kind of event and another cannot does not count; this view presumes an artificially "objective" and random quality of the external stimuli. The idea of stress is reduced to discrete individualized units (see A. Young 1980). One need not consider social, cultural, or historical circumstance; these are irrelevant when viewed against the background of individual constitutional factors.

This kind of orientation in analyzing disease risk underlies much of Western, especially American, scientific thinking. It drives, as Allan Young (1980) notes, the social production of conventional knowledge.* More precisely, the individualistic view reflects a long tradition in Western medicine that has increasingly assigned responsibility for ill-health to the victim (see Ratcliffe et al. 1984; Ryan 1976). In a comment in the mainstream scientific publication *Science*, Knowles (1977), proclaims:

---

* Ample and well-founded criticism has been leveled at research that attempts to objectify stress. Allan Young (1980), for example, has argued persuasively that "empirical facts" about stress are, in effect, discovered as a consequence of different beliefs about society, its composition, and the role of the individual within that society. Ultimately, the criticism comes down to a question of whether the idea of stress can be considered apart from sociohistorical context and whether society can be "decomposed" into units that can be scrutinized scientifically.

Clearly, stress occurs in context, and that context is located in a web of psychological, social, cultural, and historical factors. The goal of this book has been to direct the reader's attention to the many strands of this "contextual web." Yet, also clearly, I have decomposed Samoan society into a few elements that have been empirically objectified as "things," or "measures" that have a demonstrable psycho-physiological salience. I do so, however, cognizant of the pitfalls in assuming that stress can be so objectified, and in a very real intellectual struggle to connect the complex interactional dimensions of Samoan social reality to individual experience. Further, this research is founded clearly on the notion that patterns do exist and are discoverable, that one can speak of social "facts" in a Durkheimian sense. To deny that social or cultural principles exist independent of some interactional, negotiated "reality" is taking a rather extreme and ultimately solipsist stance.

I suggest that stress does exist, that it is relevant for understanding the health of individuals, and that it is necessary to place the idea of stress in a particular temporal and cultural moment. It is precisely this idea of ethnographic context that makes the anthropological approach to epidemiologic problems a particularly valid one.

Prevention of disease means forsaking the bad habits which many people enjoy. . . . Or put another way, it means doing things that require special effort—exercising regularly, improving nutrition, going to the dentist, practicing contraception, ensuring harmonious family life, submitting to screening examinations.

So powerful is this idea that individuals are solely and exclusively responsible for their own health that, invariably, when I present the Samoan data discussed here to students, someone suggests that Samoans need only stop contributing so much money and behave in an economically responsible manner to decrease their stress. Not only do students tend to overlook the positive aspects of social participation—which for many Samoans still outweigh the costs—they mostly ignore the sociopolitical foundations of poverty in our society.

Yet when it comes to looking at overall mortality and morbidity characteristics in modern societies, it is difficult to escape the conclusion that social organization and economic structure bear a closer relationship to the distribution of chronic diseases than any set of "lifestyle" factors. Brenner (1977), for example, has shown that mortality from heart disease, infant mortality in general, and mental hospital admissions vary as a function of upturns and downturns in the national economy. Further, the unemployment rate is directly related to overall mortality.

It would be absurd to assert that stress does not have psychological reality. In fact very creative work has been done by anthropologists trying to bridge the conceptual gap between stress as a structural factor and stress as an experiential process (e.g., Dressler 1980, 1982; O'Neil 1986). The point here is that stress cannot be conceived simply as an individual response to random or nearly universal external events. The source of stress is located in the social environment, and it occurs because of patterns of economic distribution, political change, and historical circumstance. The results of this study show this quite clearly. The paradox that leads to stress in Samoans has its origins in national and worldwide economic changes; it cannot be imputed solely to the nature of the Samoan community, still less to individual Samoans.

The conceptual shift entailed by this theoretical orientation is to the social and cultural features of a particular situation, that is, to place stress in its wider environmental context. I have argued elsewhere that the anthropological approach is ultimately the most useful one for this task, for it involves a scrutiny of disease risk from the "ground up," an articulation of events and processes that the subjects of the research themselves find distressing (Janes 1986). Further, placing the idea of stress in social and cultural context puts it where one can make logical statements about how it can be prevented. Individuals do not fail at coping; they find themselves in situations, often not of their own doing, where they do the best they can. Surely the most appropriate avenue for primary prevention is to understand, remove, and/or mitigate those situations, paradoxes, and contradictions that get people into trouble. McKinlay (1979: 9) tells the following story to make this same point:

> Imagine a person walking alongside a river who sees someone drowning. This person jumps in, pulls the victim out and begins artificial resuscitation. While this is going on, another drowning person calls for help; the rescuer jumps into the water again and pulls the new victim out. This process repeats itself several times until the rescuer gets up and begins to run upriver. A bystander, surprised to see the rescuer moving away from the victims, calls out, "Where are you going?" The rescuer replies, "I'm going upstream to find out who's pushing all these people in and to see if I can stop it or teach them how to swim."

The challenge is not to make people better "copers," but to scrutinize those environmental processes that put people in harm's way—to refocus our efforts "upstream." In view of the structural stresses described here, this is no mean challenge; it involves nothing less than directed social change. In the Samoan case, and doubtless in the case of other migrant groups, the keys to health seem to turn on the migrants' and the host society's ability and motivation to avoid the paradoxes that arise when communal institutions become embedded in market-economic structures.

Reference Matter

Interview Form

I originally incorporated many different types of questions into the interview instrument. Many questions were discarded as the research progressed when they proved to elicit little variation among the sample or yielded nothing of interest. I present here only the questions that were asked of all participants. I include Samoan translations for some questions, especially those concerning health symptoms and life-event stressors, so readers familiar with the language may evaluate the quality of the translation.

Several parts of this instrument are based on a similar one that Graves and Graves (1985) devised for their survey of stress and health among Pacific Islander groups in New Zealand. I thank them for providing their form for use in this research.

Interview Schedule

Date: _____

Household ID: _____   Individual ID: _____

    1. Date of birth: _____   2. Sex: _____

    3. Do you now hold a matai title?

    4. (If yes) What type of title is it? Tulafale? _____ Ali'i? _____
       Comments:

    5. From which side of your family does this title come (specify descent)?

    6. From which village does this title come?

    7. What are some of the senior title names in your family?

    8. (If no to #3 above) What is the name of the person who heads your family ('aiga)?
       a. Is this person a matai?
       b. What is his/her name?
       c. Where is this person now living?

    9. Marital status:

10. Age of spouse: _____
    a. Spouse's 'aiga name:
11. Is this your only marriage?
    a. If no, sketch details of previous marriage(s), children, etc.
12. Where did you meet your (present) husband/wife?
13. Where were you married?
14. In what year was this?
15. What village are you from?
16. Is this your mother's or your father's village? Other relative?
17. How many brothers do you have (living)?
    a. Where are they living now?
18. How many sisters do you have (living)?
    a. Where are they living now?
19. What number (place) are you in the family (oldest, second, etc.)?
20. How many children do you have?
    a. Sketch from oldest to youngest, the following information regarding children: sex, ages, marital status, ethnicity of spouse, and where they are now living.
21. I know that many Samoans have large families and like to live with many relatives. Could you tell me about the other people that live in your house besides you, your husband/wife, and children?
22. How long have you lived in this house/apartment?
    a. If purchased, when and how much paid?
    b. If rented, monthly payment?
23. Where did you live before this?
    a. Sketch housing history since arriving on mainland.
24. What do you think about this house/apartment (probe for housing satisfaction)?
25. What do you think about the neighborhood, the people, traffic, etc.?
26. Do you talk with or visit your neighbors?
27. Have you ever had any troubles with your neighbors (noise, disagreements, etc.)?
28. Have you ever thought about moving somewhere else? Reasons?
29. Now let's talk about your life when you were growing up. You told me you were from the village of _____; how many years did you live in this village?
30. In what year did you first leave your village?
    a. Where did you go at that time? Detail migration history.
31. How much schooling did you get?
    a. Where did you go to school?
32. Any other skills or qualifications (training programs, service, on the job training)? Details.
33. Have you been back to visit or live in Samoa?
    a. How many times have you been back?
    b. When was the last time you returned?
    c. What was the occasion?
34. Thinking back to when you first left Samoa, what were some of the impor-

tant reasons you decided to come to the mainland? What were some of the things which happened just before you left?

35. Did anyone help you decide to move here?

36. When you came to California (or Hawaii), who paid your fare?

37. Do you ever think about returning to the islands for good?

38. How about your children; do you think that they will ever go back to Samoa, or want to go back? Why, why not?

39. Did you know anyone (friend or relative) living here before you decided to move? Who was this person? Did they help you out when you got here?

40. When you first came to California, who did you live with? Describe relationship.

41. How long did you live with relatives before getting your own place?

42. I would now like to talk to you a little about all the relatives you have living in this area (San Francisco).
    a. How many relatives do you have living in San Francisco who are related to you through your father (those known)?
    b. Of these relatives, who do you see or talk to the most often? (Relationship, when seen, context, how often?)
    c. How many relatives do you have living on your mother's side?
    d. Of these relatives, who do you see the most often?
    e. Does your husband/wife have many relatives living in this area?
    f. How often do you visit these relatives?
    g. You told me about your brothers and sisters already. How often do you visit with members of your close family (brothers, sisters, nieces, nephews)?

43. About how many good friends do you have here in the San Francisco area? (*E tusa e fia ni 'au uo e iai i'inei i San Francisco?*)

44. Are these friends Samoan? Describe.

45. How often do you see these friends of yours? (Do you visit in each other's homes?)

46. When you are feeling upset or something is troubling you, who do you talk to about it? (*Afai 'ua 'e lagona sou fa'alavelave, po'o se mea 'ua 'e mafatia ai, o ai 'e te talanoa iai e uiga ma lou fa'alavelave?*) Describe in order mentioned.

47. Now let's talk a little about your church. Do you belong to a church?

48. About how often do you attend services? (Every week or more, twice a month, once a month, etc.)

49. Do you belong to the choir?

50. Do you hold any church office (deacon, moderator, secretary, etc.)?

51. I would now like to ask you some more questions about who you visit and who visits you.
    a. During the past two weeks, who came to your house to visit you? Adults, not children. First tell me who visited you, and how many times in the past two weeks.
    b. Now, who have you gone to visit during the past two weeks? First tell me who you have gone to visit, then tell me how many times you visited them in the past two weeks.

52. How often do you keep in touch with your friends or relatives in other ways, such as phone calls or letters?
53. (Refer to chart below): Now I'm going to ask you about different kinds of help that people give each other. Could you tell me about how many times in the last year you gave these kinds of help to relatives not living with you?
54. And how many times has a relative given you these kinds of help in the past year?
55. How many times in the past year have you given these kinds of help to a friend?
56. How many times have you received these kinds of help from a friend in the past year?

| | Relative | | Friend | |
Type of help	Given	Received	Given	Received
Child minding				
Food gifts				
Work around the house, yard				
Help in an emergency				
Help in finding a job/housing				
Loan of a valuable object				
Going with them/you to see a person in authority				
Providing transportation				
Loan of money				

57. Do you contribute money for *fa'alavelave fa'asamoa?* Do you think this is important for people to do over here on the mainland? (Probes and discussion)
58. When was the last time you contributed to a fa'alavelave? What was the fa'alavelave, and how much did you give?
59. (Where appropriate) If you are a matai, how many households do you contact when there is a fa'alavelave?
60. During the past year, about how much money have you spent or contributed for weddings, funerals, or other family obligations? (*I le tausaga taluai, e tusa e fia se tupe na 'e fa'aaogaina pe na 'e fesoasoani ai fo'i i ni fa'aipopoga, maliu, po'o ni isi fa'alavelave fa'apitoa a lou 'aiga?*)
61. Did you help support any of your relatives last year, either here or overseas?
    a. If yes, how much did you give to relatives last year (not including fa'alavelave-related expenses)? Here in California? Back in Samoa?
62. About how much money do you like to give each month for your church? About how much did you give last year?
63. Do you play bingo?
    a. How much do you usually spend for bingo in a week?
64. Do you regularly put money in a savings account?
    a. If yes, how much do you like to put aside each month?
    b. What kinds of things are you saving for?

65. Now let's talk about your work. Are you working now? Where?
66. Do they pay you pretty well there? About how much do you get in a month (average)?
67. How did you get this job? (*E fa'apefea ona 'e maua lenei galuega?*) (Self, parents, siblings, other relatives, friends, etc.)
68. Did anyone go with you when you were interviewed? (*Sa iai seisi na lua o i le fa'atonuga o lau galuega?*)
69. Why did you choose this job?
70. If you are not working now, do you receive any sort of public assistance?
    a. How much public assistance do you receive in a month? (If AFDC, include food stamps and payments for each child.)
71. Where did you work before your present job, or if no present job, describe job history? Include Samoa.
72. How did you get your first job here in California? (Who helped you or told you about the job? Siblings, parents, friends, others?)
    a. Describe situation.
73. Did anyone go with you when you were interviewed?
74. How many times have you been unemployed for a long period, say for a month or more?
75. How do you like the job you have now?
    a. Is there anything you do not like about it?
    b. What are the best things about working there?
    c. Do you hold a position of responsibility or authority at work? Describe.
    d. Would you like to hold a position of authority? Why? Why not?
76. How many friends do you have at work?
77. How many of these friends do you get together with outside of work (bars, homes, church, restaurants, sports, etc.)?
78. How many other people living in your household have jobs and contribute to expenses? (Relationship, age, where working, monthly wages.)
79. Everyone runs out of money sometimes. If you really needed money for some reason, what would you do? (*O tagata uma lava e iai le taimi e leai ai sana tupe. Afai 'ua 'e matua mana'omia lava se tupe, o le a le mea 'e te faia?*)

Now we are going to talk about some of the things that can make a person feel upset or disturbed. Often these things can make you feel sick. If one of these things happened to you in the last year, could you please tell me how often it happened to you? (*Se'i ta talanoa i ni mea e mafua ai ona ita le tagata, pe fa'aletonu ma fa'ma'a'a ai. Afai sa tupu se mea o nei mea ia te 'oe i le tausaga taluai, fai mai e fa'afia ona tupu lenei mea?*) (Use scale: 0=never; 1=one, two times last year; 2=several times last year; 3=about once per month; 4=about once per week; 5=more than once a week / every day.)

80. Running out of money (*Le lava se fasitupe*)?
81. Having troubles at work (*Ni fa'alavelave e tutupu i le galuega*)?
82. The death of someone close to you (*Le oti o seisi e pele ia 'oe*)?
    a. Describe.
83. A divorce or separation (*Tete'a po'o le nofo eseese*)?

84. A change of job (*Suia o le galuega*)?
85. Visitors or relations staying in your home (*Ni malo po'o 'ou 'aiga o tou nonofo*)?
86. Unexpected expenses (*Fa'alavelave fa'afuase'i*)?
87. A bad accident or illness in the family (*Se fa'alavelave matautia, po'o se mai i le 'aiga*)?
88. Loss of a job (*Lusi o le galuega*)?
89. Moving to a new house (*Tapega i se fale fou*)?
90. Loss of a friend (*Se uo ua leiloa*)?
91. Birth of a child (*Fanau mai o le pepe*)?
92. Problems with your children in school or elsewhere (*Fa'alavelave e tutupu i lau fanau i 'aoga po'o nisi mea*)?
93. A child leaving home, getting married, or so forth (*Se tamaitiiti ua tu'ua le 'aiga pe fa'aipoipo, ma mea fa'apena*)?
94. What things in your life worry or trouble you the most? Discuss.

Now let's talk about how you spend your time when you are not at work. (*Se'i talanoa e uiga i le fa'aaogaina o 'ou taimi avanoa pe a e le faigaluega.*)

95. How often do you do each of these things? (Use scale: o=never; 1=few times per year; 2=several times a year; 3=monthly; 4=weekly; 5=nearly every day; refer to chart below)
    a. (For each activity) Do you do this by yourself, with your wife and children, with other relatives, or with friends?

Activity	Frequency	Alone	Nuclear family	Other relatives	Friends
Playing a sport					
Jobs around the house					
Movies, dances					
Church activities					
Hobbies/crafts (sewing, reading)					
Going to races, other sports					
Going to a bar/club					
Playing bingo					

96. Do you drink alcohol?
    a. (If yes) About how many drinks do you have in a day, or week?
    b. (If yes) How often do you drink at home? (every day, etc.)

    c. When you drink at home, do you usually drink alone, with your husband/wife and children, with other relatives, or with friends?

    d. How often do you drink in other places, such as at a friend's house, a club, or so forth?

97. What language do you speak most of the time at home, English or Samoan?

98. When your children grow up, do you want them to speak English, Samoan, or both?

99. Would you be happy if one of your children married a palagi or person from another group?

100. I would now like to ask your opinion about a few things. Thinking now about raising your children, which of the following ways of bringing up kids do you think is best?

    a. To bring up kids as their parents and grandparents were brought up, teaching them about the ways of the past.

    b. To teach children some of the ways of older people, but also have them take on whatever new ways will help them get along in California.

    c. Teach children to want to find out new ways of doing things to replace the old ways of fa'asamoa. Why? Discuss.

101. If a man lost his job and needed money, who do you think he should go to for help?

    a. To close family members.

    b. To the county for welfare.

    c. To the family matai or the head of the family over here on the mainland. Why? Discuss.

102. If you won $500 one day in a raffle, what would you do with the money? (Would you use it for yourself, other relatives, your children, etc.)

103. Now to finish up, I would like to ask questions about your health. How has your health been over your whole life? Have you ever had to go to the hospital, or felt so bad you had to stay at home from work or school for a long time?

104. (If appropriate) How about your children? Have any of them been very sick? (If some are deceased: you told me that _____ of your children died; how did they die, and how old were they?)

105. When was the last time you went to see a doctor? Why did you go?

106. Do you have any medical insurance that helps you pay doctor bills? How about MediCal or Medicare?

107. Do you feel well enough to do all of the things that you like to do? Do you have any pain (*tiga*) which slows you down?

108. Has a doctor ever told you that there may be something wrong with your heart (*ma'i fatu*)?

109. Has a doctor ever told you that you have high blood pressure (*toto maualuga*)?

    a. Are you taking any medicines for high blood pressure?

110. Has a doctor ever told you that you have diabetes (*ma'i suka*)?

Even though you may not be ill enough to go to the doctor or miss work, we all have some physical complaints we have to put up with. How often have you had each of these problems in the past year? (*E ui lava ina le tetele sou mai ua mana'omia ai se foma'i pe tiai aso faigaluega ai, o tatou uma lava e maua i nei tino vaivai, 'ae taumafai pea. E fa'afia ona e maua i nei fa'alavelave i le tausaga ua mavao?*) (Use scale: 0=never; 1=few times; 2=several times; 3=monthly; 4=weekly; 5=nearly daily.)

111. Bad pains in your arms and legs (*Tiga tele ou lima po'o lou vae*)?
112. Bad pains in your back (*Tiga tele lou tua*)?
113. Stiff joints (*Ma'a'a so'oga o lou tino*)?
114. Bad pains in your stomach (*Tiga tele lou manava*)?
115. Upset stomach or nausea (*Ma'i manava pe fa'afaofau*)?
116. Loss of appetite (*Le manogi mea 'ai*)?
117. Asthma (*ma'i sela*)?
118. Bitter-tasting saliva (*O'ona ou faua*)?
119. Chest pains (*Tiga lou fatafata*)?
120. Your heart beating hard enough to bother you (*E tata malosi lou fatu ua e popoleina ai*)?
121. Arms and legs feeling numb or going to sleep easily (*Pepe gofie ou lima ma vae*)?
122. Dizziness or faintness (*E te niniva pe fia matapogia*)?
123. Trembling hands (*Tetete ou lima*)?
124. Chills or fevers (*Ma'alili ma fiva*)?
125. Colds (*Isu mamafa*)?
126. Headaches (*E tiga lou ulu*)?
127. Feeling completely exhausted (*Matua le lava tele*)?
128. Difficulty sleeping at night (*Faigata ona moe i le po*)?
129. Bad dreams (*Miti leaga*)?
130. How often do you worry about something in the future (*E masani ona e popole i ni mea i lumana'i*)?

References Cited

Ablon, Joan. 1970. The Samoan Funeral in Urban America. *Ethnology* 9: 209–27.

———. 1971a. The Social Organization of an Urban Samoan Community. *Southwestern Journal of Anthropology* 27: 75–96.

———. 1971b. Retention of Cultural Values and Differential Urban Adaptation: Samoans and American Indians in a West Coast City. *Social Forces* 49: 385–93.

Antonovsky, Aaron. 1979. *Health, Stress, and Coping.* San Francisco: Jossey-Bass.

Baker, Paul T., and Douglas E. Crews. 1986. Mortality Patterns and Some Biological Predictors. In Paul T. Baker, Joel M. Hanna, and Thelma S. Baker, eds., *The Changing Samoans.* New York: Oxford University Press.

Baker, Paul T., and Joel M. Hanna. 1981. Modernization and the Biological Fitness of Samoans. In Cara Fleming and Ian A. M. Prior, eds., *Migration, Adaptation, and Health in the Pacific.* Wellington, N.Z.: Wellington Hospital.

———. 1986. Perspectives on Health and Behavior of Samoans. In Paul T. Baker, Joel M. Hanna, and Thelma S. Baker, eds., *The Changing Samoans.* New York: Oxford University Press.

Baker, Paul T., Joel M. Hanna, and Thelma S. Baker, eds. 1986. *The Changing Samoans: Behavior and Health in Transition.* New York: Oxford University Press.

Banton, Michael. 1965. Social Alignment and Identity in a West African City. In Hilda Kuper, ed., *Urbanization and Migration in West Africa.* Berkeley: University of California Press.

Barth, Frederik. 1969. Introduction. In Frederik Barth, ed., *Ethnic Groups and Boundaries.* Boston: Little, Brown.

Beiser, M., H. Collomb, J. L. Ravel, and C. J. Nafziger. 1976. Systemic Blood Pressure Studies Among the Serer of Senegal. *Journal of Chronic Diseases* 29: 371–80.

Berkman, Lisa F. 1984. Assessing the Physical Health Effects of Social Networks and Social Support. *Annual Reviews of Public Health* 5: 413–32.

————. 1985. The Relationship of Social Networks and Social Support to Morbidity and Mortality. In Sheldon S. Cohen and S. Leonard Syme, eds., *Social Support and Health*. New York: Academic Press.

Berkman, Lisa, and S. Leonard Syme. 1979. Social Networks, Host Resistance, and Mortality: A Nine-Year Follow-up Study of Alameda County Residents. *American Journal of Epidemiology* 109: 186.

Bindon, James R. 1981. Genetic and Environmental Effects on Morphology of Samoan Adults. Ph.D. dissertation, Pennsylvania State University.

————. 1984. An Evaluation of the Diet of Three Groups of Samoan Adults: Modernization and Dietary Adequacy. *Ecology of Food and Nutrition* 14: 105–15.

Bindon, James R., and Shelley Zansky. 1986. Growth and Body Composition. In Paul T. Baker, Joel M. Hanna, and Thelma S. Baker, eds., *The Changing Samoans*. New York: Oxford University Press.

Brenner, M. Harvey. 1977. Health Costs and Benefits of Economic Policy. *International Journal of Health Services* 7: 581–623.

Broadhead, W. Eugene, Berton H. Kaplan, Sherman A. James, et al. 1983. The Epidemiologic Evidence for a Relationship Between Social Support and Health. *American Journal of Epidemiology* 117: 521–37.

Brown, Vanessa, Joel M. Hanna, and Gary E. Severson. 1984. A Quantitative Dietary Study of Native and Migrant Samoans. *American Journal of Physical Anthropology* (abstract) 63: 142.

Caldwell, John. 1969. *African Rural-Urban Migration: The Movement to Ghana's Towns*. New York: Columbia University Press.

California. 1983. *Annual Planning Information, 1983*. Sacramento: State Employment Development Department.

Caplan, Gerald. 1974. *Support Systems and Community Mental Health*. New York: Behavioral Publications.

Cassel, John. 1974. Hypertension and Cardiovascular Disease in Migrants: A Potential Source for Clues. *International Journal of Epidemiology* 3: 204–6.

————. 1975. Studies of Hypertension in Migrants. In Oglesby Paul, ed., *Epidemiology and Control of Hypertension*. New York: Stratton.

————. 1976. The Contribution of the Social Environment to Host Resistance. *American Journal of Epidemiology* 104: 107–23.

Caudill, William. 1958. *Effects of Social and Cultural Systems in Reactions to Stress*. New York: Social Science Research Council.

Chance, Norman A. 1974. Acculturation, Self-Identification, and Personality Adjustment. *American Anthropologist* 67: 372–93.

Cobb, Sidney. 1976. Social Support as a Moderator of Life Stress. *Psychosomatic Medicine* 38: 300–314.

Cohen, Jacob, and Patricia Cohen. 1975. *Applied Multiple Regression/Correlation Analysis for the Behavioral Sciences*. Hillsdale, N.J.: Laurence Erlbaum.

Cohen, Sheldon S., and S. Leonard Syme, eds. 1985. *Social Support and Health*. New York: Academic Press.

Cohen, Sheldon S., and Thomas A. Wills. 1985. Stress, Social Support and the Buffering Hypothesis. *Psychological Bulletin* 98: 310–57.

Colson, Anthony. 1970. The Differential Use of Medical Resources in Developing Countries. *Journal of Health and Social Behavior* 12: 226–37.

Cook, Jonathon M. 1983. Samoan Patterns in Seeking Health Services—Hawaii, 1979–1981. *Hawaii Medical Journal* 42: 138–42.

Cronin, Constance. 1970. *The Sting of Change*. Chicago: University of Chicago Press.

Dennett, Glenn, and John Connell. 1988. Acculturation and Health in the Highlands of Papua New Guinea: Dissent on Diversity, Diets, and Development. *Current Anthropology* 29: 273–99.

Desowitz, Robert. 1976. *New Guinea Tapeworms and Jewish Grandmothers: Tales of Parasites, Places and People*. New York: Norton.

Dohrenwend, Bruce, and Barbara Dohrenwend, eds. 1974. *Stressful Life Events: Their Nature and Effects*. New York: Wiley.

Dressler, William W. 1980. Coping Dispositions, Social Supports, and Health Status. *Ethos* 8: 146–71.

———. 1982. *Hypertension and Culture Change: Acculturation and Disease in the West Indies*. South Salem, N.Y.: Redgrave.

———. 1983. Blood Pressure, Relative Weight and Psychosocial Resources. *Psychosomatic Medicine* 45: 527–35.

———. 1985. Psychosomatic Symptoms, Stress, and Modernization: A Model. *Culture, Medicine, and Psychiatry* 9: 257–86.

———. 1988. Social Consistency and Psychological Distress. *Journal of Health and Social Behavior* 29: 79–91.

Dressler, William W., José Ernesto Dos Santos, Philip N. Gallagher, Jr., and Fernando E. Viteri. 1987a. Arterial Blood Pressure and Modernization in Brazil. *American Anthropologist* 89: 398–409.

Dressler, William W., Alfonso Mata, Adolfo Chavez, and Fernando E. Viteri. 1987b. Arterial Blood Pressure and Individual Modernization in a Mexican Community. *Social Science and Medicine* 24: 679–87.

Dunn, Frederick L., and Craig R. Janes. 1986. Medical Anthropology and Epidemiology. In Craig R. Janes, Ron Stall, and Sandra M. Gifford, eds., *Anthropology and Epidemiology*. Dordrecht: D. Reidel (Kluwer).

Ember, Melvin. 1964. Commercialization and Political Change in American Samoa. In Ward H. Goodenough, ed., *Explorations in Cultural Anthropology*. New York: McGraw-Hill.

Epstein, A. L. 1961. The Network and Urban Social Organization. *Rhodes-Livingstone Journal* 29: 29–62.

———. 1967. Urbanization and Social Change in Africa. *Current Anthropology* 8: 275–96.

Fleming, Cara, and Ian A. M. Prior, eds. 1981. *Migration, Adaptation, and Health in the Pacific*. Wellington, N.Z.: Wellington Hospital.

Foster, George M. 1976. Disease Etiologies in Non-Western Medical Systems. *American Anthropologist* 78: 773–82.

Fox, Robin. 1967. *Kinship and Marriage*. Harmondsworth, Eng.: Penguin Books.

Franco, Robert. 1978. Samoans in California: The 'Aiga Adapts. In Cluny Macpherson, Bradd Shore, and Robert Franco, eds., *New Neighbors . . . Islanders in Adaptation*. Santa Cruz: Center for South Pacific Studies, University of California, Santa Cruz.

Freeman, Derek. 1983. *Margaret Mead and Samoa: The Making and Unmaking of an Anthropological Myth*. Cambridge, Mass.: Harvard University Press.

Gluckman, Max. 1961. Anthropological Problems Arising From the African Industrial Revolution. In Aidan Southall, ed., *Social Change in Modern Africa*. London: Oxford University Press.

Gmelch, George. 1980. Return Migration. A Review. *Annual Review of Anthropology* 9: 135–59.

Gore, Susan, and Thomas W. Mangione. 1983. Social Roles, Sex Roles and Psychological Distress: Additive and Interactive Models of Sex Differences. *Journal of Health and Social Behavior* 24: 300–312.

Graves, Theodore D. 1967. Acculturation, Access, and Alcohol in a Tri-ethnic Community. *American Anthropologist* 69: 306–21.

Graves, Theodore D., and Nancy B. Graves. 1980. Kinship Ties and the Preferred Adaptive Strategies of Urban Migrants. In Stephen Beckerman and Linda S. Cordell, eds., *The Versatility of Kinship*. New York: Academic Press.

———. 1985. Stress and Health Among Pacific Islands Immigrants to New Zealand. *Journal of Behavioral Medicine* 8: 1–19.

Gray, J. A. C. 1960. *Amerika Samoa: A History of American Samoa and Its United States Naval Administration*. Annapolis: U.S. Naval Institute.

Greksa, Leonard P., David L. Pelletier, and Timothy Gage. 1986. Work in Contemporary and Traditional Samoa. In Paul T. Baker, Joel M. Hanna, and Thelma S. Baker, eds., *The Changing Samoans*. New York: Oxford University Press.

Gutkind, Peter. 1969. African Urbanism, Mobility, and the Social Network. In Gerald W. Breese, ed., *The City in Newly Developing Countries*. Englewood Cliffs, N.J.: Prentice-Hall.

Hackenberg, R. A., B. H. Hackenberg, H. F. Magalit, et al. 1983. Migration, Modernization, and Hypertension: Blood Pressure Levels in Four Philippine Communities. *Medical Anthropology* 7(1): 45–71.

Haenszel, William, ed. 1970. Symposium on Cancer in Migratory Populations. *Journal of Chronic Diseases* 23: 289–448.

Haenszel, W., and M. Kurihara. 1968. Studies of Japanese Migrants, I: Mortality from Cancer and Other Diseases Among Japanese in the United States. *Journal of the National Cancer Institute* 40: 45–71.

Haenszel, W., M. Kurihara, M. Segi, and R. K. C. Lee. 1972. Stomach Cancer Among Japanese in Hawaii. *Journal of the National Cancer Institute* 49: 969–88.

Hanna, Joel M., and Paul T. Baker. 1979. Biocultural Correlates to the Blood Pressure of Samoan Migrants in Hawaii. *Human Biology* 51: 480.

Hanna, Joel M., David L. Pelletier, and Vanessa J. Brown. 1986. The Diet and Nutrition of Contemporary Samoans. In Paul T. Baker, Joel M. Hanna, and Thelma S. Baker, eds., *The Changing Samoans*. New York: Oxford University Press.

Hayes, Geoffrey, and Michael J. Levin. 1984a. How Many Samoans? An Evaluation of the 1980 Census Count of Samoans in the United States. Unpublished ms. Northwest Regional Educational Laboratory.

———. 1984b. A Statistical Profile of Samoans in the United States. Part 1: Demography; part 2: Social and Economic Characteristics. Unpublished ms. Northwest Regional Educational Laboratory.

Hecht, Julia, Martin Orans, and Craig R. Janes. 1986. Social Settings of Contemporary Samoans. In Paul T. Baker, Joel M. Hanna, and Thelma S. Baker, eds., *The Changing Samoans*. New York: Oxford University Press.

Henry, James P., and John Cassel. 1969. Psychosocial Factors in Essential Hypertension. *American Journal of Epidemiology* 90: 171–200.

Hirsch, Susan. 1958. The Social Organization of an Urban Village in Samoa. *Journal of the Polynesian Society* 67: 266–303.

Holland, Linda M. 1989. Migration and the Status of Women in an Urban Samoan Community. Master's thesis, San Francisco State University.

Holmes, Lowell D. 1958. *Ta'u: Stability and Change in a Samoan Village*. The Polynesian Society. Originally published in 1957 in *Journal of the Polynesian Society* 66: 301–38, 398–435.

———. 1964. Leadership and Decision Making in American Samoa. *Current Anthropology* 5: 446–49.

———. 1974. *Samoan Village*. New York: Holt, Rhinehart & Winston.

Hope, Kenneth. 1975. Models of Status Inconsistency and Social Mobility Effects. *American Sociological Review* 40: 322–43.

Hornick, Conrad. 1979. Heart Disease in a Migrating Population. Ph.D. dissertation, University of Hawaii.

Hornick, Conrad, and Joel M. Hanna. 1982. Indicators of Coronary Risk in a Migrating Samoan Population. *Medical Anthropology* 6: 71–80.

House, James S., and Robert L. Kahn. 1985. Measures and Concepts of Social Support. In Sheldon S. Cohen and S. Leonard Syme, eds., *Social Support and Health*. New York: Academic Press.

Howard, Alan. 1986. Samoan Coping Behavior. In Paul T. Baker, Joel M. Hanna, and Thelma S. Baker, eds., *The Changing Samoans*. New York: Oxford University Press.

Hughes, Everett C. 1944. Dilemmas and Contradictions of Status. *American Journal of Sociology* 50: 353–59.

Hull, Diane. 1979. Migration, Adaptation, and Illness. *Social Science and Medicine* 13: 25–36.

Jacobson, David. 1987. The Cultural Context of Social Support and Support Networks. *Medical Anthropology Quarterly* 1: 42–67.

James, S. A., and D. G. Kleinbaum. 1976. Socioecologic Stress and Hypertension-Related Mortality Rates in North Carolina. *American Journal of Public Health* 7: 634–39.

Janes, Craig R. 1986. Migration and Hypertension: An Ethnography of Disease Risk in an Urban Samoan Community. In Craig R. Janes, Ron Stall, and Sandra M. Gifford, eds., *Anthropology and Epidemiology*. Dordrecht: D. Reidel (Kluwer).

Janes, Craig R., and Ivan G. Pawson. 1986. Migration and Biocultural Adaptation: Samoans in California. *Social Science and Medicine* 22: 821–34.

Kahn, R. L., and T. C. Antonucci. 1980. Convoys Over the Life Course: Attachment, Roles, and Social Support. In Paul B. Baltes and Orville G. Brim, Jr., eds., *Life-Span Development and Behavior*, vol. 3. New York: Academic Press.

Kandel, Denise B., Mark Davies, and Victoria Reveis. 1985. The Stressfulness of Daily Social Roles for Women: Marital, Occupational, and Household Roles. *Journal of Health and Social Behavior* 26: 64–78.

Kannel, W. B., and P. Sorlie. 1975. Hypertension in Framingham. In Oglesby Paul, ed., *Epidemiology and Control of Hypertension*. New York: Stratton.

Kaplan, Berton H., John Cassel, and Susan Gore. 1977. Social Support and Health. *Medical Care* 15 (supplement): 47–58.

Kasl, Stanislav V. 1984. Stress and Health. *Annual Reviews of Public Health* 5: 319–41.

Kasl, Stanislav V., and Lisa Berkman. 1983. Health Consequences of the Experience of Migration. *Annual Reviews of Public Health* 4: 69–90.

Keesing, Felix. 1934. *Modern Samoa*. Stanford, Calif.: Stanford University Press.

Kleinman, Arthur. 1980. *Patients and Healers in the Context of Culture*. Berkeley: University of California Press.

Knowles, J. 1977. Responsibility for Health. *Science* 198: 1103.

Knudson, A. G. 1977. Genetic and Environmental Interactions in the Origin of Human Cancer. In John J. Mulvihill, Robert W. Miller, and Joseph F. Fraumeni, Jr., eds., *Genetics of Human Cancer*. New York: Raven.

Kunitz, Stephen. 1983. *Disease Change and the Role of Medicine: The Navajo Experience*. Berkeley: University of California Press.

Lazar, Ineke M. 1985. *Ma'i Aitu*: Culture-Bound Illnesses in a Samoan Migrant Community. *Oceania* 55: 161–81.

Lazar, Thomas F. 1985. Indigenous Curing Patterns in a Samoan Migrant Community. *Oceania* 55: 288–302.

Lazarus, Richard S. 1966. *Psychological Stress and the Coping Process*. New York: McGraw-Hill.

Lee, E. S. 1966. A Theory of Migration. *Demography* 3: 47–57.

Leighton, Dorothea. 1978. Sociocultural Factors in Physical and Mental Breakdown. *Man-Environment Systems* 8: 33–37.

Leighton, Dorothea, et al. 1963. *The Character of Danger*. New York: Basic Books.

Lenski, Gerhard E. 1954. Status Crystallization: A Non-Vertical Dimension of Social Status. *American Sociological Review* 19: 405–13.

Levine, Sol, and Norman A. Scotch. 1970. *Social Stress*. Chicago: Aldine.

Lewthwaite, Gordon R., Christine Mainzer, and Patrick J. Holland. 1973. From Polynesia to California: Samoan Migration and Its Sequelae. *Journal of Polynesian History* 8: 133–57.

Little, Kenneth. 1965. *West African Urbanization: A Study of Voluntary Associations in Social Change*. Cambridge, Eng.: Cambridge University Press.

Lukaski, H. C. 1977. Some Observations on Coronary Risk Status of Male Samoan Migrants on Oahu, Hawaii. M.A. thesis, Pennsylvania State University.

MacDonald, John S., and Leatrice D. MacDonald. 1964. Chain Migration, Ethnic Neighborhood Formation, and Social Networks. *Milbank Memorial Fund Quarterly* 42: 82–97.

Mackenzie, Margaret. 1977. More North American Than the North Americans: Medical Consequences of Migrant Enthusiasm, Willing and Unwilled. In B. Velimirovic, ed., *Modern Medicine and Medical Anthropology in the United States–Mexico Border Population*. Washington, D.C.: Pan-American Health Organization.

———. n.d. The Fear of Fat. Unpublished ms.

Mancuso, T. F., and T. D. Sterling. 1974. Relation of Place of Birth and Migration in Cancer Mortality in the U.S. *Journal of Chronic Diseases* 27: 459–74.

Marmot, Michael, and S. Leonard Syme. 1976. Acculturation and Coronary Heart Disease in Japanese-Americans. *American Journal of Epidemiology* 104: 225–47.

Marshall, Mac. 1981. Introduction: Approaches to Siblingship in Oceania. In Mac Marshall, ed., *Siblingship in Oceania*. ASAO monograph no. 8. Ann Arbor, Mich.: University Microfilms.

Mayer, Phillip. 1961. *Townsmen or Tribesmen*. Cape Town: Oxford University Press.

McGarvey, Stephen T., and Paul T. Baker. 1979. The Effects of Modernization and Migration on Samoan Blood Pressures. *Human Biology* 51: 461–80.

McGarvey, Stephen T., and Diane E. Schendel. 1986. Blood Pressures of Samoans. In Paul T. Baker, Joel M. Hanna, and Thelma S. Baker, eds., *The Changing Samoans*. New York: Oxford University Press.

McKinlay, J. B. 1979. A Case for Refocussing Upstream: The Political Economy of Illness. In E. Gartley Jaco, ed., *Patients, Physicians and Illness: A Sourcebook in Behavioral Science and Health*. 3d ed. New York: Free Press.

Mead, Margaret. 1928. *Coming of Age in Samoa*. New York: William Morrow.

———. 1930. *The Social Organization of Manu'a*. Bulletin no. 6. Honolulu: Bernice P. Bishop Museum.

Mechanic, David. 1974. Social Structure and Personal Adaptation. In G. V. Coelho, David A. Hamburg, and John E. Adams, eds., *Coping and Adaptation*. New York: Basic Books.

Merton, Robert K. 1949. *Social Theory and Social Structure*. Glencoe, Ill.: Free Press.

Mestrovic, Stjepan, and Barry Glassner. 1983. A Durkheimian Hypothesis on Stress. *Social Science and Medicine* 17: 1315–1327.

Mitchell, J. Clyde. 1959. The Causes of Labour Migration. *Bulletin of the Inter-African Labour Institute* 6: 12–47.

———. 1966. Theoretical Orientations in African Studies. In Michael Banton, ed., *The Social Anthropology of Complex Societies*. London: Tavistock.

———. 1969. The Concept and Use of Social Networks. In J. Clyde Mitchell, ed., *Social Networks in Urban Situations: Analyses of Personal Relationships in Central African Towns*. Manchester, Eng.: Manchester University Press.

Moore, Lorna G., Peter W. Van Arsdale, JoAnn E. Glittenberg, and Robert A.

Aldrich. 1987. *The Biocultural Basis of Health.* Prospect Heights, Ill.: Waveland.

Morrill, W. T. 1967. Immigrants and Associations: The Ibo in Twentieth Century Calibar. In L. A. Fallers, ed., *Immigrants and Associations.* The Hague: Mouton.

NOSA (National Office of Samoan Affairs). n.d. Samoan Americans in Employment and Training. San Francisco: Mimeo.

Oliver, Douglas. 1961. *The Pacific Islands.* 2d ed. New York: Natural History Press.

O'Neil, John D. 1986. Colonial Stress in the Canadian Arctic: An Ethnography of Young Adults Changing. In Craig R. Janes, Ron Stall, and Sandra M. Gifford, eds., *Anthropology and Epidemiology.* Dordrecht: D. Reidel (Kluwer).

O'Nell, Carl, and Henry Selby. 1968. Sex Differences in the Incidence of Susto in Two Zapotec Pueblos: An Analysis of the Relationships Between Sex Role Expectations in a Folk Illness. *Ethnology* 7: 95–105.

Park, Chai Bin. 1979. *The Population of American Samoa.* Country Monograph Series no. 7.1. Economic and Social Commission for Asia and the Pacific. Noumea, New Caledonia: South Pacific Commission.

Parker, Seymour, and Robert J. Kleiner. 1966. *Mental Illness in the Urban Negro Community.* New York: Free Press.

Pawson, Ivan G. 1986. The Morphological Characteristics of Samoan Adults. In Paul T. Baker, Joel M. Hanna, and Thelma S. Baker, eds., *The Changing Samoans.* New York: Oxford University Press.

Pawson, Ivan G., and Craig R. Janes. 1981. Massive Obesity in a Migrating Population. *American Journal of Public Health* 71: 508–13.

———. 1982. Biocultural Risks in Longevity: Samoans in California. *Social Science and Medicine* 16: 183–90.

Pelletier, David L. 1984. Diet, Activity and Cardiovascular Disease Risk Factors in Western Samoan Men. Ph.D. dissertation, Pennsylvania State University.

Pelletier, David L., and Conrad A. Hornick. 1986. Blood Lipid Studies. In Paul T. Baker, Joel M. Hanna, and Thelma S. Baker, eds., *The Changing Samoans.* New York: Oxford University Press.

Pilisuk, Marc, and Charles Froland. 1978. Kinship, Social Networks, Social Support and Health. *Social Science and Medicine* 12B: 273–80.

Pitt, David, and Cluny Macpherson. 1974. *Emerging Pluralism: The Samoan Community in New Zealand.* Auckland, N.Z.: Longman Paul.

Plotnicov, Leonard. 1967. *Strangers to the City: Urban Man in Jos, Nigeria.* Pittsburgh: University of Pittsburgh Press.

Prior, I. A. M. 1979. Hypertension Risk Factors: A Preventive Point of View. In F. Gross and T. Strasser, eds., *Mild Hypertension: Natural History and Management.* Turnbridge-Wells, Eng.: Pitman Medical.

Prior, I. A. M., J. G. Evans, H. P. Harvey, et al. 1968. Sodium Intake and Blood Pressure in Two Polynesian Populations. *New England Journal of Medicine* 279: 515.

Rahe, Robert H. 1974. The Pathway Between Subjects' Recent Life Changes and Their Near-Future Illness Reports: Representative Results and Methodological

Issues. In Bruce S. Dohrenwend and Barbara P. Dohrenwend, eds., *Stressful Life Events: Their Nature and Effects*. New York: Wiley.

Ratcliffe, John, Lawrence Wallack, Francis Fagnani, and Victor G. Rodwin. 1984. Perspectives on Prevention: Health Promotion vs. Health Protection. In Jean de Kervasdoue, John R. Kimberly, and Victor G. Rodwin, eds., *The End of an Illusion*. Berkeley: University of California Press.

Reed, Dwayne, and Ruel Stallones. 1970. Health Effects of Westernization and Migration Among Chamorros. *American Journal of Epidemiology* 92: 94–112.

Reis, H. T. 1984. Social Interaction and Well-Being. In S. Duck, ed., *Personal Relationships*, vol. 5. London: Academic Press.

Reis, H. T., L. Wheeler, M. H. Kernis, et al. 1985. On Specificity in the Impact of Social Participation in Physical and Psychological Health. *Journal of Personality and Social Psychology* 48: 456–71.

Rolff, Karla. 1978. Fa'asamoa: Tradition in Transition. Ph.D. dissertation, University of California, Santa Barbara.

Romanucci-Ross, Lola R. 1969. The Hierarchy of Resort in Curative Practices: The Admiralty Islands, Melanesia. *Journal of Health and Social Behavior* 10: 201–9.

Rose, R. M. 1980. Endocrine Responses to Stressful Psychological Events. *Psychiatrica Clinica North America* 41: 147–64.

Ryan, William. 1976. *Blaming the Victim*. New York: Vintage.

Sanua, Victor D. 1970. Immigration, Migration and Mental Illness. In Eugene B. Brody, ed., *Behavior in New Environments*. Beverly Hills, Calif.: Sage.

Scotch, Norman A. 1963. Sociocultural Factors in the Epidemiology of Zulu Hypertension. *American Journal of Public Health* 53: 1205–1213.

Scudder, Thayer, and Elizabeth Colson. 1980. Conclusion. In Art Hansen and Anthony Oliver-Smith, eds., *Involuntary Migration and Resettlement*. Boulder, Colo.: Westview.

Selye, Hans. 1956. *The Stress of Life*. New York: McGraw-Hill.

Shankman, Paul. 1976. *Migration and Underdevelopment: The Case of Western Samoa*. Boulder, Colo.: Westview.

Shore, Bradd. 1982. *Sala'ilua: A Samoan Mystery*. New York: Columbia University Press.

Shu, Ramsay, and Adele Satele. 1977. *The Samoan Community in Southern California: Conditions and Needs*. Occasional Paper no. 2. Los Angeles: Asian American Mental Health Research Center.

Stack, Carol B. 1974. *All Our Kin: Strategies for Survival in a Black Community*. New York: Harper and Row.

Syme, S. L., M. M. Hyman, and P. E. Enterline. 1964. Some Social and Cultural Factors Associated with the Occurrence of Coronary Heart Disease. *Journal of Chronic Diseases* 16: 277–89.

Szapocznik, M., and W. Kurtines. 1980. Acculturation, Biculturalism and Adjustment Among Cuban Americans. In A. M. Padilla, ed., *Acculturation, Theory, Models, and Some New Findings*. Boulder, Colo.: Westview.

Theorell, T. 1976. Selected Illnesses and Somatic Factors in Relation to Two Psychosocial Stress Indices. *Journal of Psychosomatic Research* 20: 7–20.

Tiffany, Sharon W. 1974. The Land and Titles Court and the Regulation of Customary Title Successions and Removals in Western Samoa. *Journal of the Polynesian Society* 83: 35–57.

———. 1978. The Politics of Denominational Organization in Samoa. In James Boutilier, Daniel Hughes, and Sharon Tiffany, eds., *Mission, Church, and Sect in Oceania*. ASAO monograph no. 6. Ann Arbor, Mich.: University of Michigan Press.

Tofaeono, Bert. 1978. The Role of the Church in California Samoan Communities. In Cluny Macpherson, Bradd Shore, and Robert Franco, eds., *New Neighbors . . . Islanders in Adaptation*. Santa Cruz: Center for South Pacific Studies, University of California, Santa Cruz.

Verbrugge, Lois M. 1983. Multiple Roles and Physical Health of Women and Men. *Journal of Health and Social Behavior* 24: 16–30.

Vingerhoets, A. J. J. M., and F. H. G. Marcelissen. 1988. Stress Research: Its Present Status and Issues for Further Development. *Social Science and Medicine* 26: 279–91.

Walsh, Anthony. 1980. The Prophylactic Effect of Religion on Blood Pressure Levels Among a Sample of Migrants. *Social Science and Medicine* 14B: 59–64.

Wessen, A. F. 1971. The Role of Migrant Studies in Epidemiological Research. *Israel Journal of Medical Science* 7: 1584–1591.

Wirsing, Rolf. 1985. The Health of Traditional Societies and the Effects of Acculturation. *Current Anthropology* 26: 303–22.

Wolff, H. G. 1953. *Stress and Disease*. Springfield, Ill.: Charles Thomas.

Young, Allan. 1980. The Discourse on Stress and the Reproduction of Conventional Knowledge. *Social Science and Medicine* 14B: 133–46.

Young, Franklin A. 1972. Stability and Change in Samoa. Ph.D. dissertation, University of Oregon, Eugene.

Zimmet, P., S. Faaiuso, J. Ainuu, et al. 1981. The Prevalence of Diabetes in the Rural and Urban Polynesian Society of Western Samoa. *Diabetes* 30: 45–51.

Zimmet, P., and S. Whitehouse. 1980. The Price for Modernization in Nauru, Tuvalu, and Western Samoa. In H. Trowell and D. Burkitt, eds., *Western Diseases*. London: Edward Arnold.

Index

In this index an "f" after a number indicates a separate reference on the next page, and an "ff" indicates separate references on the next two pages. A continuous discussion over two or more pages is indicated by a span of page numbers, e.g., "pp. 57–58." *Passim* is used for a cluster of references in close but not consecutive sequence.

Library of Congress Cataloging-in-Publication Data

Janes, Craig R. (Craig Robert), 1953–
  Migration, social change, and health : a Samoan community in urban
California / Craig R. Janes.
    p.   cm.
ISBN 0-8047-1789-3 :
    1. Samoan Americans—California—Social conditions. 2. Samoan
Americans—Health and hygiene—California. I. Title.
F870.S17J36   1990   90-9457
305.8'994—dc20   CIP

⊗ This book is printed on acid-free paper